COLLEGE TYPEWRITING

THIRD EDITION

By

D. D. LESSENBERRY

Director, Courses in Commercial Education
University of Pittsburgh

Published by

SOUTH-WESTERN PUBLISHING COMPANY

CINCINNATI   NEW YORK   CHICAGO   DALLAS   SAN FRANCISCO

T28—H1048

INDEX

PREFACE

THE work of research students and the experimental studies of psychologists have added much to our understanding of how learning to type takes place. The development of maximum typewriting power in a minimum of time is now an easier and happier experience for students. It is because of the recognition of the importance of well-organized and carefully constructed practice materials that COLLEGE TYPEWRITING has been revised. In writing this book, full use has been made of the improvements in teaching and in the organization of practice materials to the end that students using COLLEGE TYPEWRITING, Third Edition, will be assured of a thoroughly tested content that will inevitably lead to the development of good typewriting power.

Many of the features of former editions of COLLEGE TYPEWRITING have been retained in the present book. The keyboard is developed rapidly, but with due regard for the necessity of relating new learning situations to the successful completion of preceding lessons. Right technique is recognized as fundamental at all times. Rapid stroking is emphasized from the first lesson. Accurate work habits as well as accurately typed materials are stressed through the use of exercises that call for typing from problem situations. Remedial practice materials based on error studies are provided for those students who must have special learning exercises.

Speed in the typing of straight copy has only limited value, but speed in the typing of office material is of great importance. This book, therefore, stresses the doing of office work in an office situation, creating as nearly as possible through the material given in the typing problems the typical office atmosphere.

The letters represent cross sections of several different businesses. Successive stages of development in the correspondence are shown so that the typist can see how the business situations are developed through the medium of the business letter. Other sections of letters show the completed file of correspondence relating to a particular business transaction, giving the letters from both correspondents in sequence so that the budget, when completed, will represent a file of correspondence exactly as it would appear in the office from which these letters have been taken. Rough draft problems are given with many of the budgets.

The experience of the past few years has demonstrated better ways of teaching typewriting and the experimental use of materials has revealed better ways of organizing drills and exercises. Thus, the new is blended with the old and this revision marks another step in the progress of providing effective materials to meet the needs of those who know that measurable improvement in learning to typewrite can be made when right practice procedures and materials are used.

This revision has many new features that will commend the book to students and teachers. Two special features that have been used with marked success in experimental classes are called for at appropriate intervals throughout the textbook. These new features are: (1) calling the throw; (2) guided writing. These devices are effective for building speed and equally effective for building control.

It is impossible to include in the acknowledgments the names of all the teachers and business workers who have contributed to the content and the organization of the teaching materials included in this book. The author acknowledges that no one person can ever write an effective textbook in typewriting—the task calls for the co-operation of teachers and business workers. This book is the product of such co-operative work.

D. D. LESSENBERRY

OPERATIVE PARTS OF THE TYPEWRITER

A part that is common to two or more different typewriters is given the same number in the illustrations on the following pages. Parts that are found on one typewriter and not on others are indicated by letters of the alphabet.

No.	Name	Function
1.	Backspacer	Used to bring the typewriter carriage to the proper position for inserting omitted letters, for making corrections, or for tabulating or centering.
2.	Ribbon Reverse (Hand Control)	Used to change the movement of the ribbon.
3.	Carriage-Position Indicator	Indicates the printing position of the carriage.
4.	Removable Platen Bracket	Used to lift out platen from machine.
5.	Carriage-Release Lever, Left	Permits operator to move carriage easily to any point on scale.
6.	Carriage-Release Lever, Right	Permits operator to move carriage easily to any point on scale.
7.	Cylinder (or Platen)	The rubber roll around which the paper is inserted and held in position for typing.
8.	Platen Knob, Left	Used to turn the cylinder by hand when paper is inserted or removed.
9.	Platen Knob, Right	Used to turn the cylinder by hand when paper is inserted or removed.
10.	Margin or Platen Scale	Used to determine the position of the carriage.
11.	Line-Space and Carriage-Return Lever	Used in returning the carriage and automatically spacing between lines.
12.	Line-Space Disengaging Lever	Permits writing between lines without resetting the line.
13.	Line-Space Regulator	Used to adjust the typewriter for single, double, or triple spacing.
14.	Margin Release	When depressed, this release permits writing outside the margin.
15.	Alignment Scale	Used as a guide when reinserting a partially completed page.
16.	Margin Stop, Left	Used to set the beginning of the writing line.
17.	Margin Stop, Right	Used to set the length of the writing line.
18.	Paper Clamp (or Finger), Left	Holds the paper firmly against the cylinder.
19.	Paper Clamp (or Finger), Right	Holds the paper firmly against the cylinder.
20.	Paper Guide	Guides the left edge of the paper as it is inserted into the typewriter.
21.	Paper-Guide Scale	Used in determining the correct position for the paper guide.
22.	Card and Label Holder	Used for holding cards, labels, or envelopes against the cylinder.
23.	Paper Release	Used when the paper is straightened or removed.
24.	Paper Table (or Rest)	Supports the paper after it is in place.
25.	Ribbon Spool, Left	Spool on which the ribbon automatically winds and unwinds as keys are struck.
26.	Ribbon Spool, Right	Spool on which the ribbon automatically winds and unwinds as keys are struck.
27.	Shift Key, Left	Used when capitals controlled by the right hand are typed.
28.	Shift Key, Right	Used when capitals controlled by the left hand are typed.
29.	Shift Lock	Used when a number of consecutive upper-case (or capital) characters are typed.
30.	Space Bar	Used to space between letters or words.
31.	Tabulator Key or Bar	Used for indenting for paragraphs, tabulated reports, or the like.
32.	Touch Control Selector	Adjusts the key tension.
33.	Tabulator Stops	Used for indenting for paragraphs, tabulated reports, or the like.
34.	Tabulator-Stop Set Key	To set inbuilt tabulator stops, depress the set key.
35.	Tabulator-Stop Clear Key	Used to clear the tabulator rack of all stops set in position.
36.	Thumb Piece	Used to control the carriage by hand when the carriage-release lever is operated.
37.	Type Bar Guide	Indicates the point at which the type strikes the paper.
38.	Variable Line Spacer	Used to reset the line at any desired point.
39.	Ribbon Indicator and Stencil Lever	Permits using upper half or lower half of ribbon or disengages ribbon for stenciling.
40.	Paper-Holder Bail	Holds the paper firmly against the cylinder.
41.	Paper-Holder Bail Lever	Used in operating the paper-holder bail.
42.	Ribbon Carrier	The "needle" through which the ribbon moves.
43.	Ribbon Spool Cover	Cover which protects the ribbon spools from dust.
44.	Margin Stop Rack	Rack along which the margin stops are moved.
45.	Margin Control Lever	Mechanism for setting the margin stops.

UNDERWOOD STANDARD

PARTS NOT SHOWN			ADDITIONAL PARTS
4	33	44	A. Left Margin Stop Release
18	37	45	B. Envelope Arm Holder
19	42		
26	43		

UNDERWOOD NOISELESS

PARTS NOT SHOWN			
4	17	41	45
12	33	42	
13	36	43	
16	38	44	

ROYAL

PARTS NOT SHOWN			ADDITIONAL PART
3	18	36	A. Ribbon-Feed Release
4	19	37	
5	25	42	
16	26	44	
17	33		

SMITH

PARTS NOT SHOWN			ADDITIONAL PARTS
4	19	41	A. Platen Lock
16	25		B. Tabulator Stop Universal
18	36		Clear Lever
			C. Carriage Scale
			D. Paper Gauge Indicator

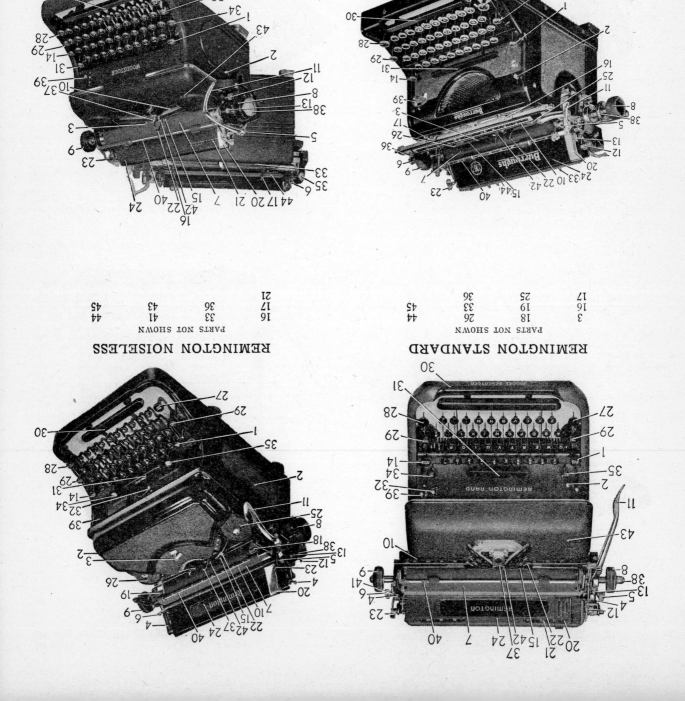

CONTENTS

PART I
FOUNDATIONS OF TYPING POWER

You can learn to type; but the extent to which you develop the typing power that you need for effective personal or vocational use depends on your efforts to acquire the right techniques. The suggested time given for the different portions of each lesson will enable you to use your practice periods effectively. Hold to the program as closely as possible, but do not permit yourself to feel that you cannot vary the time slightly if it seems best to do so.

UNIT I—*INITIATING KEYBOARD CONTROL*

LESSON 1

PAPER INSERTION

5 minutes

Explanation. Insert a full-sized sheet of paper, 8½ by 11 inches. The *right* way to handle the paper calls for the use of certain machine parts and for definite hand movements. Remove the paper and study Illustrations Nos. 1 and 2 to learn the best procedure for inserting the paper into the typewriter.

The paper is twirled around the cylinder (No. 7)* with a quick movement of the fingers and the thumb.

Illustration No. 1 — Paper Insertion

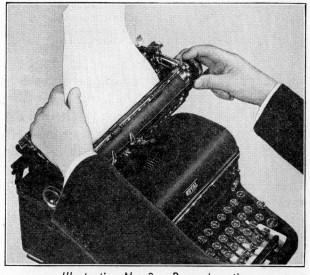

Illustration No. 2 — Paper Insertion

Manipulation Drill. 1. Study Illustration No. 1. Place the paper on the desk at the left of, and turned endwise to the typewriter.

2. Grasp paper with the left hand, placing left thumb under paper and fingers on top.

3. Study Illustration No. 2. Bring the paper to the carriage and drop it behind the cylinder (No. 7) with the left edge against the paper guide (No. 20); *at the same time* bring the right hand to the right cylinder knob

(No. 9). Place the thumb well under the knob and the first and second fingers on top.

4. Twirl the cylinder knob with a quick movement of the fingers and the thumb. Hold the elbow almost motionless; let the movement be made with the fingers and the thumb. The first writing line should be 3 or 4 spaces below the top edge of the paper.

5. Adjust the paper clamps (Nos. 18 and 19) or paper bail (No. 40) to hold the paper firmly.

---

* Learn the use of the typewriter parts as they are needed in your work. A part that is common to the different typewriters is given the number shown on the list of operative parts on page iv and in the illustrations on the following pages.

TIMED WRITING

Applying for work is something of an ordeal. The applicant does not know | 74
what to do with his hat, his hands, or his feet. He does not know how much to | 153
talk or how long to stay. It is just about as hard on the employer, too, as on | 233
the would-be employee. In a brief time, and frequently with very meager | 306
information about the training, the experience, and the interests of the appli- | 384
cant, an employer must select from a group of young men and women the per- | 457
son who will best fit into his organization. There may be some men who can | 533
appraise a person at a glance, but most men who are looking for a new worker | 610
feel the need for more than a glance at a prospective employee. | 675

There are two sides to the business of position-hunting. I have heard both | 751
sides of the question recently. The applicant says he gets scant courtesy and | 830
little or no consideration unless he has "pull" or the "inside track" in some | 908
way. Getting a place to work has come to be a matter of influence, so some say. | 990
The employer has a long list of complaints. He says that too many young peo- | 1066
ple think only of the beginning salary and do not realize that, as a rule, they | 1146
fail to earn during the first six months of their working life even the small pay | 1228
they get. Even one who is trained for the work and who has the personal qual- | 1305
ities that make for success has to have time in which to make the necessary | 1381
adjustments and to learn the routine of the new work. It takes time for a per- | 1459
son to learn how to serve an organization, even when he is willing to work | 1534
hard. A position involves much that no school seems able to teach. | 1603

Why is one person rejected in the first few minutes of an interview while | 1677
another is chosen for the place when both seem to have equal ability? The | 1752
men who do the hiring for a number of business houses were asked to explain | 1828
the basis on which they hire workers. They said there are three types of per- | 1905
sons who apply for work. There is the obvious misfit in personal qualities, | 1982
though not in point of preparation perhaps. Skill is just one of the things | 2059
wanted by employers, although young workers do not always know this to be | 2133
true. In this misfit group are the boys who are too often sloppy in looks and | 2212
lacking in poise. In this same group are the girls whose lips and fingernails | 2291
make the red, red rose blush to paleness, and who do not recognize the fact | 2367
that manners either stagey or coyly familiar are out of place in business. | 2443

The second type of applicant gives the employing manager the most trou- | 2513
ble. In this group are those greatly in need of work, eager to do their best, but | 2596
untrained. Experience may be the best teacher, but the employer often finds | 2673
it too costly to take over the task of giving the training that should be had in | 2754
school. Still, out of this second group of persons, some fine workers are some- | 2833
times found. It takes time and patient quizzing to select from the great num- | 2910
ber who belong to this group those who show promise of being able to do the | 2986
work and make the adjustments that the position demands. | 3044

The third group of those seeking work includes those who are well trained | 3118
and who are blessed with a pleasing manner, natural or acquired. They do not | 3196
like to work just for the pay that comes as a result; but they know that work | 3274
gives them many chances to learn, to grow, and to advance toward that full | 3349
life and social safety that is the aim of every worker. | 3404

PAPER REMOVAL

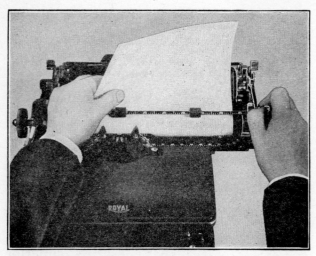

Illustration No. 3 — Removing the Paper

Explanation. Correctly done, removal of the paper from the machine is a quiet and rapid manipulation. Hold the paper release lever down until the paper is out of the machine. Then replace the lever in its proper position. If the lever is not returned to its original position, a new sheet of paper cannot be inserted efficiently.

Directions. 1. Operate the paper-release lever (No. 23) and remove the paper with the hand not controlling the lever.

2. Study Illustration No. 3. Return the lever to its first position after the paper has been removed.

Manipulation Drill. Reinsert the paper as directed in the discussion on paper insertion.

FINGER POSITION

Explanation. The first step in learning to type is to associate the controlling finger with the reach to be made. The writing position from which strokes are made is known as the *typing position.* The fingers of the left hand cover the **a s d f** keys; the fingers of the right hand, the **; l k j** keys.

Directions. 1. Look at the keyboard.

2. Place the little finger of the left hand on the first key in the second row. This is the *a* key controlled by the *a finger.*

3. Let the other fingers of the left hand cover the three succeeding keys, the *s, d, f* keys.

4. Look at the fingers of your left hand as they rest lightly on the keys and name them from the little to the index finger, **a s d f.**

5. Look at the keyboard again.

6. Place the little finger of the right hand on the key that is *next to the end key* in the second row. This is the *;* (*semicolon*) key.

7. Let the other fingers cover the three preceding keys, the *l, k,* and *j* keys.

8. Look at the fingers of your right hand as they rest lightly on the keys and then name them from the little to the index finger, **; l k j.**

Illustration No. 4 — Finger Position

Illustration No. 5 — Finger Position

Manipulation Drill. 1. Place the hands in the correct keyboard position with the fingers curved and poised lightly on the keys.

2. Remove your hands from the keyboard. Replace the hands in correct position and repeat the drill once or twice.

EXERCISE 175

Directions: Type a letter of application for a position with the Barnhart-Mosby Company, 1106 C Street, your city. Call the letter to the attention of Mr. C. W. Thompson, the manager. Your letter of application is to be written for a position with the following job specifications, the letter to precede a personal interview:

Job Specifications

Nature of work:
Typist and general clerk.

Worker wanted:
Man, 19 to 23 years of age.

Skill required:
Minimum typing speed, 55 words. Ability to set up tabulated reports, to copy rough drafts, to type letters, and to operate common office machines.

EXERCISE 176

Directions: After the receipt of your letter of application, you are called for a personal interview and a placement test. The test consists of the following unset business letter, rough-draft tabulated report, and timed writing.

LETTER

mr l d brewer 492 huntington drive springfield illinois dear mr brewer (P) in accordance with your request of march 29 we are giving you detailed information about the latest schedules between chicago and spokane on superior airlines (P) leave chicago 7:30 a m 8:30 p m cst arrive spokane 5:50 p m 6:40 a m pst leave spokane 10:05 a m 8:25 p m pst arrive chicago 11:50 p m 10:30 a m cst (P) the fare for one way is $86.50 and that for a round trip is $144 the fare necessary to make a stopover at los angeles before going to spokane is $277.93 from chicago back to chicago (P) we are enclosing a folder and a correction sheet that describe superior airlines de luxe service with the new ten passenger twin engine lockheed electras we hope that we shall have the pleasure of serving you in the near future (P) very truly yours superior airlines inc (f j bixler) division traffic manager enclosures 2

ROUGH DRAFT

(all caps,) sp. in full **Bulletin No. 28** *(Sales Bulletin No. 26-A)*

The Dept. of Sales has issued a special bulletin, showing the increase in sales of new cars, used cars, for the fiscal year ending June 30. This report is an index of the growth of our company and of the fine loyalty and salesmanship of our men, and a barometer of our future business. sales possibilities, too, for we can do better now that business is definitely on the upswing than we were able to do in the time of great business uncertainty. The following is taken from the report and will be of interest to all of our salesmen:

The report can be taken as

	Last Year	Present Year
New Cars:		
Passenger	1,075	1,786
Trucks	492	831
Used Cars:	1,562	1,684
Passenger		
Trucks	250	396

X

Indent 5

(car salesman)

The items here presented do not show the sales of automobile accessories. These sales are reported by another department. Each of the men in this department should, however, use every opportunity to mention to car and truck owners the good excellent line of supplies accessories we carry. This is a co-operative piece of work that will benefit the company directly and all of us indirectly.

STROKE AND RELEASE OF KEYS

5 minutes

Explanation. A good typing movement is made with a quick, controlled blow of the finger directed to the center of the key, with little movement of the wrist or forearm.

Directions. 1. Get the *feel* of a light, forceful key stroke and of a quick key release. Hit the keys covered by the fingers of the left hand; begin with the *f finger* (index finger) and then strike the keys with the other three fingers.

fdsaf

2. Strike the keys covered by the fingers of your right hand: **jkl;j**

3. Type the letters several times. Use a light, forceful finger stroke with little hand motion. Release the key quickly. Hold the hands steady. Let the fingers do the work

fdsafjkl;j

4. Study the illustrations and directions for returning the carriage.

CARRIAGE RETURN

3 minutes

Explanation. The carriage return must be a quick throw, made through the use of the line-space and carriage-return lever (No. 11). When the carriage is returned, the paper is automatically spaced forward for the next line of typing. Learn the right way to return the carriage and to space the paper forward to continue typing. Study the illustrations and directions that follow.

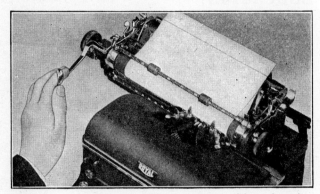

Illustration No. 6 — Carriage Return (short lever)

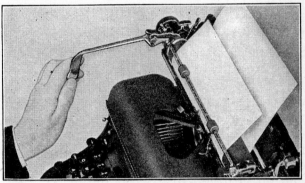

Illustration No. 7 — Carriage Return (extended lever)

Directions. 1. Extend the left hand, palm down and turned slightly sidewise, fingers bracing one another, to the line-space and carriage-return lever (No. 11). Move the elbow as little as possible.

2. Operate the lever with the first finger between the first and second joints, the other fingers bracing one another against the first finger. Throw with a wrist movement.

3. Return the hand to writing position quickly; start typing without delay.

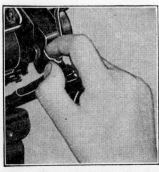

Illustration No. 8
Carriage-Release Lever and Thumb Piece

Manipulation Drill. 1. Depress the right carriage-release lever (No. 6) and move the carriage to the left. If your machine has a thumb piece, use the technique shown in Illustration No. 8; otherwise, use that shown in Illustration No. 9.

2. Place your hands in typing position.

3. Throw the carriage quickly. Use a forceful wrist movement.

4. Return the hand to typing position by the time the throw is completed; strike *f*.

5. Repeat the drill. Use the technique given in the directions.

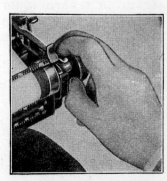

Illustration No. 9
Carriage-Release Lever and Right Cylinder Knob

UNIT XIII — *APPLYING FOR A POSITION*

It is customary for many businesses to request a written letter of application for a position, even when a personal interview has been held. The written letter of application gives information that can be filed for reference.

A letter of application should be concise, clear, and complete. Include in the letter of application reference to the type of work for which you are applying, the nature of your preparation and business experience, and other pertinent facts. If you enclose a data sheet, you may make the letter itself brief and may omit specific mention of information given on the data sheet.

A data sheet should be typed in outline form. Give complete personal information, including a statement of formal education and of business experience, if any. List at least three character and work references. Do not list the names of references unless permission to do so has been obtained.

EXERCISE 174

Directions: This letter was written by a young man who was an applicant for a position as typist and general clerk. Type the letter in a single-spaced modification of the block style with all the lines of the inside address and the body of the letter blocked at the left margin and with the closing lines blocked in the position for the complimentary close. Use mixed punctuation.

Schuster Construction Company 1800 Metcalf Street Baltimore, Maryland Attention Mr. B. C. Locke Gentlemen: (P) In this morning's conference concerning a position with your company as typist and general clerk, I outlined briefly my training for this type of work. At your request I enclose a data sheet on which this information is given in greater detail. (P) At the end of this month I am to be graduated from the School of Business Administration of this city. I am interested in immediate employment, of course; even more, however, I am interested in establishing a connection with a progressive business in which I can grow in ability to serve and in earning power. (P) If you will give me an opportunity to demonstrate my ability to do acceptable work, I shall be glad to take the test at your convenience. Very truly yours, (Robert N. Lockwood) Enclosure (*Strokes, 873; words, 123.*)

DATA SHEET

NAME:
  Robert N. Lockwood

ADDRESS:
  429 West 125th Street, Baltimore
  Telephone: LI 4020-J

PERSONAL DATA:
  Age, 21. Single. Member of Fifth Baptist Church
  Weight, 163 pounds. Height, 5 ft. 11 in.

EDUCATION:
  Graduate of Western High School
  Two years at Johns Hopkins University
  One year at School of Business Administration

BUSINESS EXPERIENCE:
  Part-time clerk at Dodson's Grocery, West Market Street, during three years of my high school training
  Messenger for First National Bank during the summer following my graduation from high school

SKILL:
  Typing rate, between 65 and 70 words a minute
  Shorthand dictation rate, 110 words a minute on unfamiliar material
  Working knowledge of the operation of (1) the Mimeograph, (2) the Comptometer, (3) adding machines, and (4) the Dictaphone

REFERENCES:
  Mr. E. C. Dodson
    President, Dodson's Grocery
    West Market Street
    Baltimore
  Mr. T. Morris Redworth, President
    First National Bank
    Baltimore
  Miss Mary C. Simpson
    Head, Typewriting Department
    School of Business Administration
    Baltimore

SPACE-BAR CONTROL

Explanation. In the material you have typed, you probably have all letters written solid—without space between groups of letters, as in the copy. The space between groups of letters is made through the use of the space bar (No. 30). This space bar is operated by the right thumb only.

Manipulation Drill. Hit the bar in the center with a forward motion of the right thumb; raise the thumb quickly.

f d fd j k jk f s fs j l jl f a fa j ; j;

You are now ready to learn to make the reaches to *r, u, g, h.*

LOCATION PRACTICE 1

10 minutes

Reaches to *r, u, g, h*

Study Illustration No. 10, which shows the reaches to *r* and to *u*. The *f finger* strikes *r*; the *j finger* strikes *u*.

Look at your fingers. Extend the *f finger* slightly and make the reach to *r* without a forward movement of the hand. Flick **rf** quickly and lightly. Watch your *j finger* reach *u*. Close your eyes and rapidly type **rf uj** several times.

Type the following drill two or three times with your eyes on this copy:

frf rf juj uj rf uj fur fur rf uj fur

Study Illustration No. 11, which shows the reaches to *g* and to *h*. Move your *f finger* to *g without moving the other fingers* from their typ-

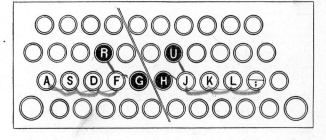

ing position. Touch **gf** quickly and lightly. Watch your *j finger* reach *h*.

Close your eyes and type **gf hj** several times rapidly.

Type the following drill two or three times with your eyes on this copy:

fgf jhj gf hj hug hug hj gf hug fur hug

Illustration No. 10 — Reaches to r and u

Illustration No. 11 — Reaches to g and h

tained in these presents shall inure to the benefit of and be binding upon the respective heirs, executors, administrators, successors, and assigns of the parties hereto.

IN WITNESS WHEREOF, The said Nicholas D. Stahlman and Clara P. Stahlman, husband and wife, have hereunto set their hands this .... day of ...., 194...

_____

_____

Signed and acknowledged
in presence of

_____

_____

_____

The State of Ohio   ⎱ ss.
County of Hamilton ⎰

BE IT REMEMBERED, That on this .... day of ...., in the year of our Lord one thousand nine hundred and ...., before me, the subscriber, a notary public in and for said County, personally came Nicholas D. Stahlman and Clara P. Stahlman, the grantors in the foregoing Mortgage, and acknowledged the signing thereof to be their voluntary act and deed.

IN TESTIMONY WHEREOF, I have hereunto subscribed my name and affixed my official seal on the day and year last aforesaid.

_____
Notary Public

EXERCISE 173
SATISFACTION OF MORTGAGE

Directions. Type one copy with double spacing. Use the following dates:

Date of mortgage—current date.
Date of recording of mortgage—one week after date of mortgage.
Date of satisfaction of mortgage and date of acknowledgment—three years after date of mortgage.

KNOW ALL MEN BY THESE PRESENTS:

That Matthew A. Dillinger of Cincinnati, Ohio, does hereby certify that a certain mortgage deed, dated the .... day of ...., 194.., and recorded on the .... day of ...., 194.., in record of mortgages, Volume 179, page 3472, in the office of the recorder of Hamilton County, Ohio, executed by Nicholas D. Stahlman and Clara P. Stahlman, husband and wife, to Matthew A. Dillinger on the following described real estate, situated in the city of Cincinnati, county of Hamilton, and state of Ohio, to-wit:

Lot thirty-one (31) on the plat of Edgemont First Subdivision, as per plat thereof recorded in Plat Book 50, page 1772, of the records of Hamilton County, Ohio,

has been fully paid and satisfied, and the recorder is authorized to discharge the same of record.

IN WITNESS WHEREOF, the said Matthew A. Dillinger has hereunto set his hand this .... day of ...., 194...

_____

Signed and acknowledged
in presence of

_____

_____

The State of Ohio   ⎱ ss.
County of Hamilton ⎰

Before me, a notary public in and for said county, personally appeared the above named Matthew A. Dillinger, who acknowledged that he did sign the foregoing instrument, and that the same is his free act and deed.

IN TESTIMONY WHEREOF, I have hereunto subscribed my name and affixed my official seal at Cincinnati, Ohio, this .... day of ...., 194...

_____
Notary Public

Practice Procedures. 1. Keep the fingers curved in the typing position.

2. Make the reach without changing the hand position. Let the fingers do the work.

3. You have seen the fingers make the reaches. You have the *feel* of the stroke. You do not need to look at your fingers as you type; therefore, keep your eyes on the copy. THINK the letter; the right finger will make the right movement.

4. Bring the finger quickly toward the palm of the hand after the stroke is made.

Directions. 1. Hold your eyes on the copy throughout the entire typing. Guard against the tendency to lift the eyes to check the writing or to return the carriage. It is important to keep the carriage moving steadily.

2. Type the drill twice. Type the lines as nearly as possible without pause.

```
r r r u u u rfuj fur fur rfuj fur fur fur

gf gf hj hj jug fur jug fur jug fur hug hug
```

EXERCISE 1   *7 minutes*

Directions. Type the drill twice. Type without pause. Hold your eyes on the copy. Keep the carriage moving steadily.

```
jug fur fur jug jug fur jug had fur jug had

fur jug fur jug rug rug fur jug rug fur fur
```

(Space once after a semicolon.)
```
ask a lad; a lad had a fur; a lad has a rug;
```

Look at your typed material. Probably it is not arranged as shown in Exercise 1. Your typing probably is not with uniform left and right margins and the spacing may be different from that shown in the book. In the next lesson you will learn how to arrange your work accurately.

Move your carriage so that it is approximately centered in order that the machine may be easily covered if your teacher instructed you to cover the typewriter at the end of each period.

LESSON 2

RECONSTRUCTION PRACTICE   *3 minutes*

You have learned the control of certain machine parts and how to strike certain letters. Recall the feel of the typewriter through a reconstruction practice.

Directions. 1. Insert a sheet of paper so the first line of typing will be three or four spaces below the top edge of the sheet. Study Illustrations Nos. 1 and 2, page 1.

2. Depress the carriage-release lever and move the carriage to the left. Study Illustration No. 8 or No. 9, page 3.

3. Place the hands in the correct typing position with the fingers curved and poised lightly on the keys. Study Illustrations Nos. 4 and 5, page 2.

4. Throw the carriage. Study Illustration No. 6 or 7, page 3.

5. Type the following lines:

```
frf juj fgf jhj frf juj fgf jhj fdsaf jkl;j

rf uj rf uj gf hj rf uj gf hj rf uj gf hj
```

premises, and have full power to convey the same; and that the title so conveyed is clear, free, and unencumbered; and further, that they do warrant and will defend the same against all claim or claims of all persons whomsoever.

The condition of this mortgage is such that whereas, the said Nicholas D. Stahlman and Clara P. Stahlman, grantors, have executed and delivered unto the said Matthew A. Dillinger, grantee, their certain promissory note of even date herewith for the sum of three thousand dollars ($3,000), with interest at the rate of six per cent per annum, payable semiannually, due three years after date at the First National Bank, Cincinnati, Ohio, and

Whereas, said grantors hereby covenant and agree with said grantee that they will immediately insure the buildings on said premises for the sum of at least three thousand dollars ($3,000) against loss or damage by fire, tornado, or cyclone, by and under policies approved by and deposited with the grantee and which shall provide for the payment of any loss under the same to the grantee, his heirs, executors, administrators, or assigns as his or their interest may appear; and at least forty-eight (48) hours prior to the expiration of any such policy to deposit with the grantee an approved renewal policy of like tenor and amount; and further, that said grantors shall pay at maturity all taxes and assessments which shall be assessed or levied against said premises.

Now, if the said grantors shall well and truly pay, or cause to be paid, said promissory note according to its tenor to said grantee, and shall pay said taxes and assessments and shall insure said buildings and keep the same insured, as herein provided, then these presents shall be void; otherwise to remain in full force and effect.

The grantors further covenant with said grantee as follows, to-wit:

(1) That if said grantors shall fail to insure said buildings, or to keep the same insured, or to deliver said policies of insurance to said grantee, or to pay said taxes and assessments, as herein provided, then said grantee may insure said buildings, and pay said taxes and assessments, and the amount so paid for insurance premiums and for said taxes and assessments shall be immediately repaid by said grantors to said grantee, and in default thereof, the same shall be added to and be a part of the sum secured by this mortgage, and shall bear interest at the same rate as the principal sum secured hereby.

(2) That if default be made in the payment of said principal sum, or of any installment of principal or interest thereon, or in the payment of said taxes and assessments, or of said insurance premiums, when the same become due, or if default be made in the performance or observance of any of the covenants and agreements herein contained on the part of the grantors to be performed or observed, then, and in any such case, the entire principal sum of said promissory note shall immediately become due and payable at the option of said grantee, notice of said option being hereby expressly waived; and, further, that upon any such default, said grantee may take possession of said premises, rent the same, collect and realize on the rents, issues, and profits thereof and therefrom, and, after deducting all reasonable expenses and charges, apply the same to the payment and satisfaction of the debts and obligations secured by these presents.

(3) That in any action that may be brought to foreclose this mortgage, the court may at any time and without notice to said grantors, appoint a receiver for the benefit of said grantee to preserve said property, rent the same, and collect and realize on the rents, issues, and profits of the property, and to apply the same to the payment and satisfaction of the debts and obligations secured by these presents.

(4) That no building or improvement on said premises shall be removed or demolished without the written consent of the grantee; nor shall any other waste be committed or suffered by the grantors.

(5) That all the covenants, agreements, terms, conditions, and obligations con-

At the end of the last class period, you were asked to inspect your typed material to see if you had uniform left and right margins and double spacing. Study the illustrations and instructional material that follow so you can make accurate adjustments as directed for further work.

PAPER-GUIDE PLACEMENT
2 minutes

Explanation. The paper guide (No. 20) guides the left edge of the paper as it is inserted into the typewriter.

Directions. 1. Place the paper guide (No. 20) so the indicator is at 2 below 0 on the paper-guide scale. Study Illustration No. 12.

2. Determine whether you are using a machine with pica or elite type. There are 10 spaces to a horizontal inch of pica type; 12 spaces to a horizontal inch of elite type. If your margin scale (No. 10) reads 0-85 or 90, you are operating a machine with pica type; if it reads 0-100 or 110, you have an elite-type machine.

Illustration No. 12
Placement of Paper Guide

MARGIN-STOP ADJUSTMENT
3 minutes

Explanation. The margin stops (Nos. 16 and 17) control the width of the left and right margins. To set the stops, move the carriage so the position indicator (No. 3) is at the point on the scale at which the writing is to begin; then move the stop that controls the left margin to that point. Until otherwise directed, move the stop that controls the right margin to the end of the scale.

Directions. 1. Move the carriage so the position indicator is at 20 for a pica-type machine or at 30 for an elite-type machine.

2. Move the stop for the left margin along the scale until it is stopped by the mechanism. This will set the left margin stop at 20 on the pica-type machine and at 30 on the elite-type machine.

Illustration No. 13 — Setting the Margin Stop—Underwood

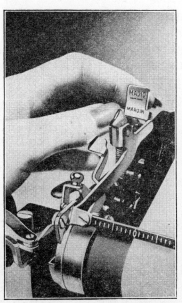

Illustration No. 14 — Setting the Margin Stop—Royal

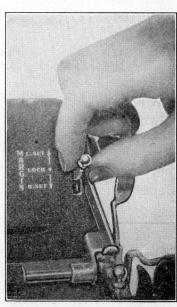

Illustration No. 15 — Setting the Margin Stop—L C Smith

Plaintiff says he has performed each and all the conditions of said contract and lease to be kept and performed by him, that he paid each and every installment of rent in advance as provided in said contract and lease, and that on the 1st day of September, 1939, the same being more than thirty days prior to the end of the third year of said term, he notified defendant in writing that he elected to purchase said premises and real estate for the said agreed price of ten thousand dollars ($10,000), and that he would assume and pay the valid existing mortgage on said premises in the sum of seven thousand five hundred dollars ($7,500) as a part of said purchase price, and then and there tendered to defendant in cash the difference between said agreed purchase price and the amount of said valid mortgage on said premises in the sum of seven thousand five hundred dollars ($7,500), and requested defendant to execute and deliver to plaintiff his warranty deed with release of dower for said real estate and premises, which defendant refused to do, and defendant still refuses and continues to refuse to comply with the terms of said contract and lease, although plaintiff has been and is now ready and willing to comply with all the terms of said contract, lease, and said election.

WHEREFORE, plaintiff prays that said contract be specifically performed, that defendant be ordered to execute and deliver to plaintiff his warranty deed with release of dower for said premises, and for such other and further orders and relief as the court may direct.

———————————

Attorney for Plaintiff

The State of Ohio } ss.
County of Hamilton }

ARTHUR W. LANG, being first duly sworn, says that he is the plaintiff in this action, and that the facts stated and allegations contained in the foregoing pleading are, as he believes, true.

———————————

Sworn to before me and subscribed in my presence this .... day of ...., 194...

———————————

Notary Public

If this petition was being filed with a court of record, a copy of the lease would be attached and made a part of the pleading.

EXERCISE 172
MORTGAGE

Directions. Type one copy with double spacing. Use the current date. Provide a backing sheet, and type the indorsement. Bind the pages together, and fold them for filing.

KNOW ALL MEN BY THESE PRESENTS:

That Nicholas D. Stahlman and Clara P. Stahlman, husband and wife, of Cincinnati, Ohio, grantors, in consideration of the sum of three thousand dollars ($3,000) to them paid by Matthew A. Dillinger, the grantee, the receipt whereof is hereby acknowledged, do hereby GRANT, BARGAIN, SELL, AND CONVEY to the said Matthew A. Dillinger, his heirs and assigns forever, the following described real estate, situated in the city of Cincinnati, county of Hamilton, and state of Ohio, and known as

Lot thirty-one (31) on the plat of Edgemont First Subdivision, as per plat thereof recorded in Plat Book 50, page 1772, of the records of Hamilton County, Ohio,

and all the estate, title, and interest of the said Nicholas D. Stahlman and Clara P. Stahlman, grantors, either in law or in equity of, in and to the said premises; together with all the privileges and appurtenances to the same belonging, and all the rents, issues, and profits thereof; to have and to hold the same to the only proper use of the said Matthew A. Dillinger, his heirs and assigns forever.

And the said grantors, for themselves and their heirs, executors, and administrators, do hereby covenant with the said grantee, his heirs and assigns, that they are the true and lawful owners of the said

LINE-SPACE REGULATOR

1 minute

Explanation. Typewriters have mechanisms for setting the machine for single, double, or triple spacing. The spacing between lines is controlled by the line-space regulator (No. 13). •

Directions. Set the line-space regulator for double spacing.

Woodstock

Underwood

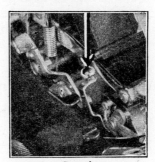

Royal

L C Smith

Illustration No. 16 — Setting the Line-Space Regulator

TECHNIQUE PRACTICE 2

10 minutes

Directions. Type the drill twice.

		STROKES
(Release the key quickly.)	r r u u rf uj ur fur fur fur frf juj fur	40	(Hold your eyes on the copy.)
	gf gf hj hj ug ju jug fur jug hag fur hag	41	
(THINK the letter.)	fur jug fur jug rug jug had fur had fur	39	
	has fur lad fur has rug ask ask fur lad	39	
	fur jug rug has fur had jug lad fur ask	39	

EXERCISE 2

10 minutes

Directions. 1. Type this exercise once on the same sheet of paper that you used for the preceding technique practice. Use the same margins and double spacing. Operate the line-space and carriage-return lever twice; this will separate the typing you have done from the lines of this exercise.

2. Return the carriage rhythmically and without looking up. Start typing the next line without pause.

		STROKES	
(Move only the controlling finger in making the reach.)	fur jug fur jug rug jug rug fur fur jug	39	(Hold your eyes on the copy.)
	jug jar fur jar hag jar had jug had fur	39	
	had fur had jug has fur has jar fur jug	39	
	dug jar had fur had jug has fur ask ask	39	
(Space once after a semicolon.)	ask dad; dad had a fur; a lad has a jug;	40	
	fur ask rug lad jug had fur ask rug has	39	
	dad has a rug; a lad had a jar; ask dad;	40	

H. D. Phillips, defendant in the foregoing action, says that the promissory note set forth in the petition was given to plaintiff on condition that plaintiff would deliver to defendant on the 21st day of February, 1941, twelve (12) NEWTONE RADIOS at defendant's place of business, 101 West Fourth Street, Cincinnati, Ohio, which defendant was then and there willing to accept; but said plaintiff then and there failed to deliver said radios and still refuses to deliver the same or any part thereof, and the consideration for said promissory note has failed, and the same should be ordered returned to this defendant.

Sworn to before me and subscribed in my presence this 30th day of October, 1941.

_____

_____
Notary Public

EXERCISE 171

PETITION FOR SPECIFIC PERFORMANCE OF CONTRACT

Directions. Type one copy with double spacing. The description of the real estate should be typed with single spacing. Use the current date.

COURT OF COMMON PLEAS, HAMILTON COUNTY, OHIO

ARTHUR W. LANG,
4430 South Cummings Ave.,
Cincinnati, Ohio,
    Plaintiff

vs.

JACOB S. DURANT,
12 Lincoln Parkway,
Cincinnati, Ohio,
    Defendant

No. ....

PETITION FOR SPECIFIC PERFORMANCE OF CONTRACT

Plaintiff says that at the times hereinafter named the defendant was and is now the owner in fee simple of the following described real estate, to-wit:

Situated in the city of Cincinnati, county of Hamilton, and state of Ohio, and being known, numbered, and designated as Lot fifty (50) on the plat of Brookwood First Subdivision, as per plat thereof recorded in Plat Book 30, page 56, of the records of Hamilton County, Ohio.

That on the 12th day of September, 1936, the plaintiff and defendant entered into a written contract and lease whereby the plaintiff leased said real estate and premises from defendant for the term of four years from the 15th day of October, 1936, at the annual rental of fifteen hundred dollars ($1,500), payable in equal monthly installments of one hundred twenty-five dollars ($125), on the 10th day of each month in advance, that said contract and lease was duly acknowledged by the parties, and recorded in Volume 292 at page 1364 of the lease records of said Hamilton County, Ohio, a copy of which lease is hereto attached, filed herewith, and marked "Exhibit A."

Plaintiff says that said contract and lease contains a provision whereby plaintiff was given the right and option to purchase said premises from defendant at the end of the third year of said term for the sum and purchase price of ten thousand dollars ($10,000), and to assume and pay as a part of said purchase price the amount of any valid mortgage or mortgages that may exist on said real estate and premises at the end of said third year on condition that plaintiff keep the terms of said lease as to the payments of rent as in said lease specified, and notify defendant of his election to purchase said real estate and premises thirty days prior to the end of said third year of said term; thereupon said defendant agreed to execute and deliver to plaintiff his warranty deed with release of dower for said real estate and premises.

Reaches to *e, n, t*

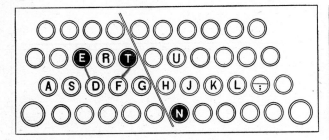

Illustration No. 17 — Reaches to e and **n**

Use a full sheet of paper for this practice. Your margins are set for the right length line.

The uniform method of initiating the new reach will be as follows:

1. Study the illustration.
2. Watch your finger make the movement from the typing position to the new key to be controlled.
3. Close your eyes and practice the reach several times.
4. Type the experimental practice line.

The letter *e* is controlled by the *d finger.* Lift the *f finger* slightly to give the controlling *d finger* complete freedom in making the reach.

Pull the finger quickly toward the palm of the hand after the stroke has been made.

ded ed he ded ed he he she ded he she

The letter *n* is below and slightly to the left of the *j* location and it is controlled by the *j finger.* Move the *j finger* slightly to the left in making this reach to *n.*

Avoid change of hand position and arm or elbow movement.

jnj nj an jnj jn an an and jnj an and

Illustration No. 18 — Reach to **t**

The *f finger* controls *t.* Straighten the finger slightly and strike the center of the key.

If the fingers are in proper position, you will make the reach to *t* without hand movement.

ftf ftf tf the ftf the ftf the ftf the

STRAIGHTENING AND REMOVING THE PAPER

When it is necessary to straighten the paper, grasp it with the forefinger and the thumb of each hand and square the edges of the paper. In order to do this, use the paper release (No. 23). Follow the instructions given below for the typewriter that you are using.

UNDERWOOD. Partially depress the paper release with the heel of the right hand.

ROYAL and WOODSTOCK. Pull paper release forward with the little finger of the right hand.

REMINGTON and NOISELESS MACHINES. Push back the paper release by using the backs of the second and third fingers of the left hand.

L C SMITH. Pull the paper release forward with the little finger of the left hand.

After straightening the paper, return the paper release to its regular position.

To remove the paper, operate the paper release. Remove the paper with the hand not controlling the paper release.

three hundred dollars ($300), with interest thereon at the rate of six per cent (6%) per annum from the fourteenth day of February, 1941.

_____
Attorney for Plaintiff

The State of Ohio   )
                     : ss
County of Hamilton   )

    Basil D. Wingate, being first duly sworn, states that he is the attorney of record for the plaintiff herein, and that this pleading is founded on a written instrument for the payment of money which is in affiant's possession, and that the facts and allegations contained therein are true, as he verily believes.

_____

    Sworn to before me and subscribed in my presence this ____20th____ day of ____October____, 1941__.

_____
Notary Public

Illustration No. 90—Petition on Note (Concluded)

EXERCISE 170
ANSWER OF DEFENDANT

Directions. H. D. Phillips, the defendant in the petition on a promissory note (see Exercise 164), filed his answer to said petition alleging failure of consideration. Type one copy with double spacing.

IN THE MUNICIPAL COURT OF CINCINNATI,

HAMILTON COUNTY, OHIO

MARSHALL RADIO CORPORATION, 16 Marshall Boulevard, Cincinnati, Ohio, Plaintiff	) :) :)	No. 1062
vs.	:)	
H. D. PHILLIPS, doing business as PHILLIPS RADIO SHOPPE, 101 West Fourth Street, Cincinnati, Ohio, Defendant	:) :) :	ANSWER OF DEFENDANT

Directions. 1. Operate the line-space lever an extra time to set off the drill from the preceding practice.

2. Type this drill twice on the same sheet of paper that you used for the preceding experimental practice.

STROKES

ded ed he he ded he she led he ded he she	41
jnj an jnj an and jnj and and fun hen and	41
he ran; he and she ran; she had run far;	40
ftf the the ftf the let ftf let jnj net	39
he us he an he the he she an and he the	39

(Space once after a semicolon.)

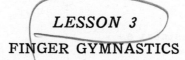

LESSON 3

FINGER GYMNASTICS   *1 minute*

You need flexible fingers for rapid and accurate typing. A minute or two of finger-gymnastic practice each day will help you to develop good control of your fingers. Begin with the drills pictured and described below:

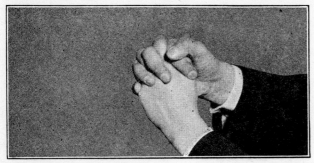

Drill 1. Interlace the fingers of the two hands and wring the hands, rubbing the heels of the palms together.

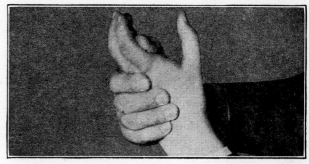

Drill 2. Rub the palms of the hands vigorously; then flex the fingers by closing and opening them a few times.

RECONSTRUCTION PRACTICE   *5 minutes*

Explanation. The reconstruction practice at the beginning of each practice period will aid you in getting the right mind-set for the work that will follow. Type each reconstruction practice with even rhythm and with attention to a quick stroke and release of the key.

Directions. 1. Check to see that the paper guide is placed 2 points below 0 on the scale; this will give 40 as the centering point for pica- and 50 as the centering point for elite-type machines.

2. Move the carriage so the position indicator is at 20 for a pica-type machine or 30 for an elite-type machine.

3. Move the stop for the left margin along the scale toward the carriage-position indicator until it is stopped by the mechanism of the indicator.

4. Move the stop for the right margin to the end of the scale.

5. Set the line-space regulator for double spacing.

6. Insert a sheet of paper. Have a top margin of three or four lines. Type the drill from the book or from the dictation of your teacher. Before typing, study the technique emphasis.

EXERCISE 169

PETITION ON NOTE

Directions. Type with double spacing one copy of the following form. Use the current date. Provide a backing sheet and type the indorsement as it is shown in Illustration No. 82 on page 219.

IN THE MUNICIPAL COURT OF CINCINNATI,

HAMILTON COUNTY, OHIO

MARSHALL RADIO CORPORATION,
16 Marshall Boulevard,
Cincinnati, Ohio,
    Plaintiff

No. _____

  vs.

H. D. PHILLIPS, doing business as
PHILLIPS RADIO SHOPPE,
101 West Fourth Street
Cincinnati, Ohio,
    Defendant

PETITION ON NOTE

Plaintiff states that there is due and owing to it from the defendant the sum of three hundred dollars ($300), with interest at the rate of six per cent (6%) per annum from the fourteenth day of February, 1941, upon a note, a copy of which, with all credits and endorsements thereon, is as follows:

$300.00   February 14   1941

_____ Six months _____ after date ___ I ___ promise to pay to

the order of _____ Marshall Radio Corporation _____

Three hundred and no/100 - Dollars

Payable at _____ Merchants Trust Company, Cincinnati, Ohio _____

Value received with interest at six per cent (6%) per annum.

No. _____ Due _____   (SIGNED) H. D. PHILLIPS

Plaintiff further states that there are no credits or endorsements thereon.

WHEREFORE, plaintiff prays for judgment against defendant in said sum of

Illustration No. 90—Petition on Note

[232]

Technique Emphasis. 1. Hit the center of the key with the ball of the fingertip and release the key quickly.

2. Keep the fingers curved.

3. Hold the arms practically motionless.

4. Make each reach without changing the hand alignment with the keyboard.

5. Bring the finger toward the palm of the hand as soon as it has delivered the blow to the center of the key.

```
u u r r ur ur fur j u ju jug jug fur fur

frf juj fgf jhj fur fur jug fur jug fur

fur jug hag ded jnj ded jnj she and she

ed he he she nj an and tf the the let
```

TECHNIQUE PRACTICE 3
7 minutes

Directions. 1. Operate the line-space lever twice; this will separate the preceding lines from the lines of the technique practice.

2. Type the drill once.

	STROKES
`ftf jnj ftf jnj ded juj fgf jhj ded jnj`	39
`ed he he she nj an he an and he she and`	39
`he th the the an and the she and he the`	39
`he she fur he the let an and the and let`	40
`he ran; he and she ran; she had run far;`	40

EXERCISE 3
10 minutes

Directions. 1. Operate the line-space lever twice.

2. Type the exercise once.

	STROKES
`she had fun; he ran; he ran and she sang;`	41
`she has a fur; he has a rug; he had a jug;`	42
`he had a sale; he had a sale near a lake;`	41
`ask the lad; the lad has the fan and fur;`	41
`he had a hard fall here; the lad fell;`	38
`she heard that he had land near the lake;`	41
`he heard the lark at the lake as usual;`	39

dorsement for deposit as cash or for collection in the said bank,

3. To accept all drafts or bills of exchange that may be drawn on me;
giving and granting unto the said attorney full power and authority to do and perform all and every act and thing whatsoever, requisite and necessary to be done in and about the premises, as fully to all intents and purposes as I might or could do, if personally present, with full power of substitution and revocation; hereby ratifying and confirming all that the said attorney or his substitute shall lawfully do, or cause to be done, by virtue thereof.

IN WITNESS WHEREOF, I have hereunto set my hand this .... day of .... in the year one thousand nine hundred and ....

_____

Signed and acknowledged in the presence of us:

_____

_____

_____

_____

The State of Illinois }
County of Clark } ss.

I, John M. Goodman, notary public, do hereby certify that Morris Edwards, personally known to me to be the same person whose name is subscribed to the foregoing instrument, appeared before me this day in person and acknowledged that he signed, sealed, and delivered the said

instrument as his free and voluntary act, for the uses and purposes therein set forth.

Given under my hand and official seal, this .... day of ....,
A. D. 19....

_____

Notary Public

Know All Men by These Presents:

That I, Morris Edwards, of the city of Marshall, county of
Clark, state of Illinois
have made, constituted, and appointed, and by these presents do make, constitute,
and appoint, J. Edgar Lee, of the city of Marshall, county of
Clark, state of Illinois, my
true and lawful attorney , for me and in my name, place, and stead,
to act as follows in connection with my business of general merchandising
at Marshall:

1. To draw checks against my account in the First National Bank,

2. To indorse notes, checks, drafts, or bills of exchange that may require my indorsement for deposit as cash or for collection in the said bank,

3. To accept all drafts or bills of exchange that may be drawn on me;

giving and granting unto the said attorney full power and authority to do and perform all and every act and thing whatsoever, requisite and necessary to be done in and about the premises, as fully to all intents and purposes as I might or could do, if personally present, with full power of substitution and revocation; hereby ratifying and confirming all that the said attorney or his substitute shall lawfully do, or cause to be done, by virtue hereof.

In Witness Whereof, I have hereunto set my hand this twelfth day of June in the year one thousand nine hundred and forty

Signed and acknowledged
in the presence of us:

_____ | _____
_____ |
_____ |

The State of ILLINOIS County of CLARK ss.
I, John M. Goodman, notary public, do hereby certify that
Morris Edwards, personally known to me to be the same person whose name is subscribed to the foregoing instrument, appeared before me this day in person and acknowledged that he signed, sealed and delivered the said instrument as his free and voluntary act, for the uses and purposes therein set forth.
Given under my hand and official seal, this twelfth day of
June A. D. 19 40.

_____
Notary Public

Illustration No. 89—Power of Attorney

BUDGET XXI

It is customary to type three copies of all legal pleadings. Frequently more than three copies are required. In your school work, however, one copy will be sufficient. Be careful in your typing; check all completed work.

Reaches to *i*, *v*, . (period)

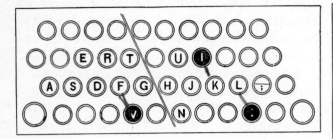

Illustration No. 19 — Reaches to i and v

Illustration No. 20 — Reach to . (period)

The keyboard chart is given with each location practice so you can quickly see the relation between the new keys to be controlled and the typing position of the controlling fingers. All keys that have been taught in preceding lessons appear on the chart; but the new controls are shown on a black background for emphasis.

Look at the chart when you are identifying the exact location of the new key to be learned, and determine the exact finger pathway that must be used in making the new reach. You will not need to refer to the chart frequently as you type. If you feel that this is necessary, you will be permitting the chart to become a crutch instead of a help. Once you have initiated the reach and the finger has made its pathway movement, it will be unnecessary for you to look at your fingers or at the keyboard chart in order to have the finger make the right movement. Hold your hand in correct alignment with the keyboard, *think* the letter, and the finger will make the right movement without the necessity of your looking at the chart.

To initiate the new reaches in this and subsequent lessons, use the uniform method that was given with Location Practice 2 and that is repeated below:

1. Study the illustration.

2. Watch your finger make the movement from the typing position to the new key to be controlled.

3. Close your eyes and practice the reach several times.

4. Type the experimental practice line.

The letter *i*, controlled by the *k* finger, is above the letter *k*.

In making the reach to *i*, raise the *j finger* slightly to give greater freedom to the controlling *k finger*.

Keep the fingers curved and poised lightly in typing position. When the reach is made, return the controlling finger to typing position quickly.

`kik kik kid fir his kid fir his this is`

The letter *v*, controlled by the *f finger*, is below and to the right of *f*.

Make the reach without moving the elbow and without changing the hand position.

`fvf fvf van fvf five five give five have`

The period, which is beneath and slightly to the right of the *l* key, is controlled by the *l finger*.

Hold the little finger in its typing position, lift the other fingers of the hand slightly, and strike the period without changing the hand position.

`l.l l.l fvf kik l.l frf l.l fvf l.l l.l`

not to use said premises or any part thereof in violation of any law relating to intoxicating liquors; and at the expiration of this lease, to surrender said premises in as good condition as they now are or may be put by said lessor, reasonable wear and unavoidable casualties, condemnation or appropriation, excepted. Upon nonpayment of any of said rent for ten days after it shall become due and without demand made therefor, or the bankruptcy or insolvency of lessee or assigns, or the appointment of a receiver or trustee of the property of lessee or assigns, or if this lease pass to any person or persons by operation of law, or the breach of any of the other agreements herein contained, the lessor may terminate this lease and re-enter and repossess said premises.

SAID LESSOR AGREES (said lessee having performed his obligations under this lease) that said lessee shall quietly hold and occupy said premises during said term without any hindrance or molestation by said lessor, her heirs, or any person lawfully claiming under them.

Signed this ...... day of ...., A. D. 19....

_____

_____

In the presence of:

_____

_____

State of Minnesota ⎰
County of Hennepin ⎱ ss.

This day, before me, a notary public in and for said county, personally came Elizabeth Seanor and William C. Nickol, the parties to the foregoing Lease, and acknowledged the signing thereof to be their voluntary act.

WITNESS my hand and official seal this...... day of............, A.D. 19....

_____
                        Notary Public

EXERCISE 168

A formal written document in which an agent is appointed is called a *power of attorney*. A power of attorney need not be acknowledged unless it is to be recorded.

The appointment of an agent may sometimes be implied from the acts and conduct of the principal. If a person, knowingly and without dissent, permits another to act as his agent, or, if by affirmative action he leads others reasonably to believe that a particular person is his agent, he will be held liable as a principal to third persons who have relied upon the apparent agency.

When a person purports to act as the agent of another, without real or apparent authority, or when one who is really an agent exceeds his authority, he does not bind the person for whom he assumes to act, unless the supposed principal later expressly assents to the act, or impliedly assents, as, for example, by knowingly accepting the benefits of the act.

The power of attorney illustrated here authorizes one person to indorse and accept negotiable instruments for another.

KNOW ALL MEN BY THESE PRESENTS:

THAT I, Morris Edwards, of the city of Marshall, county of Clark, state of Illinois, have made, constituted, and appointed, and by these presents do make, constitute, and appoint, J. Edgar Lee, of the city of Marshall, county of Clark, state of Illinois, my true and lawful attorney, for me and in my name, place, and stead, to act as follows in connection with my business of general merchandising at Marshall:

1. To draw checks against my account in the First National Bank,

2. To indorse notes, checks, drafts, or bills of exchange that may require my in-

LOCATION DRILL 10 minutes

Directions. 1. Operate the line-space lever an extra time to set off the drill from the preceding practice.
2. Type the drill twice.

STROKES

kik kid kik fir is this if if it is if 38

if it is an if us it is an if it is if 38

fvf fvf five have give have fvf five give 41

give have five live dive vine five river 40

kik fvf kik l.l l.l fvf l.l kik l.l l.l 39

SHIFTING FOR CAPITALS 5 minutes

Explanation. To type a capital controlled by a finger of the right hand, depress the left shift key (No. 27) with the *a finger*. To type a capital controlled by a finger of the left hand, depress the right shift key (No. 28) with the *; finger*.

Illustration No. 21 — Control of the Left Shift Key   Illustration No. 22 — Control of the Right Shift Key

Directions. 1. *Stretch* the little finger to the shift key. Keep the other fingers hovering near the typing position.
2. Hold the shift key down until the key for the capital has been struck and released; then release the shift key and return the controlling finger immediately to its typing position.
3. Depress the left shift key with the *a finger* (lines 1 and 4); the right shift key with the *; finger* (lines 2 and 3).
4. Type the drill once.

STROKES

Ja Ja Jane Jane Ja Jake Jake Jane 33

F; F; Flag Flag Alf Alf Sue Alf 31

(Space twice after a period at the end of a sentence.)

Alf has a jug. Sue and he sang. 32

He is here. Jane and he are here. 34

subscriber, a notary public in and for said county, personally came Walter C. Westwood, and acknowledged the within instrument to be his voluntary act and deed.

IN TESTIMONY WHEREOF, I have hereunto subscribed my name, and affixed my official seal, on the day and year last aforesaid.

_____
Notary Public

EXERCISE 167

The agreement that establishes the relation of landlord and tenant is known as a *lease*. Consequently, the landlord is often called the *lessor;* and the tenant, the *lessee*. A lease may be oral or written if there is no statute prescribing a particular form. Leases that are to exist for periods longer than a specified time, however, are usually required to be in writing. In some states a lease must be in writing if it is to run for three years or more. In other states a lease for one year or more must be written.

A particular form of language is generally not necessary in a lease. Any words that express the intention of the persons creating the particular tenancy are sufficient. The lease, however, should state in plain language all material terms of the agreement so that a misunderstanding may not arise later. A formal lease usually contains:

1. The date of execution.
2. An identification of the parties.
3. A description of the property.
4. The length of the period during which the tenancy is to exist.
5. The amount of the rent and the manner of paying the rent.
6. A statement of covenants and conditions.
7. The signatures of the parties.

In some states leases for specified periods of time must be under seal, witnessed, acknowledged, and recorded.

Illustration No. 88—Lease

THIS LEASE WITNESSETH:

THAT Elizabeth Seanor does hereby lease to William C. Nickol the premises situate in the city of Minneapolis in the county of Hennepin and state of Minnesota, described as follows: Dwelling House, No. 3979 Braxton Street, Minneapolis, Minnesota, with the appurtenances thereto, for the term of two years commencing May 1, 1940, at a rental of Ninety (90) dollars per month payable monthly.

SAID LESSEE AGREES to pay said rent, unless said premises shall be destroyed or rendered untenantable by fire or other unavoidable accident; not to commit or suffer waste; not to use said premises, or any part thereof, or permit the sale of his interest therein by legal process, without the written consent of said lessor;

LESSON 4

FINGER GYMNASTICS

1 minute

Drill 3. Clench the fingers, bending them at the first and second joints only. Hold this position for a short time; then extend the fingers, relaxing the muscles of the fingers and the hand. Repeat the movements slowly several times. Exercise both hands at the same time.

RECONSTRUCTION PRACTICE

6 minutes

Directions. 1. Move the carriage so the position indicator is at 20 for the pica-type machine or 30 for an elite-type machine. Slide the stop for the left margin toward the carriage-position indicator until it is stopped by the mechanism of the carriage-position indicator.

2. Move the stop for the right margin to the end of the scale.

3. Set the line-space regulator for double spacing.

```
rf uj ed nj tf ik vf hj ed .l .l tf nj ik

u r ur fur h e he he she he t h the the

n j an and i k if it is if v f five five

Jane is in.  Alf and Sue have the rug.
```

(Space twice after a period at the end of a sentence.)

TYPING POSTURE

3 minutes

Explanation. When you are typing, sit in an alert manner and let the body lean slightly forward from the hips with the back away from the chair. When you remove your hands from the typewriter, take the at-rest or relaxed posture, with your back resting against the chair.

Illustration No. 23 — Position at the Typewriter

A *bill of sale* transfers the title to goods. It is valuable evidence of what has been done. A document of this kind is particularly desirable when the goods have not been actually delivered to the buyer.

Know All Men by These Presents:

That I, Walter C. Westwood, of Knoxville, Tennessee, in consideration of the sum of Three Hundred Dollars ($300) to me paid by M. S. Barton, residing at 2246 Mound Street in the city of Knoxville, state of Tennessee, the receipt whereof is hereby acknowledged, have bargained, sold, granted, and conveyed, and by these presents do bargain, sell, grant, and convey, unto the said M. S. Barton, his executors, administrators, and assigns, one Chrysler coach, manufactured by Chrysler Corporation, manufacturer's number 7555425, motor number C18-25579, H. P. 27.34

To Have and to Hold the same unto the said M. S. Barton, his executors, administrators, and assigns forever.

And I for myself and for my heirs, executors, and administrators do hereby covenant with the said M. S. Barton, his executors, administrators, and assigns, that I am the true and lawful owner of the said described goods hereby sold, and have full power to sell and convey the same; that the title, so conveyed, is clear, free, and unencumbered; and further, that I do warrant and will defend the same against all claims of all persons whomsoever.

In Witness Whereof, I have hereunto set my hand this sixteenth day of September in the year of our Lord one thousand nine hundred and forty-one

Signed and delivered in the presence of

____________________ (SEAL)

____________________ (SEAL)

The State of Tennessee, County of Knox, ss.

Be It Remembered, That on the sixteenth day of September in the year of our Lord one thousand nine hundred and forty-one before me, the subscriber, a notary public in and for said county, personally came Walter C. Westwood the grantor in the foregoing Deed, and acknowledged the instrument to be his voluntary act and deed.

In Testimony Whereof, I have hereunto subscribed my name, and affixed my official seal, on the day and year last aforesaid.

____
Notary Public

Illustration No. 87—Bill of Sale

KNOW ALL MEN BY THESE PRESENTS:

THAT I, Walter C. Westwood, of Knoxville, Tennessee, in consideration of the sum of Three Hundred Dollars ($300) to me paid by M. S. Barton, residing at 2246 Mound Street in the city of Knoxville, state of Tennessee, the receipt whereof is hereby acknowledged, have bargained, sold, granted, and conveyed, and by these presents do bargain, sell, grant, and convey, unto the said M. S. Barton, his executors, administrators, and assigns, one Chrysler coach, manufactured by Chrysler Corporation, manufacturer's number 7555425, motor number C18-25579, H.P. 27.34.

TO HAVE AND TO HOLD the same unto the said M. S. Barton, his executors, administrators, and assigns forever.

AND I for myself and for my heirs, executors, and administrators do hereby covenant with the said M. S. Barton, his executors, administrators, and assigns, that I am the true and lawful owner of the said described goods hereby sold, and have full power to sell and convey the same; that the title, so conveyed, is clear, free, and unencumbered; and further, that I do warrant and will defend the same against all claims of all persons whomsoever.

IN WITNESS WHEREOF, I have hereunto set my hand this ...... day of .... in the year one thousand nine hundred and ....

____

____

Signed and acknowledged in the presence of us:

____

____

____

____

The State of Tennessee }
County of Knox } ss.

BE IT REMEMBERED, That on the .... day of .... in the year of our Lord one thousand nine hundred and ...., before me, the

CHECK-UP ON TYPING POSTURE

Directions. 1. Place the chair so the front of your body will be 8 to 10 inches from the base of the typewriter and slightly to the right of the center of the keyboard.

2. Place the textbook at the right of the typewriter. (If you are operating a typewriter with a right carriage throw, place the textbook at the left of the machine.)

3. Sit well back on the chair. Lean slightly forward from the hips.

4. Let the arms hang easily at your sides. If the little fingers are short, hold the elbows away from the body; if they are of normal proportion to the other fingers, hold the elbows near (not against) the body.

5. There should be a slope from the back of the hands to the elbow. The position calls for a distance of approximately 7 or 8 inches between the top of the knee, when the typist is seated, and the under frame of the typewriter.

6. Curve the fingers until the tips are approximately 1½ inches from the palm of the hand.

7. Hold the right thumb above, not on, the space bar. The left thumb is not used in operating the keyboard. Keep it out of the way of the fingers and the right thumb.

8. Place the feet on the floor in front of the chair, one foot slightly in advance of the other. This posture aids in maintaining body balance.

TECHNIQUE PRACTICE 4

7 minutes

Directions. 1. Operate the line-space lever twice; this will separate the preceding lines from the lines of this practice.
2. Type the drill once.

	STROKES
he the she an and he the then than then	39
if it is he us an it is as in he if it	38
this king five live five dine five this	39
Hal and she sang. Hal gave Jane a ring.	40
Alf has fine land; he lives near a lake.	40

(Space twice after a period at the end of a sentence.)

EXERCISE 4

10 minutes

Directions. Type the exercise once.

	STROKES
I had the fur. I had the fur and the rug.	42
Jane and I have the fine line and fish net.	43
Sue is fine. She lives near Dan and Alfred.	44
He had a gun. Jane ran. He heard her run.	43
Jake heard Jane as she sang and laughed.	40
Frank had Nan and the lad send the file.	40
He heard a lark sing near this fine lake.	41

hereby acknowledged, do hereby GRANT, BARGAIN, SELL AND CONVEY to the said Robert Reilly, his heirs and assigns forever, Lot Twelve (12), Block Six (6), in the Rosedale Subdivision of Norfolk, Norfolk County, Virginia, and all the estate, title, and interest of the said Grantors, either in law or in equity, of, in and to the said premises; together with all the privileges and appurtenances to the same belonging, and all the rents, issues and profits thereof; to have and to hold the same to the only proper use of the said Grantee, his heirs and assigns forever;

AND the said Larry J. Boothe and Vivian Boothe, for themselves and for their heirs, executors and administrators, do hereby covenant with the said Robert Reilly, his heirs and assigns, that they are the true and lawful owners of the said premises, and have full power to convey the same; that the title, so conveyed, is clear, free and unencumbered; and further, that they do warrant and will defend the same against any claim or claims of all persons whomsoever.

IN WITNESS WHEREOF, the said Larry J. Boothe and Vivian Boothe have hereunto set their hands this ...... day of .... in the year of our Lord one thousand nine hundred and.........

_____

_____

Signed and acknowledged in the presence of us:

_____

_____

The State of Virginia
County of Norfolk } ss.

BE IT REMEMBERED, That on the .... day of .... in the year of our Lord one thousand nine hundred and ...., before me, the subscriber, a notary public in and for said county, personally came Larry J. Boothe and Vivian Boothe, the grantors in the foregoing Deed, and acknowledged the signing thereof to be their voluntary act for the uses and purposes therein mentioned.

IN TESTIMONY WHEREOF, I have hereunto subscribed my name, and affixed my official seal, on the day and year last aforesaid.

_____

Notary Public

EXERCISE 166

Sales of goods constitute the most common form of business transactions. It is virtually a daily experience of each of us to buy or to sell some article. The relation of vendor and vendee is involved in the buying of a piece of candy, a book or a pencil, clothes, food, real estate, or an automobile.

The *Uniform Sales Act,* a statute prepared by a commission for the purpose of getting uniformity in the rules and principles applicable to sales in the United States, has been adopted by a majority of the state legislatures. The other states will probably soon enact similar legislation, and thus bring about substantial uniformity in the laws applicable to sales.

A sale of goods is an agreement whereby one party transfers the property in goods (the title) to another for a consideration called the price. The transferor is known as the *seller* or *vendor,* and the transferee is called the *buyer* or *vendee.*

A distinction is made between a sale of goods and a contract to sell goods. The latter is an agreement whereby the seller promises to transfer the property in goods to the buyer for a consideration called the price. As both a sale of goods and a contract to sell goods are based upon valid agreements, they contain the essential elements of a contract.

LOCATION PRACTICE 4

Reaches to *o, c, m*

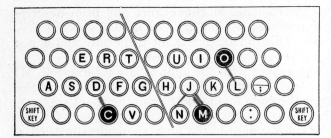

Illustration No. 26 — Reach to m

Illustration No. 24 — Reach to o

Illustration No. 25 — Reach to c

The *l* finger controls *o*. In making the reach, raise the *j* and *k fingers* slightly to give the controlling *l finger* greater freedom.

lol lol lol old fold gold fold told old

The *d finger* controls *c*. Lift the *f finger* slightly so that the controlling finger will have freedom of movement.

Hold the *a finger* on the *a* key, but let the other fingers of the left hand move slightly with the *d finger*. Make the reach without twisting the elbow or wrist.

dcd dcd cad can dcd cut cot dcd cad cot

The letter *m* is controlled by the *j finger*. Make the reach without twisting the hand or moving the other fingers from typing position.

jmj jmj mad rim vim dim ham some move

LOCATION DRILL

10 minutes

Directions. Operate the line-space lever an extra time to set off the drill from the preceding practice. Type the drill twice.

	STROKES
he the them them or for form form them	38
came come home move deck dock sick such	39
I can go. I can go for them. I can go.	40
She has gone for it. He gave cash for it.	42
Joe had the old rod and the net for her.	40

BUDGET XX

The exercises in this budget contain forms of instruments of conveyance and brief descriptions of the forms. Type the descriptions of the forms on plain paper. Use double spacing.

Each legal form is shown in a small illustration. This illustration is for form only and is not to be used as copy. The complete copy for each form is given in large type.

If blank legal forms are available, fill in the blank spaces with the appropriate information. If blank legal forms are not available, type all the copy on legal paper. In that case, follow the style of the printed form, but do not attempt to type the copy line for line or in the exact arrangement used on the printed form.

Use the current date. In Exercise 165, type the indorsement in the form shown in Illustration No. 82 on page 219 for the warranty deed.

EXERCISE 165

In the transfer of the title to real property, certain formalities are required by law. Because of the technical and precise rules governing the transfer of real property, the details of conveyancing should be entrusted to a person who is skilled in real-estate law. Everyone should possess, however, an appreciation of the problems involved in a transaction of this nature. These problems generally involve the contents of a deed of conveyance, the execution of the deed, and the rights of the parties to the deed and of third parties.

A transfer of the title to real property by means of a properly executed written instrument is called a *deed*. The instrument by means of which the conveyance is made is also known by this term. The one who transfers the property is called the *grantor*. The one to whom it is transferred is called the *grantee*.

There are two kinds of deeds. *A quitclaim deed* purports to convey merely the interest that the grantor may have in the property, and nothing more. The grantee assumes the risk that the grantor may not have a good title or that he may not have any title at all. *A warranty deed* not only purports to convey the specified interest of the grantor, but also contains stipulations in which one or both of the parties covenant or warrant that certain facts are true or that certain things will be done. This type of deed is ordinarily used in conveying the title to real property.

Illustration No. 86—Warranty Deed

KNOW ALL MEN BY THESE PRESENTS:

THAT Larry J. Boothe and Vivian Boothe, his wife, in consideration of One Thousand (1,000) Dollars to them paid by Robert Reilly, the receipt whereof is

LESSON 5

FINGER GYMNASTICS

Drill 4. Hands open, fingers wide, muscles tense; then close the fingers into a tight "fist," with the thumb on top. Relax the fingers as you straighten them; then repeat the movement several times.

RECONSTRUCTION PRACTICE

5 minutes

Directions. 1. Set the left margin stop at 20 for a pica-type or 30 for an elite-type machine.
2. Use double spacing.

```
rf hj ed nj tf uj vf ik cd ol as mj gf ;l

uu rr nj nn us an us an ik tf ik tf it it

ol ol of of mj mm am of am do it is am go

dcd dcd cad can jmj rim ham dcd cad rim
```

TECHNIQUE PRACTICE 5

12 minutes

Directions. Operate the line-space lever twice.* Type the drill twice.

	STROKES
to go he us do so if it an or is of he an	41
he the them them or for for form form the	41
I can go. I can go for them. I can go.	40
Sam can not go for it. He had to leave.	40
Jack lives near the lake. I am going there.	44

(Easy-word drill.)

EXERCISE 5

10 minutes

Directions. Type the exercise once.

	STROKES
I can do this much in the right manner.	39
Hal and I can go for them. Hal is here.	40
Dale did not see Sam or hear him sing.	38
Some of the men like to ride in the train.	42
I can do this right if I think I can.	37
He came here to make me do this just so.	40
Vera cannot go to the train for the men.	40

---

* Hereafter when more than one part of a lesson is typed on a single sheet of paper, it will be understood that the **parts** will be separated by two extra spaces and instructions to operate the line-space lever twice will not be repeated.

Real Estate of said estate is in all respects just and true according to the best of her knowledge.

Address_____

Sworn to and subscribed before me this 1st day of June, A. D. 1941.

_____
Probate Judge and Ex-Officio Clerk

By_____
Deputy Clerk

Illustration No. 85—Final Account (Concluded)

EXERCISE 164
AGREEMENT

Directions. Type one copy with double spacing. Use the current date. Follow same general form as for Exercise 161.

AGREEMENT

THIS AGREEMENT, made this ...7th... day of ....*March*...., 194.9, between **J. L. MORRISON,** hereafter called the first party, and **H. W. LANGLEY,** hereafter called the second party, both of Dayton, Ohio,

WITNESSETH:

WHEREAS, said first party is at the present time engaged in the operation of an Automobile Stage Line for the transportation of passengers between Dayton, Ohio, and Cincinnati, Ohio, said operation having been started prior to May 1, 1917; and

WHEREAS, said first party desires to sell said operative rights in said Stage Line, and said second party desires to purchase said operative rights;

NOW IT IS, THEREFORE, AGREED that said first party will sell to said second party the said operative rights in said Automobile Stage Line, subject to the authorization of the Railroad Commission of the state of Ohio, a petition for which authorization has this day been filed by said parties with said Railroad Commission.

And said second party hereby agrees to purchase of said first party the said operative rights in said Automobile Stage Line, and to pay therefor the sum of One Dollar ($1.00) and other good and valuable consideration.

It is expressly understood and agreed between the parties hereto that the assignment from said first party to said second party of said operative rights, executed contemporaneously herewith, shall not be valid until said Railroad Commission has made its order authorizing the said transfer.

IN WITNESS WHEREOF, the said parties have hereunto set their hands and affixed their seals the day and year first above written.

_____ (Seal)
_____ (Seal)

Signed, sealed, and delivered in the presence of

_____
_____

LOCATION PRACTICE 5

Reaches to *w*, , (comma), *?* (interrogation point)

Illustration No. 27 — Reach to w

Use the uniform method that was given with Location Practice 2, page 8.

The letter *w* is above *s* and is controlled by the *s* finger. Make a direct reach from *s* to *w*. Let the *d* and *f* fingers move slightly when the *s* finger makes this reach; do not move elbow.

```
sws sws how sow now sws low how sow sws
```

The comma is below and somewhat to the right of *k* and is controlled by the *k* finger. In reaching to the comma, lift the *j* finger slightly to give freedom to the controlling *k* finger.

```
k,k if he is, k,k if so, if, therefore.
```

Illustration No. 28 — Reach to , (comma)

The *?* is the shift of the last key at the right of the first row of keys and is controlled by the *;* finger.

> On some typewriters, the *?* is the shift of the comma key.

Hold the hands steady as you shift and make the reach to the *?*.

Illustration No. 29 — Reach to ? (interrogation point)

```
;?; ;?; Is he going?  Can he work well?
```

LOCATION DRILL

10 minutes

Directions. Type the drill twice.

	STROKES
sws sws now how sws low how sws mow vow	39
wish with wish vows vows when with wish	39
He can go, too, when we leave, can he not?	42
Most of us work well if we think we can.	40
Does he work well? I work well, I think.	41

(Space once after the comma.)

(Space twice after a question mark used at the end of a sentence.)

[17]

Date		Voucher No.	Receipts	Disbursements
1940				
Dec. 7	Cash on hand per inventory		$6,370.45	
10	Taxes on real estate	1		$ 267.30
15	Rent from real estate		75.00	
20	Byron Memorial Hospital	2		295.98
1941				
Jan. 15	Rent from real estate		75.00	
15	W. T. Jones, appraiser's fee	3		3.00
15	G. M. Hock, appraiser's fee	4		3.00
15	J. A. Brady, appraiser's fee	5		3.00
20	Widow's first year's allowance	6		1,200.00
20	Surviving spouse's statutory allowance	7		1,200.00
Feb. 15	Rent from real estate		75.00	
Mar. 1	Street Assessment, Vr. 126870	8		52.40
6	Moore & Son, funeral expenses	9		450.00
15	Rent from real estate		75.00	
Apr. 10	Dr. Harold T. Watson	10		230.50
10	Dr. Paul S. Baum	11		175.00
15	Rent from real estate		75.00	
20	Treasurer of Hamilton County, inheritance tax	12		238.70
26	Daily Post, newspaper notices	13		2.75
May 10	Costs of administration	14		176.57
10	Ethel Morgan, executrix's fee	15		250.00
10	Wingate & Wingate, attorney's fee	16		250.00
15	Rent from real estate		75.00	
30	Residue to widow, Ethel Morgan	17		2,022.25
	TOTAL		$6,820.45	$6,820.45

Executrix of the Estate of Stanley
Morgan, Deceased

The State of Ohio   )
                      : ss
County of Hamilton)

Personally appeared before me, the undersigned, JUDGE OF THE PROBATE
COURT in and for said County, Ethel Morgan, executrix of the estate of
Stanley Morgan, deceased, who, upon oath, deposeth and saith, that the
annexed FINAL ACCOUNT of the Personal Property and also the income of the

Illustration No. 85—Final Account (Continued)

LESSON 6

FINGER GYMNASTICS

Drill 5. With the finger tips on the desk, extend one finger at a time as far as you can without moving the wrist. Pull the finger back toward the palm of the hand with a quick movement. Alternate the hands in this practice.

RECONSTRUCTION PRACTICE
6 minutes

Directions. 1. Set the left margin stop at 15 for a pica-type or 25 for an elite-type machine.
2. Use double spacing.

```
sws sws how now sws vow how sow now cow sws cow sws

edcd ujmj rfvf ik,k tfgf hjnj wsws ol.l cded ;?;

if he if he is to go an so am if it an it if we

such them wish turn with such wish firm then them
```

TECHNIQUE PRACTICE 6
7 minutes

Directions. Type the drill once.

	STROKES
wish form with form wish file such when work work	49
I can do the work. I can do this kind of work well.	52
All of us must give more thought to the work we do.	51
Can Will do the work? He can, if he works hard.	48
What we are means much more than what we have.	46

(Space twice after a question mark at the end of a sentence. Space once after a comma.)

TABULATOR-KEY CONTROL
5 minutes

Use the tabulator mechanism to indent for paragraphs, for special lines, and for materials to be typed in columns. Understand the use of the tabulator key or bar (No. 31), the tabulator stops (No. 33), and the tabulator set and release keys (Nos. 34 and 35).

Tab Set and Tab Clear Mechanism. Depress and hold down the tab clear key (No. 35) and move the carriage from left to right. (It is not necessary to move the carriage when the tab clear key releases all stops on the rack as is the case with the Woodstock typewriter.)

Move the carriage-position indicator to the desired writing point; depress the tab-set key (No. 34). This key automatically sets a stop at the rear of the typewriter.

Hand-Set Tabulator Mechanism. On some typewriters, the stops must be set by hand. To do this, clear the rack of all stops between the point at which the left margin ends and the point at which the first stop is to be set; then place the stops at the points desired for typing.

Tabulator Key or Bar. Locate the tabulator key or bar (No. 31). Study the illustration on the following page that shows the control of the key or bar on the typewriter you are using. When you depress the key or bar, hold it down until the carriage movement stops; then release and type. Understand the correct way to operate the tabulator key or bar, and you will add to the ease and speed of your work.

[18]

The State of Ohio)
                    : ss
County of Hamilton)

The above named Ethel Morgan being first duly sworn, says that the facts
stated and the allegations in the foregoing application contained, are true as
she verily believes.

_____

Sworn to before me and subscribed in my presence this 30th day of
November, 1940.

_____
                                                    Notary Public

Illustration No. 84—Application for Probate of Will (Concluded)

EXERCISE 163

FINAL ACCOUNT

Directions. It is necessary to prepare many forms during the administration of an estate. A typical form, however, is the final account which shows the amount of cash received and disbursed during the pendency of the estate proceedings. All claims included in this account must have been filed with the administrator (or administratrix) or executor (or executrix) and allowed by the probate court. Type one copy of the following final account.

IN THE PROBATE COURT,

HAMILTON COUNTY, OHIO

In the Matter of the   )
                                  :   No. 42756
    Estate of STANLEY MORGAN,   )
                                  :   FINAL ACCOUNT
        Deceased   )

Now comes Ethel Morgan, executrix of the estate of Stanley Morgan,
deceased, and submits the following as her final account of said estate:

Illustration No. 85—Final Account

Illustration No. 30 — Control of the Tab Bar

Illustration No. 31 — Control of Tab Key

MANIPULATION DRILL

You are to type the word *for* in three columns. Your score will be the number of words correctly typed and correctly placed in the columns.

Directions. 1. Adjust the marginal and tabulator stops as follows:

	PICA TYPE	ELITE TYPE
Marginal stop for left margin...	25	35
First tabulator stop	40	50
Second tabulator stop	60	70

2. When told to begin typing, type the word *for* at the left margin.

3. Depress and hold the tabulator key or bar until the carriage stops moving.

4. Type the word *for* again.

5. Depress the key or bar; after the carriage has moved to the third column, type the word *for* again.

6. Return the carriage with a quick wrist movement; start typing *for* in the columns. Continue the typing until time is called.

Checkup. Did you have all words correctly placed in columns? If not, you are probably not holding the tab key or bar down until the carriage has stopped moving.

EXERCISE 6   *10 minutes*

Directions. 1. Set the left margin stop at 15 for a pica-type or 25 for an elite-type machine and for double spacing.

2. Set a tabulator stop for a 5-space indention (20 for a pica-type or 30 for an elite-type machine).

3. Type the exercise once.

	STROKES
All of us want to do well in life. We can, if	47
we think right and work right. It is not enough to	99
work hard for a short time; we have to do our work	150
as well as we can week after week, month after month.	204
These sentences are the work that I must write now;	256
I must write them with ease and control. This I can	309
do if I write just as I think.	339

(Space once after a comma.)

[19]

IN THE PROBATE COURT,

HAMILTON COUNTY, OHIO

In the Matter of the

  Estate of STANLEY MORGAN,

    Deceased

)
:
)
:
)

No. _____

APPLICATION FOR PROBATE OF WILL

Your applicant respectfully represents that Stanley Morgan, late a resident of the city of Cincinnati, in said County, died on or about the 29th day of November, 1940, leaving an instrument in writing, herewith produced, purporting to be his last will and testament; that the said Stanley Morgan died leaving Ethel Morgan of the age of 40 years as his surviving spouse, who resides at 1104 Main Street, Cincinnati, Ohio, and the following named persons as his only next of kin, to-wit:

Name	Degree of Kinship	Age	P. O. Address
Estella May Morgan	Daughter	16	1104 Main Street, Cincinnati, Ohio
Douglas W. Morgan	Son	13	1104 Main Street, Cincinnati, Ohio

Your applicant offers the said will for probate and prays that a time may be fixed for the proving of the same, and that said next of kin heretofore named, who are known to be residents of this state, may be notified according to the law of the presentation of the said will for probate.

_____
Applicant

1104 Main Street, Cincinnati, Ohio
Residence

Illustration No. 84—Application for Probate of Will

LOCATION PRACTICE 6

Reaches to *b*, *y*, *q*

The letter *b* is below *g* and is controlled by the *f finger*. Make a direct reach from *f* to *b*. Let the *d* and *s* fingers move slightly when the *f finger* makes this reach.

Check to see that the hand does not change alignment with the keyboard when the reach to *b* is made.

fbf fbf bad bug fbf but bad fob rob fbf

The letter *y* is above *h* and is controlled by the *j finger*.

Straighten the *j* finger and make the reach to *y* without moving the other fingers from their typing position.

jyj day jay hay jay may jay may jay jyj

The letter *q* is above *a* and is controlled by the *a finger*.

Hold the elbow steady. Make the reach to *q* by straightening the finger; do not move the elbow in or out.

aqa aqa quit acquit quick acquire quiet

Illustration No. 32 — Reaches to b and y

Illustration No. 33 — Reach to q

LOCATION DRILL

10 minutes

Directions. Type the drill twice.

	STROKES
fbf jyj boy boy why bay rub fbf jyj bay boy fob rub	51
fib fob day say bug big rub rib rob tub lay bay may	51
quit back your quick quickly inquire acquire quickly	52
Do you like to work? I think I can work quite well.	52
He is very young, but he is a very quick worker.	48

(Space twice after a question mark at the end of a sentence.)

settle, and adjust all demands and claims in favor of or against my estate, and to sell, at private or public sale, at such prices, and upon such terms of credit or otherwise, as she may deem best, the whole or any part of my real or personal property, and to execute, acknowledge, and deliver deeds and other proper instruments of conveyance thereof to the purchaser or purchasers. No purchaser from my executrix need see to the application of the purchase money to or for the purposes of the trust, but the receipt of my executrix shall be a complete discharge and acquittance therefor. I request that no bond be required of my said executrix.

IN WITNESS WHEREOF, I, Stanley Morgan, have hereunto subscribed my name and affixed my seal to this, my last will and testament, at Cincinnati, Ohio, this 1st day of May, A. D. 1939.

_____ (SEAL)

Signed by the said Stanley Morgan and by him acknowledged to be his last will and testament, before us and in our presence, and by us subscribed as attesting witnesses in his presence and at his request and in the presence of each other this first day of May, A. D. 1939.

_____   _____
                              (Residence)

_____   _____
                              (Residence)

Illustration No. 83—Last Will and Testament (Concluded)

EXERCISE 162

APPLICATION FOR PROBATE OF WILL

Directions. After the death of the testator of a will, it is necessary first to file an application for probate of will with the probate court in the county of the state of the testator's last domicile. Type one copy of the application for probate of will on page *222*. Use double spacing.

LESSON 7

FINGER GYMNASTICS

1 minute

Drill 6. Spread the fingers apart as much as possible. Hold this position for a brief time; then relax the fingers and fold them lightly into the palm of the hand. Repeat the movement slowly several times. Exercise both hands at the same time.

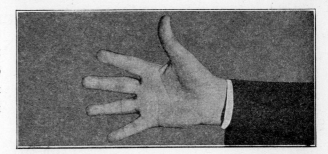

RECONSTRUCTION PRACTICE

7 minutes

Explanation. To center a line horizontally, set the stop so that half of the line to be typed will be at the left and half at the right of the center of the paper. With the paper guide set so the left edge of the paper is inserted at 2 below 0, the center point will be 40 for pica type and 50 for elite type.

Half of 50 spaces is 25. Center point is 40; therefore, $40 - 25 = 15$, the point at which the left margin will be set for pica type. For the elite type, the centering point is 50; therefore, $50 - 25 = 25$, the point at which the left margin will be set for elite type.

The typewriter is equipped with a bell that will ring from five to seven spaces before the point at which the stop for the right margin has been set. The ringing of this bell is a warning that the carriage will lock within the five or seven spaces. It is customary to add to the stop for the right margin five spaces so that the bell will ring just before the point at which the line should end.

To set the right margin stop, add 25 spaces (half of the length of the line) and 5 more spaces for the bell signal, to the center point. Thus, $40 + 25 + 5 = 70$, the point at which the right margin will be set for pica type; $50 + 25 + 5 = 80$, the point at which the right margin will be set for the elite type.

Directions. 1. Set the margin stop for a 50-space line.
2. Use double spacing.

```
ws uj cd ol ed nj gf mj tf ik bf nj qa yj qa yj bf

bf bf fob fib yj yj boy day ray rib tub jay may boy

aqa quick quickly quit acquit quire inquire acquire

did and the for win can but vow yes yet now not boy
```

TECHNIQUE PRACTICE 7

10 minutes

Directions. Type the drill twice.

	STROKES
The boy did not get the old net and the new rod.	48
They said they must move that club from this land.	50
They have that same fine view from this high site.	50
Both boys must have some time from this hard work.	50
They will have this long word read from that book.	50

You are working as a stenographer for Wingate & Wingate, attorneys at law in Cincinnati, Ohio. The following legal papers are typical of the dictation given in the offices of these lawyers.

EXERCISE 161

LAST WILL AND TESTAMENT

Directions. Type one copy of the will. Use double spacing. Space is provided for the signatures and addresses of two witnesses. In some states only one witness is required. Type the indorsement in the form shown in Illustration No. 82 on page 219. Bind the pages with a backing sheet and fold them for filing.

LAST WILL AND TESTAMENT

OF

STANLEY MORGAN

I, Stanley Morgan, of the city of Cincinnati, county of Hamilton, and state of Ohio, being of full age and of sound and disposing mind and memory, do make, publish, and declare this to be my last will and testament, hereby revoking all wills by me heretofore made.

Item I

I direct that all my just debts and funeral expenses be paid out of my estate as soon as practicable after the time of my decease.

Item II

All the property, real and personal, of every kind and description, wheresoever situate, which I may own or have the right to dispose of at the time of my decease, I give, devise, and bequeath to my wife, Ethel Morgan, absolutely and in fee simple.

Item III

I make, nominate, and appoint my wife, Ethel Morgan, to be the executrix of this, my last will and testament, hereby authorizing and empowering my said executrix to compound, compromise,

Illustration No. 83—Last Will and Testament

Directions. 1. Set a tabulator stop for a 5-space paragraph indention.
2. Type the exercise twice.

	STROKES
These are words I can write with ease and with	47
control. This will show that I command my fingers	98
and write as I am told to write. I know that I	146
must strike one letter at a time and write without	197
jerks. This can be done quite well if I look at	246
the work all the time as I write and if I return	295
the carriage with a quick throw.	327

LOCATION PRACTICE 7

3 minutes

Reaches to *x, p*

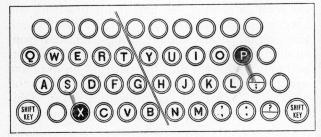

The letter *x* is below *s* and is controlled by the *s finger.*

Lift the *d* and *f fingers* slightly when making the reach to *x* with the controlling *s finger.*

Hold the hand in correct position with the keyboard and make the reach without elbow movement.

sxs sxs fix six mix six sxs six fox sxs

The letter *p* is above *;* and is controlled by the *; finger.*

Make the reach to the letter *p* by straightening the controlling finger.

Keep the elbow from swinging out. If a slight movement is necessary for you to control the letter *p*, bend the fingers and make a forward reach.

;p; pad ;p; map sip rip lap ;p; tip dip

Illustration No. 34 — Reach to x

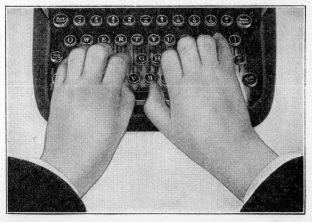

Illustration No. 35 — Reach to p

LEGAL DOCUMENTS

Many legal documents have become standardized in form and may be obtained as printed copies to be filled in. This study of legal papers must be limited to a few special forms that show the general arrangement of typical legal documents so that you can arrange other legal papers that you have to type.

The typing of legal papers requires accuracy because the context must be clear and concise to avoid misunderstanding. Erasures must be avoided. Use care in punctuation so that the meaning will be clear.

Most legal papers are typed with double spacing on legal paper 8½ by 13 or 15 inches with left and right ruled margins. Type within these vertical lines, leaving two or more spaces between the ruled line and the typing. If the paper does not have vertical rulings, set the margin stops for a 1½-inch left margin and a ½-inch right margin. The first line of typing should begin about 2 inches (12 single spaces) from the top of the paper. The first page is usually not numbered, but subsequent pages are numbered in the center at the bottom of each page.

The Indorsement. Legal documents are usually bound in a manuscript cover, or backing sheet. On the cover is typed information (called the *indorsement*) concerning the contents of the document.

Preparation of the Backing Sheet. At the top make a fold of approximately an inch. Bring the bottom edge of the backing sheet even with the top edge. Crease the fold neatly.

Place the bottom edge of the last fold even with the top of the sheet and crease. (The indorsement is to be typed on the fold facing you.) Unfold the last fold, insert the backing sheet into the typewriter, and type the indorsement.

Place the typed pages under the inch fold at the top of the backing sheet, and bind them, placing an eyelet at each side, about an inch from the top and the sides.

Frequently, a printed form of indorsement is used. Such a form has all general information printed on the back of the last sheet of the form, and provides blanks for inserting the specific information necessary to distinguish the particular instrument being prepared from similar instruments. In Illustration 82 the last will and testament and the petition on note are examples of typewritten indorsements; the warranty deed is an example of a form of indorsement that is usually partially printed.

LAST WILL AND TESTAMENT
OF
STANLEY MORGAN

WINGATE & WINGATE
Attorneys at Law
Cincinnati, Ohio

No. ————

IN THE MUNICIPAL COURT OF CINCINNATI,
HAMILTON COUNTY, OHIO

MARSHALL RADIO CORPORATION,
16 Marshall Boulevard,
Cincinnati, Ohio,
                    Plaintiff
              vs.
H. D. PHILLIPS, doing business as
PHILLIPS RADIO SHOPPE,
101 West Fourth Street,
Cincinnati, Ohio,
                    Defendant

PETITION ON NOTE

WINGATE & WINGATE
Attorneys at Law
Cincinnati, Ohio

Warranty Deed

LARRY J. BOOTHE and
VIVIAN BOOTHE, his wife,
                    Grantors

ROBERT REILLY,
                    Grantee

DATED   January 17,   19 41

Filed for Record at the Request of

————————————————————
————————————————, A. D. 19————,
at ————— *min. past* ———————— *o'clock,*
————*M., and recorded in Vol.*————————
of ———————————— *page* ————————
County Records
————————————————————
                              Recorder
By————————————————————
                              Deputy Recorder

Illustration No. 82—Indorsements of Legal Forms

Directions. Type the drill twice.

	STROKES
sxs six fix mix sxs tax fox box sxs ;p; pay pad map	51
paid next next type pale play next page paid next	49
The six men did not fix the big old box for the boy.	52
They will have that next page read from this book.	50
May I be next? I am quick. I can type quite well.	51

LESSON 8

FINGER GYMNASTICS   *1 minute*

Drill 7. Rub the hands vigorously. Let the thumb rub the palm of the hand. Rub the fingers, the back of the hand, and the wrist.

RECONSTRUCTION PRACTICE   *6 minutes*

Directions.
1. Use a 50-space line.
2. Set the machine for double spacing.

(Flick the finger from the key.)   r r q r x q r u u p u p e c p n i v r m o b u b o t p

(Think the word.)   to if he an of do us us if or it or is he to an by

(Think the letter.)   sxs six fix fox box six ;p; pay map lap sip pay map

aqa quick require question deck check rob fob tub rib

TECHNIQUE PRACTICE 8   *10 minutes*

Directions. Type the drill twice.

	STROKES
I can type. I can type quite well. Can you type?	50
How I sit at the machine has much to do with my work.	53
Each key must be struck with a quick, sharp blow.	49
My rate of typing will improve with right practice.	51
Good typing power will be of much help to all of us.	52

Indexing and filing are two of the daily tasks to be performed in all offices.
Papers must be filed according to the uniform rules that are used in all the
offices of an organization. It is not enough that records be filed in a safe place;
they must be filed so that they can be found quickly. In an office, time is
money; and the worker who can file papers and then find them quickly when
they are needed is worth much to a business. As records are important, they
must not be lost. A building that burns can be rebuilt; a worker who leaves
can be replaced; but if records are lost, it may not be possible to replace
them just as they were, because thousands of items make up the records of a
business.

The file clerk has to be accurate. She must know that the filing is done right,
just as the bookkeeper must know that his entries are correct. As a matter of
fact, the file clerk must be even more accurate than the bookkeeper. A set of
books can be proved; but when papers are filed, there is no way to check the
accuracy of the filing unless index cards are kept. Then, too, errors in book-
keeping records may be traced after work hours; but when an error has been
made in filing, it is usually discovered at the very time when the paper is
needed most. The delay in finding the paper may mean the loss of money to
the business, the slowing up of the work of the entire organization, and the
consequent irritation of all, from the president down to the file clerk.

Filing is important in all businesses, but in no other office is it more exact-
ing than in a law office. The papers of a law office are said to be the lawyer's
"stock in trade." It used to be that legal papers were folded and placed in a
document file. This way of filing papers is not used so much as it once was. In
most law offices papers are left unfolded and are filed vertically. Filed in this
way, they take up much less space and are not so easily torn or worn. In some
cases legal papers already folded to document size must be folded again for
filing. In this case a special file known as the document file may be used. The
letters in a law office may refer to a number of things: cases in court, collections, patents, other legal transactions—to name just a few of the many kinds
of problems that come within the range of the duties of a worker in a law office.

It is often best to file papers in a law office in either an active or a closed file.
All the correspondence about a case should be filed together under the client's
name and should be kept as a unit. Cross-reference cards should be made for
all letters except those addressed to the client under whose name the papers
are to be filed. As frequent use is made of the files, the papers must be placed
so that they can be found without loss of time. If the size of a legal paper
makes filing difficult unless the paper is folded, just as few folds as possible
should be made. When a case has been closed, the brief and the transcript of
the record should be removed from the files and bound. A history of each case
is kept. This history is known as the register. It is from this record that the
details for billing a client are obtained.

EXERCISE 8 *12 minutes*

Directions. Set a tabulator stop for a 5-space indention. Type the exercise twice.

STROKES

I can learn to type with speed and with ease if   48

I will back up my desire with some good hard **work.**   99

Each project must be done just right; I should not   150

expect skill to come through poor work. Habits once   203

formed are hard to change. I know this and I shall   255

guard against forming wrong habits. Right typing   305

habits will bring real typing power.   341

LOCATION PRACTICE 8 *3 minutes*

Reach to *z*

The *z* key is below *a* and is controlled by the *a finger*. Move the controlling finger to *z* without moving the other fingers from their typing position. Move the finger, not the hand.

Illustration No. 36 — Reach to z

aza haze maze lazy hazy size haze aza

LOCATION DRILL *8 minutes*

Directions. Type the drill twice.

STROKES

size prize zeal zone hazy lazy size zinc prize prize   52

realize recognize organize realize zenith organize   50

This is not the right size. What is the next prize?   52

Most of us can win the prize of good typing skill.   50

Rob is much too lazy to work with zest or zeal.   47

UNIT XII — *LEGAL DOCUMENTS*

BUDGET XIX

TECHNIQUE PRACTICE 94

Directions. Use a 70-space line; single spacing. Type each line twice. Double-space after the second typing of each line.

	STROKES
"And/or" is an expression used to denote both or either of two factors.	71
In legal papers spell sums of money and write figures in parentheses.	69
Example: We agree to pay the sum of Two Hundred Ten Dollars ($210).	68
When figures are inserted before the word "Dollars," omit the sign.	67
Example: We agree to pay the sum of Two Hundred Ten (210) Dollars.	67

SENTENCE PRACTICE

Directions. Use a 70-space line; single spacing. Type a sentence five times in each practice period; or, if your teacher so directs, use a sentence for a one-minute writing.

	STROKES
There is no proper ending without proper effort to bring it about.	66
Many know how to gain a victory, but not how to make proper use of it.	70
The only way to have a friend is to be one; this calls for thought.	67
If we cannot dignify our present station, we can dignify no other.	66
You will find an honest desire to help others a quick help to yourself.	71

CORRECTIVE DRILL PARAGRAPH

Directions. Use a 70-space line; a 5-space indention; single spacing.

(Emphasizing letters *e, o, r*)

	STROKES
The work of a stenographer in the office of a lawyer is con-	59
sidered just about the most exacting type of office work. A high	125
degree of technical skill is necessary in the taking of dictation	191
and the use of the typewriter. A worker has to familiarize him-	254
self with a terminology not used in any other kind of work.	315
There can be no guesswork in legal transcripts; the right word	378
must be used in the right place. In the copying of legal papers	443
from court records, exactness is required. Errors in typing that	509
appear in the original paper must not be corrected in a copy. The	576
typist should underscore a word in which an error occurs to show	641
that the error is in the original document. Stenographic work	704
in the office of a lawyer has been for many young men and	762
women the gateway to the practice of law. Such young men and	824
women have access to the fine libraries that most lawyers gather	889
for their specialized labors; they learn court procedure in all its	957
phases; and they are constantly adding to their store of knowl-	1019
edge through office contacts and correspondence.	1067

TIMED WRITING

Directions. Use a 70-space line; a 5-space indention; double spacing. If you complete the test before time is called, start at the beginning and continue typing. After time has been called, check the writing carefully.

LESSON 9

FINGER GYMNASTICS   *1 minute*

Drill 8. Interlace the fingers of the two hands and wring the hands, rubbing the heels of the palms vigorously.

RECONSTRUCTION PRACTICE   *6 minutes*

Explanation. When you want to type with definite control, *think* the letters of the word as you type. This practice tends to give a smooth and continuous typing rate but is not the best procedure to use for building speed.

When you want to increase your stroking rate, *think* the word. *Word typing* calls for a higher order of typing habit than letter typing, but both typing procedures are needed in typing these lessons.

Directions. Use a 60-space line. Set the machine for double spacing.

```
fvf ;p; aza jyj sxs ;p; aza jyj aqa kik sxs ;p; fbf jnj dcd

fix six mix box rob fob tub pay can win won map pal won cut

size quit next size quiz next city wish deck quit zeal zone

such with when down both file wish work half kept half kept

form then they turn hand dock sick duck lane both hand such
```

TECHNIQUE PRACTICE 9   *10 minutes*

Directions. 1. Type the drill twice.
2. In the first three sentences in this drill, you should type letter by letter—"on the letter level," as it is usually expressed. You should be able to handle most of the words in the last two sentences on the word level. Whenever you find a word too hard or too long to be handled on the word level, use the letter-level stroking.

	STROKES
Max and Nan can go to Maine or Maryland for the month of May.	61
Robert will take Spaulding to Texas for two weeks in April.	59
Do you want to excel? If so, always plan your work well.	57
Most of us can do much more work than we make ourselves do.	59
This is the kind of work I like to do and the work I do well.	61

[25]

EXERCISE 158
OUTGOING LETTER

Directions. Type this letter in the form used in Style Letter No. 6 on page 125. Use end punctuation. Type the title of Mr. Wilkinson on a separate line, and type the title of Mr. Duncan on the line that is to be used for his signature.

Mr. T. J. Wilkinson, Construction Engineer, Grayson - Wickman Company, Boulder, Colorado. Dear Sir: As you requested, I am sending you sufficient funds to cover your pay roll for the week ending on August 15. I am enclosing a distribution sheet and a cash memorandum to aid you in your withdrawal from the bank. (P) You are doing good work in your section, and your ability to get new business and push through jobs on hand is calling forth the commendation of our company. (P) I have been instructed to place $7,000 to the credit of the company in the Citizens National Bank of your city, subject to withdrawal by you for any transaction made in the name of the Grayson-Wickman Company. Very truly yours, (William F. Duncan) Cashier GRAYSON-WICKMAN COMPANY Enclosures: Check Distribution Sheet Cash Memorandum (*Strokes, 809; words, 109.*)

EXERCISE 159
PAY-ROLL DISTRIBUTION SHEET

Directions. Type a distribution sheet from the pay roll of the Grayson-Wickman Company. Arrange the data in the form shown in Illustration No. 79.

No.	Name	Total Wages		Bill and Special Memorandum							
				$10	$5	$1	50¢	25¢	10¢	5¢	1¢
1	Dudley Beecher	34	40	3		4		1	1	1	
2	Thomas Browning	37	05	3	1	2				1	
3	James Conklin	35	60	3	1		1		1		
4	Jesse Coombs	35	88	3	1		1	1	1		3
5	Charles Henry	36	40	3	1	1		1	1	1	
6	Matty Hindman	34	00	3			4				
7	Ben Jenkins	35	10	3	1				1		
8	Walter Knott	33	40	3		3		1	1	1	
9	David O'Rourke	35	00	3	1						
10	Henry Raymond	36	40	3	1	1		1	1	1	
11	Adam Reynolds	32	63	3		2	1		1		3
12	Ivan Steadman	35	60	3	1		1		1		
13	George Thurman	30	38	3				1	1		3
14	Edwin Wakefield	36	00	3	1	1					
	Totals	487	84	42	9	18	4	6	10	5	9

Illustration No. 79 — Pay-Roll Distribution Sheet

EXERCISE 160
CASH MEMORANDUM AND CHECK

Directions. Prepare a cash memorandum for the pay roll of the Grayson-Wickman Company. Arrange the data in the form shown in Illustration No. 80 at the left. Fill out a bank check for the total amount shown on the cash memorandum. The check should be similar in form to that shown in Illustration No. 81.

Bank of Moberly
Moberly, Missouri

PAY ROLL OF

The Pinker Manufacturing Company

Per L. M. Cross

March 14, 194-

42	Bills, 10s	$420	00
9	Bills, 5s	45	00
18	Bills, 1s	18	00
4	Half Dollars	2	00
6	Quarter Dollars	1	50
10	Dimes	1	00
5	Nickels		25
9	Pennies		09
	Total	$487	84

Illustration No. 80
Cash Memorandum

MOBERLY, MO._____ March 14, 19____ No. 237

BANK OF MOBERLY 80-74

PAY TO THE ORDER OF The Pinker Manufacturing Company- - - - - - - $487.84

Four Hundred Eighty-Seven and 84/100- - - - - - - - - - - -DOLLARS

The Pinker Manufacturing Company

L. M. Cross

Illustration No. 81 — Bank Check

EXERCISE 9

20 minutes

Directions. 1. Set the tabulator stop for an indention of 5 spaces.

2. Each paragraph is to be used for two three-minute writings. If your teacher cannot time you, use a watch with a second hand and time yourself as accurately as possible.

3. If you complete the paragraph before the end of the three-minute writing, throw the carriage, indent, and retype the paragraph.

Practice Procedures. 1. Type the paragraph for three minutes. Note the gross words per minute typed.*

2. For the second typing, set the ribbon lever (No. 39) for stenciling. This will give you a complete typing situation except that there will be no readable imprint of the strokes. The stencil drill will aid you in learning to stroke the keys rapidly. See to it that all stroking is as accurate as you can make it, but make all strokes rapidly.

3. Set the goal for the second typing two or three words faster than the first or ribbon typing. If, for example, you type only two lines in the first writing, let your goal be the completion of two and a half lines in the second typing. If you complete the paragraph before the end of the three-minute writing, throw the carriage, indent for the paragraph, and continue typing.

Illustration No. 37
Setting Ribbon Lever
for Stenciling

	STROKES
Good typing skill can be used with almost all kinds of	55
office work. It is worth all the hard work and the thought	115
one must give it to learn to type well.	154
I can get speed in typing if I use a quick stroke and	54
if I get rid of all the stops and the jerks that come from	113
working with a sense of hurry.	143

SPEED EMPHASIS

5 minutes

Directions. Type the drill once. Repeat the drill if you have time.

	STROKES
if if he if he is is to go if he is to go do an us us if	56
or or for for for he he the he the the the for for the the	58
an and and for the and for the and for for the and for the	58
He can go. He can go for it. He can go there for them.	56
I can work. I can work with them. I can work well with them.	62
All of us must do well the work that comes to us to be done.	60

* The column of figures gives the cumulative strokes for the paragraph. To determine gross strokes, note the figure in the column for the last completed line; then count the strokes typed for the uncompleted line. Divide by 5 to determine gross words. Divide gross words by the time (3 minutes in this case) to determine gross words per minute.

[26]

Banks furnish blank forms, or cash memorandum slips, to their depositors for use in withdrawing definite numbers of bills and coins. The forms are of the same size as deposit slips. The paymaster of a business presents to the bank a check for the full amount of money to be withdrawn for the pay roll. The bank clerk gives him the amount in the bills and the coins listed on the cash memorandum. (See page 216.)

The exercises in this budget deal with matters concerning pay rolls.

EXERCISE 156
INCOMING LETTER FROM BOULDER, COLORADO

Directions. Type this letter in the block form. Type the dictator's name in the position for the official title, and type the official title below the dictator's name. Use open punctuation.

Grayson-Wickman Company 1314 Steadman Street Denver, Colorado Gentlemen An upward trend in our line of construction work makes it necessary for me to employ ten more men. I have engaged workmen who have been on several of the big construction jobs in this section and who come highly recommended. I have agreed to pay them 65 cents an hour, a slight increase over our regular wage. As they are superior workmen, I think the increase will pay in the end. (P) I shall need funds by the time you can rush your check to me. Do not delay it. (P) I am expecting two additional construction jobs within the next few days. Very truly yours T. J. Wilkinson Construction Engineer *(Strokes, 710; words, 103.)*

EXERCISE 157
PAY ROLL

Directions. The data for the pay roll of the employees of the Grayson-Wickman Company at Boulder are given below. Type a pay roll in the form shown in Illustration No. 78.

Monday: Robert Thompson, 8 hrs.; George Henry, 8½ hrs.; Edward Brown, 9 hrs.; Clyde Williams, 9 hrs.; Russell Cooper, 9 hrs.; James Bates, 10 hrs.; Marshall Finley, 10 hrs.; Martin Ray, 7½ hrs.; Louis Black, 8 hrs.; Henry Pilson, 10 hrs.; William Cranfill, 9½ hrs.; Phillip Jenkins, 9 hrs.; Fred Smith, 8 hrs. Tuesday: Cooper, 8 hrs.; Jenkins, 8 hrs.; Williams, 5 hrs.; Bates, 9 hrs.; Finley, 8½ hrs.; Bernard Lytle, 9½ hrs.; Pilson, 10 hrs.; Thompson, 8 hrs.; Henry, 10 hrs.; Cranfill, 9 hrs.; Brown, 8 hrs.; Smith, 10 hrs.; Black, 7½ hrs. Wednesday: Lytle, 9 hrs.; Pilson, 9

No.	Name	Hours per day						Total Hours	Wages per Hour	Total Wages	
		M	T	W	T	F	S				
1	Dudley Beecher	7	7	7	7	8	4	40	.86	34	40
2	Thomas Browning	7	7	7	7	7	4	39	.95	37	05
3	James Conklin	7	7	7	7	7	5	40	.89	35	60
4	Jesse Coombs	7	7	7	7	7	4	39	.92	35	88
5	Charles Henry	8	5	8	7	8	4	40	.91	36	40
6	Matty Hindman	7	7	7	7	8	4	40	.85	34	00
7	Ben Jenkins	4	8	8	8	7	4	39	.90	35	10
8	Walter Knott	7	8	7	7	4	7	40	.83½	33	40
9	David O'Rourke	7	7	8	6	3	4	40	.87½	35	00
10	Henry Raymond	8	8	7	7	6	5	40	.91	36	40
11	Adam Reynolds	8	7	4	8	4	6½	37½	.87	32	63
12	Ivan Steadman	7	7	7	7	7	5	40	.89	35	60
13	George Thurman	8	4	8	6	4	7½	37½	.81	30	38
14	Edwin Wakefield	7	8	7	7	7	4	40	.90	36	00
							Total			487	84

Illustration No. 78 — Pay Roll

hrs.; Black, 9 hrs.; Ray, 8½ hrs.; Brown, 10 hrs.; Finley, 7½ hrs.; Cranfill, 8 hrs.; Bates, 8 hrs.; Williams, 7 hrs.; Henry, 8 hrs.; Cooper, 10 hrs. Thursday: Thompson, 9 hrs.; Lytle, 7 hrs.; Cooper, 5 hrs.; Bates, 5 hrs.; Henry, 4 hrs.; Jenkins, 8 hrs.; Ray, 8 hrs.; Williams, 7 hrs.; Brown, 8 hrs. Friday: Ray, 8 hrs.; Jenkins, 8 hrs.; Cooper, 4 hrs.; Bates, 4 hrs.; Cranfill, 7 hrs.; Smith, 9 hrs.; Williams, 8 hrs.; Thompson, 9 hrs.; Brown, 5 hrs.; Pilson, 8 hrs.; Finley, 7 hrs.; Henry, 5 hrs.; Black, 8 hrs.; Lytle, 8 hrs. Saturday: Jenkins, 7 hrs.; Bates, 4 hrs.; Cooper, 4 hrs.; Black, 7½ hrs.; Henry, 4 hrs.; Ray, 8 hrs.; Lytle, 6½ hrs.; Smith, 7½ hrs.; Williams, 4 hrs.; Finley, 7 hrs.; Cranfill, 6 hrs. Wages per hour: Thompson, Henry, Smith, Cranfill, and Ray, 60 cents; Finley, Brown, Bates, and Pilson, 66 cents; Williams, Cooper, Black, Jenkins, and Lytle, 63 cents.

LESSON 10

RECONSTRUCTION PRACTICE
5 minutes

Explanation. The words used in this drill are controlled by one hand. They represent "speed traps" until continuous stroking skill is established for them. In this typing, speed is of less importance than continuous typing.

Directions. Use a 60-space line. Set machine for double spacing.

```
a;sldkfjgh a;sldkfjgh a;sldkfjgh a;sldkfjgh a;sldkfjgh

r b r b q r u o u n r p r z a f z u g v n i p w s w l . . , y
```

(One-hand words. Type on letter level.)
```
as on we in be up was joy wax you see him fear jump dear look

were pull ever limp tear dear fear link mink card cars only
```

TECHNIQUE PRACTICE 10
16 minutes

Directions. Use each sentence for three one-minute writings. The first writing should be used to establish your writing rate; the second writing should be for a goal at least two words in excess of the base writing rate; the third writing should be for the original base writing rate so that you can have the feeling of ease and control.

Technique Emphasis. You must *feel* the difference between writing rapidly with a sense of ease and control, and writing rapidly with a sense of hurry. Whenever you feel pushed to your limit, take the next timed writing at a slower rate and give attention to the continuity of stroking.

	STROKES
`I know that I can do this work in the way it should be done.`	60
`The eyes must be held on the copy all the time I am writing.`	60
`Most of the words should be typed with ease and with speed.`	59
`It takes a little thought and effort to get the right stroke.`	60

EXERCISE 10
15 minutes

Directions. 1. Set a tabulator stop for a 5-space indention.
2. Each paragraph is to be used for two three-minute writings. Type the first writing with the ribbon set for normal typing; the second writing with the ribbon lever set for stenciling.

Technique Emphasis. 1. Relax the muscles of the shoulders and arms.
2. Hold the hands as steady as possible.
3. Avoid elbow or wrist movement; let the fingers do the work.

	STROKES
`Most men want to do a lot of big things in life; but`	53
`they must keep their minds on the little things they have to`	114
`do each day, too. Little things done well lead to big things.`	176

I wish I could tell Ted Jackson that he is his own handicap. I wish I could tell the young boy who lives next door not to discuss his company's plans with all the neighbors. I know that Ted is baffled by his inability to forge ahead. He never seems to hear himself quite as others hear him; yet if I were to tell him that even his closest associates call him a "windbag," he would be hurt instead of realizing that I was attempting to be a friend. If I were to tell the young chap next door that established principles of business say plainly, "Thou shalt keep thy mouth shut about office matters," he would call me a meddler, or worse. So they talk and pay the price for too much talking and not enough thinking; and neither friend nor enemy can do anything to help them, for they will not be helped.

Thinking, not talking, is the important thing in life. It leads to something. Our thinkers are remaking the world. They catch the music from the air; London broadcasts, and Sioux City tunes in. They build a Graf Zeppelin, and we are thrilled by a flight around the world. These are times to thrill those who have eyes to see and ears to hear. It is a time when careless talk is costly, silence is golden, and doing is fruitful beyond all dreams. Great things are in the making. Pioneer days are not over. The frontier now is in men's thinking and not in the land acquired by clearing forests or staking claims to plains. The new kind of pioneering calls for men just as alert and brave as those of homesteading days. Dynamic thinkers are needed.

From the grains of wheat the farmer sows, he reaps a crop of wheat; from the corn he plants, he gathers corn. The sower knows that he will not reap oats from wheat, nor will he harvest hay from corn; for like produces like. Just so, dynamic thinking reproduces its own kind. If you sow the seeds of kindness and of thoughtfulness, these qualities will grow and become a definite part of your character. If you sow the seeds of belief in yourself, of confidence in your own ability, of courage to meet all situations honestly and squarely, you will reap a harvest that will ennoble your life and give a greater scope to its usefulness. This is growth, and it is the prize that thinkers win. In your school life, then, talk less, think more; idle less, do more; guess less, prepare more; pretend less, excel more.

	STROKES
	1684
	1763
	1844
	1923
	1999
	2081
	2161
	2238
	2316
	2394
	2413
	2493
	2566
	2643
	2722
	2805
	2886
	2965
	3044
	3121
	3169
	3242
	3318
	3395
	3471
	3546
	3626
	3702
	3783
	3865
	3947
	3986

A pay roll shows the name of each employee, the time that each worked, the wages per hour, and the total wages. A typical pay roll is shown in Illustration No. 78. A pay roll is made up from a time record kept by a timekeeper or by the employees themselves.

A distribution sheet illustrated on page 216 is prepared from the pay roll. Several columns at the right show the denominations in which each employee is to be paid, and the totals of these columns are the amounts of various denominations needed to meet the pay roll.

```
 I can type some words without thinking the letters, but      56

some words I must spell.  Right now I must learn when to use  117

the letter level and when to use the word level in typing.    175
```

SPEED EMPHASIS

6 minutes

Directions. 1. Type the drill once.
2. If you have time, repeat the drill.
3. Follow the same directions for succeeding speed emphasis drills unless you are otherwise directed.

STROKES

(Say the word before typing it.)
```
for for the for the and and for the and for them them them    58

did man fur dig lap bid big bug rig did cow rug map sir map    59

sir dug wit sob fob rub tub rob rib fib fob sod nap dog lap    59

them them when they they what wish with wish both such such    59

He is to go.  He is to go with them.  Both of them will go.    59
```

LESSON 11

FINGER GYMNASTICS

1 minute

Drill 9. Keep the hands open, the fingers wide apart, and the muscles tense. Close the fingers into a tight fist. Relax the fingers as you straighten them. Repeat the movements several times with both hands.

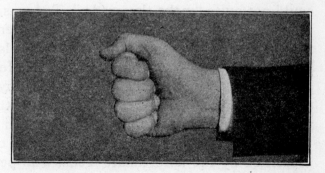

RECONSTRUCTION PRACTICE

5 minutes

Directions. Use a 60-space line. Set the machine for double spacing.

(Type rapidly.)
```
a;sldkfjgh a;sldkfjgh a;sldkfjghfjdksla; a;sldkfjghfjdksla;
```

(Type on letter level.)
```
was car hum vat wet bat lop saw cat rat lip nip rag fat pin

were jump read card only dead fear limp lump tear cart hull

quit next zeal zone both very lack paid quit zest cent quit
```

CORRECTIVE DRILL PARAGRAPH

Directions. Use a 70-space line; a 5-space indention; single spacing.

STROKES

(Emphasizing letter *b*) At the thirty-sixth convention of the American Booksellers' — 60
Association, a Nobel prize winner in literature spoke on "Ene- — 121
mies of the Book." He began his address by declaring that — 180
writers of books and dealers in books belong to the same guild, — 244
the purpose of which is to sell books. He said that he did not — 308
believe anything would supplant the printed book. Neither a — 369
nimble television apparatus nor a gadget whereby we can carry — 431
the bulky works of Balzac in a tiny bundle will take the place of — 497
books as we know them. These devices have their place in — 555
libraries, but they will be used as devices and not as substitutes — 622
for books. There are other beguilements beckoning and getting — 685
between us and our habit of quiet browsing among books—the — 745
automobile, the bridge table, and the night club. "Of the making — 811
of books there is no end," and every year brings a new band of — 874
readers who belie the jeremiad that "no one reads books any — 934
more." — 940

TIMED WRITING

Directions. Use a 70-space line; a 5-space indention; double spacing. If you complete the test before time is called, start at the beginning and continue typing. After time has been called, check the writing carefully.

STROKES

I have heard people say that talk is cheap, yet I know of nothing that costs — 77
more. It was too much talk that caused Ted Jackson to be known as one who — 152
could not quite "make the grade." Ted was a capable man and had been with — 227
the firm several years. He felt that he deserved promotion. His superiors did — 307
not fail to recognize his worth, but they also knew his weakness. When the — 383
big chance came, Ted was passed by. He felt unappreciated and thought bit- — 457
terly that, if one gave his life to a company, he should expect nothing in re- — 534
turn. He talked himself into a vicious attitude, lost favor with his fellow — 611
workers, and set his feet on the wrong path in finding a road to success. — 684

There are two aspects to this problem of talking to excess. One side is — 757
presented by the unfortunate Teds, who permit their tongues to chain them — 831
within the zone of the mediocre. With their ceaseless flow of words, they — 906
overwhelm all who come within their range. Too much talk is costly, too, — 980
when secret information is carelessly passed about by idle chatter. Many a — 1056
business transaction has failed to develop just because of what is called a — 1132
"leak in the department." The leak does not come from a desire to harm but, — 1209
rather, from a failure to quit the paths of thoughtless talk. No matter what — 1287
the intent may be, the result is the same—to the company a loss of business — 1364
and to the worker the loss that comes from lack of steady growth in power. — 1440
In every council room heed is given to the men who achieve instead of chatter — 1518
—to those whose words bear weight, because they have thought more than — 1590
they have talked. — 1607

TECHNIQUE PRACTICE 11 *16 minutes*

Directions. Use each sentence for three one-minute writings. Use ribbon typing for the first and third writings. Set the ribbon lever for stenciling when typing the sentence the second time.

Technique Emphasis. You want to increase your stroking rate, but the increase in speed must be gained *WITH right technique*.

1. Lift the fingers from the keyboard; then place them lightly in typing position—barely touching the keys.

2. Have a minimum of hand, wrist, and arm movement; let the fingers do the work.

3. Hold the eyes on the copy throughout the typing; the throw is made at the end of the printed line and there is no necessity for you to look up when returning the carriage.

STROKES

A sense of hurry will cause men to do poor work when typing.	60
I shall not fail if all of my work is done right each day.	58
He who works with fear does only half the work he could do.	59
It is right for all of us to think and do as well as we can.	60

EXERCISE 11 *15 minutes*

Directions. Set a tabulator stop for a 5-space indention. Use each paragraph for two three-minute writings. Type the first writing with the lever set for ribbon typing; the second writing with the lever set for stenciling.

Technique Emphasis. Note the ease with which letters may be struck when the muscles of the arm and shoulder are relaxed and the fingers are poised lightly in typing position. The hands must never rest like a weight on the keys. Hit the key with a quick, forceful blow and remove the finger even more quickly than the finger moved in striking the key. Equalize the power behind the strokes.

HANDS MUST BE QUIET SO THE FINGERS CAN DO THEIR WORK RAPIDLY AND ACCURATELY.

STROKES

The hands must be quiet so the fingers can do the work	55
well. The stroke must be light but forceful. A heavy stroke	117
is a slow stroke; a light and forceful stroke is made with	176
ease and speed and adds to typing power.	216
All of us have to work. That is sure. Some people work	57
with a sense of joy in what they do; others do their work	115
just as though it had been given to them to make them suffer.	177
The way we work means a lot when it comes to the final check	238
on our effort.	252

[29]

EXERCISE 154

The Marvin Hardware Company issues a check for $3.26 to pay the freight charges on the shipment.

Directions. Type one copy of the check in a form similar to the one illustrated below.

No. 196　　　Milwaukee, Wisconsin,　June 26,　194-

Merchants National Bank 13-19

Pay to the order of Chicago & North Western Railway Co.------- $3.26

Three and--26/100 Dollars

For　Freight Charges　　　Marvin Hardware Company

V B Mitchell

Treasurer

Illustration No. 77 — Check

EXERCISE 155

On June 26 the Marvin Hardware Company issues a check in payment of Invoice No. 24183 of the Clark-Peters Hardware Company, which is given in Exercise 151. The amount of the invoice is $606.60, but a 2% discount is allowed for cash within ten days. The check is for $594.47.

Directions. Make one copy of the check.

BUDGET XVIII
TECHNIQUE PRACTICE 93
Emphasizing Figures

Directions. Use a 70-space line; single spacing. Type each line twice. Double-space after the second typing of each line.

	STROKES
In 1920, 518,493 cars were shipped f.o.b. Detroit to the Canal Zone.	68
Mr. Tobin worked 925 men on a project that was planned to employ 600.	69
"Form No. 194," he explained, "will tell you of the new route 46-W."	68
An explanation of Schedule B is in Vol. VIII, Chap. XI (see Fig. 1).	68
On February 28 he reported the sale of 36,582 copies of the brochure.	69

SENTENCE PRACTICE

Directions. Use a 70-space line. Use the sentences for one-minute writings and for drill on calling the throw.

	STROKES
The world bestows its big prizes upon the ones who do their work well.	70
Have a desire to do the right thing without being told or watched.	66
The past is of no value only as it can make the life of today fuller.	69
Getting ahead is largely a matter of just keeping ahead of the times.	69
It makes a difference whether you go into a thing to win or to drift.	69

if or it is he or he if an us am us do it so go us an is he   59

lay lid may for tug man dog fit lap sit and cut vow did may   59

sick form they they burn burn turn firm make lake make laid   59

He has the form. They will make them take it. He is sick.   59

LESSON 12

FINGER GYMNASTICS

1 minute

Drill 10. Clench and relax the fingers several times; then shake the hands with the fingers thoroughly relaxed.

RECONSTRUCTION PRACTICE

5 minutes

Technique Emphasis: Shifting for Capitals.
1. If a capital letter is above the line of writing, the shift key was not depressed firmly or it was released too quickly.

Remedial Procedure. Depress the shift key more firmly and time the release to follow the stroke and release of the key for the capital letter.

2. If the reach to the shift key causes the hand to move far from the typing position, there will be considerable hesitancy in typing after the capital is made.

Remedial Procedure. Use the "hinge" wrist motion; stretch the little finger, but hold the other fingers near the typing position. Be very certain not to move the elbow.

Directions. Use a 60-space line. Set the machine for double spacing.

(Type on letter level.)

rfvf ujmj tfbf yjnj wsxs ol.l qaza p;?; edcd ik,k gfbf hjnj

regarded minimum greater opinion exceeded monopoly weaved

(Shift-key practice.)

Mary and Jack will go in March. Is Jane in Maryland now?

Sue and Sally left for Spain in April. Fred is in Algiers.

TECHNIQUE PRACTICE 12

10 minutes

Directions. Type the drill once; then select for repetition practice the sentence or sentences that provide the drill for your weak controls. Type on the letter level. The goal is continuous and smooth typing. If you find letter combinations or words that cause hesitancy in your stroking, practice the difficult combinations or words until you learn how to type them with sureness.

Drill
STROKES

(a) April days may be as gay as May days, but I prefer May days.   60

(b) Robert Barbour brought his brother to see the Boston bridge.   60

(c) Charles has the canceled check which the Clinic clerk cashed.   61

(d) Did Dick decide to direct the squad to depend on radio beams?   61

(e) Each effort expended for the sake of science will be blessed.   61

EXERCISE 152

The bill of lading shown in this exercise is the original copy of that prepared by the Clark-Peters Hardware Company. It shows the name of the railroad to which the merchandise billed on the invoice in the preceding illustration was delivered for shipment. This bill of lading was prepared in triplicate, and the original was mailed to the Marvin Hardware Company.

(Uniform Domestic Straight Bill of Lading Adopted by Carriers in Official, Southern and Western Classification Territories, March 15, 1922, as amended August 1, 1930.)

UNIFORM STRAIGHT BILL OF LADING--ORIGINAL--NOT NEGOTIABLE Shipper's No.______

CHICAGO & NORTH WESTERN RAILWAY **Company** Agent's No.______

RECEIVED, subject to the classifications and tariffs in effect on the date of the issue of this Bill of Lading.

June 20, 194- From **CLARK-PETERS HARDWARE CO.**

the property described below, in apparent good order, except as noted (contents and condition of contents of packages unknown), marked, consigned, and destined as indicated below, which said company (the word company being understood throughout this contract as meaning any person or corporation in possession of the property under the contract) agrees to carry to its usual place of delivery at said destination, if on its own road or its own water line, otherwise to deliver to another carrier on the route to said destination. It is mutually agreed, as to each carrier of all or any of said property over all or any portion of said route to destination, and as to each party at any time interested in all or any of said property, that every service to be performed hereunder shall be subject to all the conditions not prohibited by law, whether printed or written, herein contained, including the conditions on back hereof, which are hereby agreed to by the shipper and accepted for himself and his assigns.

(Mail or street address of consignee—For purposes of notification only)

Consigned to Marvin Hardware Company . 768 Main Street

Destination Milwaukee **State of** Wisconsin **County of**______

Route______

Delivering Carrier______ **Car Initial**______ **Car No.**______

No. Packages	Description of Articles, Special Marks and Exceptions	*WEIGHT (Subject to Correction)	Class or Rate	Check Column
2	cases hardware	255#		
1	case cutlery	150#		

Subject to Section 7 of conditions, if this shipment is to be delivered to the consignee without recourse on the consignor, the consignor shall sign the following statement
The carrier shall not make delivery of this shipment without payment of freight and all other lawful charges.

______
(Signature of Consignor)

If charges are to be prepaid, write or stamp here, "To be Prepaid."

Received $______
to apply in prepayment of the charges on the property described hereon
Agent or Cashier

Per______
(The signature here acknowledges only the amount prepaid.)

Charges Advanced. $______

*If the shipment moves between two ports by a carrier by water, the law requires that the bill of lading shall state whether it is "carrier's or shipper's weight." Note—Where the rate is dependent on value, shippers are required to state specifically in writing the agreed or declared value of the property. The agreed or declared value of the property is hereby specifically stated by the shipper to be not exceeding______ per ______

Clark-Peters Hardware Co., *Shipper, Per* R.O.C. ______ *Agent, Per*______

Permanent post-office address of shipper 619 Wabash Ave., Chicago

***Illustration No. 75* — Bill of Lading**

EXERCISE 153

The freight bill in this exercise shows the transportation charges on the merchandise billed on the invoice and listed on the bill of lading prepared in the preceding exercises. This freight bill indicates that the merchandise delivered to the transportation company by the Clark-Peters Hardware Company is now at the freight station of the Marvin Hardware Company. It also serves to notify the Marvin Hardware Company of the amount due for freight charges. The Marvin Hardware Company must pay this freight bill before receiving the merchandise from the railroad agent.

Make checks payable to

FREIGHT BILL

CHICAGO AND NORTH WESTERN RAILWAY COMPANY **CHICAGO, ILL.**

Dr., For Charges on Articles Transported:

DATE June 25, 19 4- FREIGHT BILL NO. 386752

SECTION 31 X

ROUTE ______ (Point of Origin to Destination)

CONSIGNEE Marvin Hardware Co.

DESTINATION Milwaukee, Wisconsin

Way-Billed From / Point and Date of Shipment	Way-Bill Date and No. / Connecting Line Reference	Full Name of Shipper / Previous Way-Bill Reference	Car Initials and No. / Original Car Initials and No.
Chicago	1983 June 20	Clark-Peters Hdw. Co.	C 29475

NUMBER OF PACKAGES, ARTICLES AND MARKS	WEIGHT	RATE	FREIGHT	ADVANCES	TOTAL
2 cases hardware	255#	.80½	2.05		
1 case cutlery	150#	.80½	1.21		3.26
TOTAL PREPAID					

RECEIVED PAYMENT ______ 19____ TOTAL 3.26

L C Kole FREIGHT AGENT

Original paid freight bills must be surrendered for overcharges to be refunded and must accompany claims for overcharge, loss or damage.

***Illustration No. 76* — Freight Bill**

Directions. Type one copy of the freight bill, using a form similar to the one illustrated. If such a form is not available, do not type the printed form, but arrange the typewritten **material** in the same order as that in which the insertions are shown on the printed form.

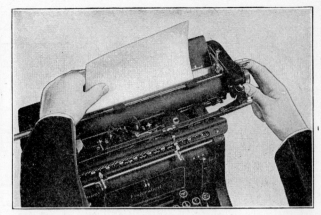

Illustration No. 38 — Inserting a Half Sheet of Paper   Illustration No. 39 — Inserting a Half Sheet of Paper

EXERCISE 12

12 minutes

Directions. 1. Remove the paper for the technique practice from the machine.
2. Study Illustrations Nos. 38 and 39 which show how to insert a half sheet.
3. Insert a half sheet. Set a tabulator stop for a five-space indention. Have a top margin of 10 spaces. Type this exercise once on the stroke level.
4. When you have completed the exercise, remove the paper, insert another half sheet, and retype the exercise.

All letters of the alphabet are used in this exercise.

STROKES

If you expect to find a job as soon as you complete your   56

school work, you will have to answer the question, What skill   118

have you that a businessman will prize? You must be able to   179

do some things so well that you will be given the work even   239

though others want that work too. The power to type well is   300

one skill you can use with most kinds of office work. You   359

must be a good typist, though, to use the skill in business.   419

The scale at the left shows the vertical inches and line spaces on a half sheet of paper.

In line 2, the question is not a direct quotation; therefore, quotation marks are not used. The capital is used, however, because there is a complete interrogative sentence used as a part of the longer declarative sentence.

EXERCISE 151

This invoice of the Clark-Peters Hardware Company is the result of the purchase order shown in the preceding exercise. The notation "Shortage—Back-ordered 2 doz #97." is typed on the bottom of the invoice to indicate that only four dozen of this item were in stock and that the other two dozen have been back-ordered and will be shipped later.

CLARK-PETERS HARDWARE COMPANY
619 WABASH AVENUE
CHICAGO

Invoice No. 24183

Date June 19, 194-   Cust. Order No. 457

Sold to   Marvin Hardware Co.   Shipped to   Marvin Hardware Co.
          Milwaukee   Milwaukee
          Wisconsin   Wisconsin

Shipped Via   C. & N. W. R. R.   Terms: 2%   10 days; 30 days net

AMOUNT ORDERED	AMOUNT SHIPPED	PIECE NUMBER	DESCRIPTION	PRICE	PER	AMOUNT
5 doz	5 doz	#16	24" Hand Saws	22.90	doz	114.50
5 "	5 "	#17	26" Hand Saws	26.00	"	130.00
5 "	5 "	#18D	24" Panel Saws	24.75	"	123.75
3 "	3 "	#60	Scissors	10.40	"	31.20
5 "	5 "	#2008	Knives & Forks	29.75	"	148.75
6 "	4 "	#97	Pocket Knives	14.60	"	58.40
						606.60

Shortage—Back-ordered 2 doz #97

Illustration No. 74 — Invoice

BILLS OF LADING

When a shipment is to be made by freight, a bill of lading is prepared at the time the merchandise is turned over to the carrier. A bill of lading is a contract between the shipper and the transportation company. The printed form, made out in triplicate, provides space for entering:

(1) the name of the transportation company receiving the merchandise (unless the name is printed on the form)
(2) the date
(3) the name of the shipper (unless the name is printed on the form)
(4) the name and the address of the buyer, or consignee
(5) the names of all other transportation companies that must handle the shipment
(6) a list of the cases or other containers in the shipment
(7) the signatures of the shipper and the agent for the transportation company
(8) the address of the shipper.

The railroads in the United States are under the jurisdiction of the Interstate Commerce Commission. The Commission has set up certain regulations regarding bills of lading. These regulations deal with (1) size, (2) number of copies to be prepared, and (3) color of paper to be used in printing the blanks. The size of the bill of lading and the color of the paper are regulated according to the convenience of the buyer, the seller, and the transportation company. Three copies are prepared: the *original* is mailed to the buyer; the *shipping order* is retained by the railroad; and the *memorandum* is retained by the seller. The printed forms for bills of lading are prepared in such a way that three copies may be made at one time through the use of carbon paper.

The buyer, or consignee, gets the original copy of the bill of lading as evidence that the shipment has been accepted by the carrier for delivery to him. If the consignee is not known to the local agent of the transportation company, the original of the bill of lading will be required before the shipment will be released.

A straight bill of lading is used when the buyer pays for the merchandise in advance or buys it on account. The order bill of lading is used when goods are shipped C. O. D. When an order bill of lading is used, the shipper usually sends it to a bank in the customer's city with a commercial draft attached. By paying the draft, the customer obtains the bill of lading and hence the title to the goods. The bank then sends the shipper the amount of the invoice, less a collection charge, by means of a cashier's check or a bank draft. The buyer must endorse the bill of lading and present it to the transportation company in order to obtain the goods.

Reaches to *3-#, 7-&* (ampersand)

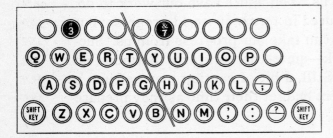

Illustration No. 40 — Reaches to 3-#, 7-& (ampersand)

The figure *3* is above *e*; the number sign (#) is the shift of *3*. The *d finger* controls these characters.

Lift the *f finger* slightly as the *d finger* makes the reach to *3-#*.

The number sign (#) is used with bill numbers and in tabulated work. In ordinary textual material, use *No.* instead of #. This symbol is also used to indicate pounds in invoice and statement work. When used to express pounds, the symbol follows the figure without a space.

de3d d3d d#d d3d d#d d3d d#d d3d#d d3d

The figure *7* is above *u*; the *&* (ampersand) is the shift of *7*. The *j finger* controls these characters.

Make the reach to *7-&* by straightening the *j finger*. Hold the other fingers in their typing position.

The symbol *&* (known as the ampersand) is the abbreviation for *and*. This symbol is used correctly in firm signatures containing personal names.

ju7j j7j j&j d3d j7j d#d j&j Mill & Hall

Figures and symbols make up a considerable part of the typewritten material that goes out of an office. The ability to type numbers and symbols rapidly and accurately will add a great deal to your job efficiency.

The finger pathway for the reach to the figure key must be reconstructed frequently after it has been established. You should mentally associate the figure and symbol with the controlling finger. Make the reach with little hand or arm movement.

You can learn to type figures with the same accuracy that you type words, but each figure must be controlled as a separate movement. This is comparable to letter-level typing and different from the word-level typing you have been doing.

LOCATION DRILL

10 minutes

Directions. Type the drill twice.

Use the small letter l for the figure 1.

	STROKES
d3d d3d j7j d3d j7j 37 13 17 31 71 73 173 13 137 d3d j7j 371	60
3d#d 7j&j 37 #37 3d#d 7j&j 173 137 3d#d 7j&j 3d#d 7j&j #173	59
We have your letter of May 13. The check is dated April 17.	60
Bill #7 must be paid June 3. Smith & Day have paid Bill #73.	61
What is the sum of 31 and 7 and 13? Is the check dated July 7?	63

ment, and obscurity. The world at large pays, too, for the progress of the world depends on the progress made by each of us. You and I have our work to do. That work may be large or small as measured in terms of world progress; but no one can do our work for us, and no one can take our progress from us. Success does not come from haphazard work—quite the contrary. Sermons on the matter of waste will not help much. Still, a bit of caution may set just a few students to thinking and may help them budget their time as they prepare for the work they plan to do.

3047
3124
3200
3277
3349
3429
3506
3535

The exercises in this budget give the forms involved in a complete transaction. You will assume that you are working for the MARVIN HARDWARE COMPANY, INC. The number of copies of each form that would be made in an office is indicated, but it will not be necessary for you to make more than one copy of each form in an exercise.

EXERCISE 149

The requisition given in this exercise is a written request made by O. M. Bagby, the stock clerk for the Marvin Hardware Company, to C. R. Laughlin, the purchasing agent, for merchandise to be ordered as specified. In the office this requisition would be issued in duplicate; the original would be given to the purchasing agent, and the duplicate would be retained by the stock clerk.

MARVIN HARDWARE COMPANY, Inc.
MILWAUKEE
Purchase Requisition

REQUISITION No. B-429

Required for Department D
Notify Mr. Foster   on delivery
Date Issued June 16, 194-
Date Required June 30, 194-

QUANTITY	DESCRIPTION
5 doz each	24" and 26" Hand Saws
5 "	24" Panel Saws
3 "	Scissors
6 "	Pocket Knives
5 " sets	Knives and Forks

Approved by_____
Requisition Placed by_____ O. M. Bagby

PURCHASING AGENT'S MEMORANDUM

Purchase Order No._____   Issued to_____
Date_____

Illustration No. 72 — Purchase Requisition

PURCHASE ORDER   No. 457

MARVIN HARDWARE COMPANY, Inc.
MILWAUKEE

Date June 16, 194-

To Clark-Peters Hardware Company   Ship Via
619 Wabash Avenue, Chicago   F.O.B. Chicago
Deliver As soon as possible   Terms 2% 10 days; 30 days net

QUANTITY		DESCRIPTION	PRICE
5 doz	#16	24" Hand Saws	22.90
5 "	#17	26" Hand Saws	26.00
5 "	#18D	24" Panel Saws	24.75
3 "	#60	Scissors	10.40
5 "	#2008	Knives & Forks	29.75
6 "	#97	Pocket Knives	14.60

C R Laughlin
Purchasing Agent

Illustration No. 73 — Purchase Order

EXERCISE 150

This purchase order is the result of the requisition given in the preceding exercise. In an office this form would be issued in triplicate. The original would be mailed to the Clark-Peters Hardware Company; one copy would be retained by the purchasing agent; and the other copy would be retained by the Receiving Department.

LESSON 13

FINGER GYMNASTICS

1 minute

Drill 11. Rub the palm of one hand with the thumb of the other. Rub the backs of the hands vigorously.

RECONSTRUCTION PRACTICE

5 minutes

Directions. Use a 60-space line. Set the machine for double spacing.

(Say the word.)

```
an he if us of is it an do he or so am it am go he or an he
```

(Type on the stroke level.)

```
d3d j7j 3d7j d#d d#d #1 #1 j7j j&j &j Hall & Mill d3d j7j 31

1 3 13 1 7 3 173 1 3 7 137 3 7 1 371 7 1 3 713 3 1 7 317 317

The order is dated March 13.  We have your letter of May 7.
```

TECHNIQUE PRACTICE 13

10 minutes

Directions. Type the drill once; then select for repetition practice the sentences that provide the drill for your weak controls. Type on the letter level.

STROKES

```
Order #73 was shipped March 13.  The check is dated May 7.    58

We wrote them on April 3.  Their answer is dated April 17.    58

Harris & Marks will pay the bill May 3 or May 7, they wrote. 60
```

Drill

```
(i) I think it is in this typing skill that I will find most joy. 61

(n) None is so futile as he who cannot control his own thinking. 60
```

EXERCISE 13

12 minutes

Directions. Set a tabulator stop for a 5-space indention. Type the exercise twice. Use a half sheet of paper for each writing. Leave 10 spaces in the top margin. Type on the stroke level.

All letters of the alphabet are used in this exercise.

STROKES

```
We are judged by how we look as well as by how we     50

act.  It takes only a little thought and effort each  103

day for us to acquire neatness in dress.  There is no 157

excuse for any of us to fail to take thought of our   209

grooming.  If we realize that our dress has much to do 264

with the impression made on others, most of us will   316

give it the attention it deserves.  Now is the time to 371

begin to improve in dress and in manner.              411
```

[33]

We are often told that we are a nation of wasters. We had great forests
once; now our acres of trees are numbered. Many of our hills, on which fine
trees stood just a few years ago, are covered with stumps and small brush. Our
rich soil, vast stores of oil, and great mineral deposits seemed to give the
nation a capital without limit. Quantity has made us careless. We grow more,
make more, sell more, buy more, eat more, and waste more than any other
nation. We are prodigal in all that we do. Our philosophy of life seems to be
based on the theory that we cannot exhaust our resources. We do not realize
that waste always causes shortage; that it is the right use of what we have
that makes for continued abundance.

If trees are planted, they will eventually cover the bare hills. Acres of waste
land can be reclaimed and made to yield abundantly. These, however, are not
the wastes that make a nation poor. A nation is made poor through the waste
of time, which leads to wasted years and wasted lives. We are all equal in the
hours we possess, though we make vastly different use of these hours. The
rich and the poor, the high and the low, the workman and the student—all
have just twenty-four hours in which to do all the things people do because
they must do them or because they desire to do them. As in the case of the
nation's great store of natural resources, we do not prize the time we have.
Some are able to do outstanding things because they exact of themselves the
wise use of their time, and others fail to rise above the doing of unimportant
things because they fritter their time in futile gestures or in fanciful planning.

The only way to save an hour is to spend it wisely. All of us have a margin
of time apart from the hours necessary for work and for recreation. How shall
we use this margin of time? If we should save just two hours a day, the saving would mean more than six hundred hours in a year. In six hundred hours
we could read at least ten great books and ponder them earnestly. In six hundred hours we could add keenness to our thinking and depth to our living.
With six hundred hours saved to be spent carefully and wisely, any of us in a
few short years could become an outstanding leader in his field of interest. It
is not lack of ability or lack of opportunity that sets us apart. The way in
which their equal numbers of hours are spent sets up zones of demarcation
between the successful workman and the one who never quite reaches the
heights.

In most typewriting classrooms there is wasted time that, if properly used,
would add a large number to the group of expert typists who have already
achieved success. Pupils do not work to their capacity. In business there is
enough time wasted by careless workers to double the entire office production.
Too many work for themselves and not for the company. We pay the price
for our waste of time; and we pay in the coin of disappointment, small achieve-

LOCATION PRACTICE 13

Reaches to *4-$, 8-'* (apostrophe)

The *f finger* controls *4-$*. Make the reach with a direct finger movement without change of hand or elbow position.

The *$* is typed before figures and without a space between the symbol and the first figure.

```
fr4f f4f f$f f$f 41 41 141 4f $f $14 $41
```

The *k finger* controls *8-'*. Lift the *j finger* slightly as the *k finger* makes the reach to *8-'*.

Illustration No. 41 — Reaches to 4-$, 8-' (apostrophe)

The apostrophe is used in the possessive of nouns and in contractions. It is also used to indicate a quotation within a quotation.

```
ki8k k8k k'k k'k 84 148 isn't don't 184
```

LOCATION DRILL

Directions. Type the drill twice.

STROKES

We have the letter of January 14. The check is dated March 8.	62
The check is for $148. The amount of the bill is $184, isn't it?	65
Mr. Long's check for $148 was cashed yesterday at ten o'clock.	62
What is the sum of 1 and 8 and 4 and 7 and 3 and 14 and 17?	59
I can type the figures 1, 3, 8, 4, and 7 with speed and ease.	61

LESSON 14

FINGER GYMNASTICS   *1 minute*

Drill 12. Hold both hands in front of you, fingers together. Hold the last three fingers still and move the first finger as far to the side as possible. Return the first finger; then move the first and second fingers together; finally move the little finger as far to the side as possible.

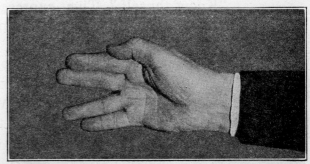

BUDGET XVII
TECHNIQUE PRACTICE 92
Emphasizing Symbols

Directions. Use a 70-space line; single spacing. Type each line twice. Double-space after the second typing of each line.

	STROKES
We sold 985 copies of his book, *Conquest,* in June; only 724, in July.	69
He paid a bill of $36.10 at Gaines's and another of 95 cents at Ross's.	71
At O'Neil's they sold 216 lbs. of Golden Gran butter @ 35 cents a pound.	72
Policy #459201 matured when I was 57 years 9 months and 28 days old.	68
Mr. North's report was included in Part VI, Section 8, pages 972-1006.	70

SENTENCE PRACTICE

Directions. Use a 70-space line. Use the sentences for one-minute writings and for drill on calling the throw.

	STROKES
When you know a thing can and should be done, you can find the way.	67
We are not here to play, to dream, to drift; we are here to work.	65
Let me not fail to be kind, for I shall never pass this way again.	66
True worth is in being, not in seeming; in doing, not in dreaming.	66
When the wrong thought appears, crowd it out with a right thought.	66

CORRECTIVE DRILL PARAGRAPH

Directions. Use a 70-space line; a 5-space indention; single spacing.

	STROKES
(Emphasizing letter *x*) Socrates and Xanthippe are excellent examples of the exist-	58
ing belief that exact extremes attract each other. Socrates was	123
a philosopher, quiet, studious, and given to excogitation.	183
Xanthippe is reported to have been an experienced virago with	245
a tongue that could excoriate like a xyster. In justice to her,	310
one must realize that she had her trials with the exalted ex-	370
pounder of theories who found exhilaration in cross-examining	432
students in the market place. Doubtlessly, he often sought that	497
exit from her exhibitions of extremism, which must have ex-	555
hausted him. Xanthippe left an unsavory reputation for quar-	615
relsomeness; Socrates left the well-known philosophic maxim:	677
"Know thyself." They expressed their lives in their own indi-	738
vidual ways. Neither was exempt from mistakes, but they have	800
come down to us through the pages of history as outstanding	860
examples of the attraction of opposites.	900

TIMED WRITING

Directions. Use a 70-space line; a 5-space indention; double spacing. If you complete the test before time is called, start at the beginning and continue typing. After time has been called, check the writing carefully.

RECONSTRUCTION PRACTICE

Directions. Use a 60-space line. Set the machine for double spacing.

f4f k8k f4f k8k f$f k'k f4f k8k d3d j7j d#d j&j f 1 8 3 7 4 8

He will be here May 14. The check is for $73, isn't it?

The note is due August 18. We can't pay it until August 31.

Has Hill & Young's order #471 been paid? It amounts to $138.

TECHNIQUE PRACTICE 14

Directions. Use each of the first three sentences for two one-minute writings. Set the goal for the second writing one word in advance of the rate of the first writing. Type the last two sentences on the letter level until you feel that you have acceptable control of the letters emphasized, letters *p* and *q*.

	STROKES
No one should let himself doubt that he can do his work well.	61
We must check our own work to know when it is right or wrong.	61
I can do the work with just a little more ease each day I type.	63
Poise, purpose, and precision help prepare one for life's work.	63
Quiz questions quite frequently require quick and apt quoting.	62

EXERCISE 14

Directions. 1. Set a tabulator stop for a 5-space indention.
2. Type the exercise twice. Use a half sheet of paper for each writing. Leave 10 spaces in the top margin.
3. Type on the stroke level.

All letters of the alphabet are used in this exercise.

	STROKES
Usage differs as to how to express numbers. There are	55
some points on which there is agreement. Regardless of size,	117
spell out numbers at the very beginning of a sentence. Use	177
figures for page numbers; as, pages 38 and 473. Dimensions	237
should be expressed in figures; as, 8 by 14 feet. Units of	297
measure should be expressed in figures; as, 7 quarts, 3 pecks.	360
These are just a few points on which there is some agreement.	421

EXERCISE 144
INCOMING LETTER

Directions. Use the single-spaced indented form; end punctuation. Type the dictator's signature in the position for the official title.

July 28, 194–. Baker-Allison Company, 349-350 Market Street, Spokane, Washington. Gentlemen: I am returning today by special-delivery truck one barrel of Superior Flour billed to me on your Invoice No. 2947. This barrel contained flour of a grade very inferior to that which you have always sent me under the label of Superior. You will readily see that it is not of so fine a quality as the other barrels delivered at the same time. (P) It will be unnecessary for you to send another barrel of flour at this time. When my present supply begins to get low, I shall place another order. (P) Please send me a credit memorandum for the flour I am returning. Yours truly, G. H. Williamson *(Strokes, 707; words, 108.)*

EXERCISE 145

The credit memorandum illustrated below is the result of the letter written in the preceding exercise. A credit memorandum is a business form that contains written information regarding a return of merchandise to the seller, or an allowance from the price of merchandise that is granted by the seller.

Directions. Type the credit memorandum in duplicate. The original copy would be mailed to Mr. Williamson, and the duplicate would be filed with the invoice after the proper record had been made to show that the amount of the sale made to Mr. Williamson had been reduced by the amount of the credit memorandum.

CREDIT MEMORANDUM

BAKER-ALLISON COMPANY	July 29, 194-
349-350 MARKET STREET	G. H. Williamson
SPOKANE, WASHINGTON	215 North Federal Street
	Spokane, Washington

WE CREDIT YOUR ACCOUNT AS FOLLOWS:

1 bbl	Superior Flour	8	16	8	16

Illustration No. 71 — Credit Memorandum

EXERCISE 146

Directions. Make the extensions and find the total of the invoice. Type one copy.

July 29, 194–   Invoice No. 2980
Sold to L. M. Evans
          1676 W. Ninth Street
                Spokane, Washington
Terms: Cash in 30 days; no discount
How shipped: Delivered

10#	Meadow Dew Butter	@ .48 per lb
5#	Pimento Loaf	.38 " "
1 doz	Pimento ½'s	2.50 " doz
1 pc	Lamberta Cheese 4½#	.70 " lb

EXERCISE 147

Directions. Issue a credit memorandum to L. M. Evans, 1676 W. Ninth Street, Spokane, Washington, to cover the return of the following items charged on Invoice No. 2980. Type the memorandum in duplicate.

10#   Meadow Dew Butter
1 pc Lamberta Cheese 4½#

EXERCISE 148

Directions. Make the extensions and find the total of the invoice. Type one copy.

July 29, 194–   Invoice No. 2981
Sold to S. R. Perkins
          56 S. Second Street
                Spokane, Washington
Terms: Cash 30 days; no discount
How shipped: Delivered

1 bx Meadow Dew Butter 30# @ .46 per lb
1 bx Meadow Dew Prints 30# @ .47½ per lb
1 cs Eggs 30 doz @ .55 per doz
1 cut Wheel Swiss 9½# @ .45 per lb

LOCATION PRACTICE 14

Reaches to *2-"*, *9-(*

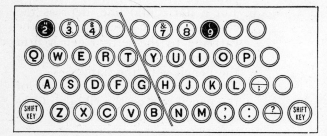

Illustration No. 42
Reaches to *2-"*, *9-(* (left parenthesis)

The figure *2* is above *w*; the shift of *2* is the quotation mark ("). The key is controlled by the *s* finger.

In making the reach, hold the *a finger* near its typing position and lift the *s* and *d fingers* to give freedom to the controlling finger *s*. Make the reach without change of hand or elbow.

```
sw2s s2s s"s He said, "Get 21 quarts."
```

The figure *9* is above *o*; the shift of *9* is the left parenthesis [*(*]. This key is controlled by the *l* finger.

In making the reach, hold the *;* finger near its typing position and lift the *k* and *j* fingers to give freedom to the controlling finger *l*. Hold the elbow steady; there must be no in-and-out movement when the reach is made.

```
lo91 191 1(1 1(1 1931 1939 1 2 1 9 1219
```

LOCATION DRILL

Directions. Type the drill twice.

	STROKES
`s2s 191 s2s 191 121 191 291 291 192 192 s2s 191 s"s 1(1 "s (1`	61
`I am 24 years old.  Joe was born in 1929.  Are you 27 yet?`	58
`He said, "There are 29 men here."  I thought there were 39.`	59
`The "(" is just a part of the complete parentheses we use.`	58
`I think "it's" is the right form to use.  "Its" is a pronoun.`	61

SPECIAL FEATURES

You have already learned many of the operative parts of typewriters. Some machines, however, have special features that you will need to know and these will be given from time to time throughout the book.

The Remington jam trip remedies the fumbles that result in collided type bars. A light touch on the jam-trip lever releases the stuck type bars and permits you to continue your typing without much more than a momentary break in the rhythm of your writing.

If the keys collide and stick when you are operating an L C Smith, just touch the shift key and the type bars will fall into place without the necessity of pulling them apart.

7. Type all invoices with single spacing unless there are only two or three items to the invoice.
8. To rule with the typewriter:
   a. Use the underscore for horizontal lines.
   b. Raise or lower the line position by resetting the carriage through the use of the variable line spacer.
   c. Use the apostrophe or the colon to make vertical lines.
9. To rule with a pencil while the paper is still in the typewriter:
   a. Rest the tip of the pencil on the ribbon mechanism at the V point above the ribbon. Hold the point of the pencil firmly against the paper.
   b. For a horizontal line, depress the carriage-release lever and move the carriage to the left. Keep a firm hold on the carriage. Do not guide the pencil with the hand.
   c. To rule vertically, let the tip of the pencil rest on the ribbon mechanism and roll the carriage forward.
10. Check all work before mailing it. Use window envelopes for invoices.

EXERCISE 141

Directions. Type the invoice as it is given. Determine the correct adjustments for the tabulator stops.

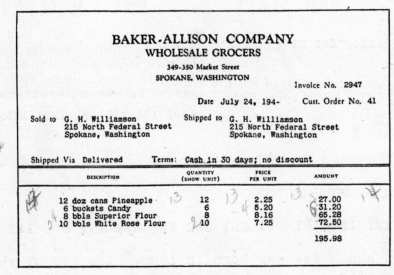

Illustration No. 70 — Invoice

EXERCISE 142

Directions. Type in invoice form, similar to the form in Exercise 141.

July 24, 194–   Invoice No. 2948
Sold to Holmes & Murdock
              Ritzville, Washington
Terms: Cash in 30 days; no discount
How shipped: Delivered

2 cs Eggs	60	doz	.50	30.00
1 bx Yellow Daisy Butter	7-3	oz	.30	2.16
1 bx Long Horn Cheese	27-9	oz	.28	7.72
1 Wheel Swiss Cheese	14-1	oz	.46	6.47
				46.35

The weight for the second item is to be read "7 pounds and 3 ounces."

EXERCISE 143

Directions. Type in invoice form, similar to the form in Exercise 141. Total the extensions.

July 24, 194–   Invoice No. 2949
Sold to F. C. Morris
              1928 King Street
              Spokane, Washington

Terms: Cash in 30 days; no discount
How shipped: Delivered

2 bx Holland Rolls Cheese	60#	.45	27.00
1 bx Holland Quarters	30#	.47	14.10
1 bx White Rose Butter	30#	.42	12.60
1 Philadelphia Cream Loaf	3#	.44	1.32
1 Brick Cheese	6¼#	.29	1.81

LESSON 15

FINGER GYMNASTICS

1 minute

Drill 13. Rub the hands vigorously. Let the thumb rub the palm of the hand. Rub the fingers, the back of the hand, and the wrist.

RECONSTRUCTION PRACTICE

5 minutes

Directions. Use a 60-space line. Set the machine for double spacing.

```
3d 7j 4f 8k 4f 8k 2s 2s 9l 9l 2s 9l 4f 8k 2s 9l 12 13 14 21

4f$f 8k'k 3d#d 7j&j 2s"s 9l(1 3 1 4 8 1 7 2 9 3 1 4 8 2 1 9

The bill is #47.  Date the check May 12.  Pay this April 9.

He quoted, "He can who thinks he can."  I owe them $294.83.
```

TECHNIQUE PRACTICE 15

10 minutes

Directions. Use each of the first three sentences for two one-minute writings. Set the goal for the second writing one word in advance of the rate of the first writing. Type the last two sentences on the letter level until you feel that you have acceptable control of the letters emphasized, letters *t* and *x*.

STROKES

```
  It is just as hard to be a good winner as to be a good loser.  61

  Do not ask for any work that you are not prepared to do well.   61

  We find that it pays to work hard if we want to progress.       57
```
Drill
```
(t) That treaty tried to temper justice with mercy but it failed.  61

(x) To excel in life, expect and exact excellent work of yourself.  62
```

EXERCISE 15

12 minutes

Directions. Set a tabulator stop for a 5-space indention. Type the exercise twice. Use a half sheet of paper for each writing. Leave 10 spaces in the top margin. Type on the stroke level.

All letters of the alphabet are used in this exercise.

STROKES

```
     Pull out of each practice project all possible meanings.      57

For example, why is a comma used after the first two words of      119

this sentence?  In each day's work there will be opportunities     182

for you to learn more than just straight copying.  Why was the     245

apostrophe used in writing the word "day's"?  Why do you put       306

the quotation mark before the question mark in the sentence        366

just typed?  Seize every chance to learn "why" and "how."          423
```

BUDGET XVI
INVOICES

The work of the invoice clerk is of vital importance. Accurate billing aids in the prompt settlement of accounts that are due. The work will not be particularly difficult for you if you have skill in operating the typewriter and if you have a "figure sense" that will help you to make extensions without error.

The columnar headings on invoice forms indicate the position for the different types of information, even though rulings are often omitted from the printed forms. (See the invoice on page 205.) Before typing an invoice, study the columnar headings. The placing of the figures in the proper columns will make it possible to interpret the figures accurately. You must be careful to see that the items and the extensions are in the proper columns.

In typing tabulated work, make full use of the special tabulator attachments on your typewriter. If your typewriter has the decimal tabulator mechanism, you can indent quickly and accurately to the exact position desired. If it does not, scan the figures that are to go into each column and set a tabulator stop so that the tabulator mechanism will give you the correct indention for the greatest number of figures in a column. You can space forward for one or two positions when necessary, or you can backspace for each additional space required. For instance, if you have a column of numbers in which the digits representing hundreds are used most frequently, set a stop for the hundreds point; then, when it is necessary to type digits representing thousands, backspace after indenting to the position for hundreds. This procedure will effect a saving in time that will greatly increase your production.

WINDOW ENVELOPES

Window envelopes have transparent or cutout openings in the lower center, through which the address typed on a letter, a statement, or an invoice can be seen. Such envelopes may be used for invoices, monthly statements, or regular correspondence.

In the folding of correspondence for the window envelope, the important thing is to keep in mind that the complete address must show through the window in the envelope. Fold a full-page invoice or letter from the top down fully two thirds the length of the paper; then fold back the required distance to make the address come to the correct position. Only two folds are usually necessary for a paper that is to be inserted into a window envelope. Fold a half sheet through the center, keeping the typewritten side on the outside. Insert the paper into the envelope with the address toward the front.

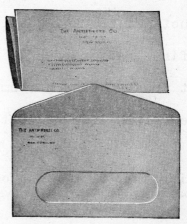

Illustration No. 69 — Window Envelope

CHECK LIST FOR INVOICE WORK

1. Use a pencil and paper for checking extensions, figuring discounts, etc.
2. Study the material so that you can type it accurately on the invoice form.
3. Set tabulator stops for all the main columns.
4. Several duplicate copies of all invoices would be made in regular office work, but only one copy will be typed for this school work.
5. After abbreviations, and in columnar tabulations where the ruling separates the dollars from the cents, you may omit all periods.
6. Use the following special abbreviations:
   " (quotation mark) for *ditto,* used as the sign of repetition.
   " (quotation mark) to express inches.
   ' (apostrophe) to express feet.
   # (number sign) to express pounds.
   C for hundreds.
   M for thousands.

Reaches to 5-%, 0-) (cipher and right parenthesis)

Illustration No. 43
Reaches to 5-%, 0-) (cipher and right parenthesis)

The figure *5* is above and to the right of the letter *r*; the shift of *5* is %, the per cent symbol. This key is controlled by the *f finger*.

Look at your finger make an experimental reach to *5*; then type the following line:

f5f f5f f%f f5f f%f Pay me $5.51, or 7%.

The cipher *(0)* is above the letter *p*; the shift of the cipher is *)* [the right parenthesis]. This key is controlled by the *; finger*.

Make the reach to *0-)* without change of elbow position. Stretch the controlling finger and move it forward to the key, keeping the other fingers as close to the home keys as possible.

;0; ;); ten 10 twenty 20 (10) (20) ;0;

LOCATION DRILL

10 minutes

Directions. Type the drill twice.

STROKES

f5f ;0; f5f ;0; f%f ;); f5f ;0; 15 50 15 150 31 30 301 103 50   61

Don't forget November 11, 1918. Jim's birthday is January 15.   62

We owe them $500. The rate of interest is 3%. Pay him $50.   60

What is the sum of 2 and 8 and 4 and 9 and 3 and 5 and 70?   58

Jack is 15 years 10 months and 8 days old. I am older than he.   63

SPECIAL FEATURE

Touch control or touch tuning is possible with many of the makes of typewriters. The purpose of the touch control mechanism is to adjust the pressure to your individual touch. The various touch control mechanisms (No. 32) are alike in that they provide for seven possible variations in the touch that can be made. These variations in adjustments are from very light to extra heavy. The Noiseless and Remington pressure dial gives a similar control of the pressure and permits writing to be done in various degrees of inking density, from very light to very dark. This is an invaluable feature in matching type for "fill-in" work.

For most classroom work, the touch adjustment mechanism should be set for a light pressure and not varied unless the nature of the work requires a heavier touch.

EXERCISE 139

Directions. Type an index card for each name on the mailing list on page 202. Type on the card, two lines below the last line of the address, the notation "Form letter mailed" and add the date. Arrange the cards in alphabetical order and file them for future use.

MAKING COPIES OF A FORM LETTER

A letter addressed to an individual may be of interest and importance to a number of others. Through the use of carbon paper and onionskin paper, or some other very thin paper, a dozen or more copies can be made at one typing. The names of those to whom carbon copies are to be sent should be typed as a mailing notation at the left margin below the reference initials and the enclosure notation. This method is used in Exercise 140.

It is equally correct to place the names of all those to whom the letter is to be sent in the position for the inside address and to use the salutation "Gentlemen." In this case the list of names may be omitted at the bottom of the letter. This form may be used when the letter is to be sent to men of the same relative official position, but the form would not be used in connection with such a letter as that in Exercise 140. In this case one man, Mr. Hall, is the manager of a branch office, and the others are working under his direction.

```
                         Yours very truly


                            Secretary

CY

Enclosure

C/c to Mr. A. C. Brownlee
       Mr. Mark L. O'Donovan
       Mr. C. V. Peterson
       Mr. James Richardson
       Mr. Leonard E. Winslow
       Mr. William O. Wundt
       Mr. P. Thomas Young
```

Illustration No. 68 — Part of a Form Letter Showing the Names of Those to Whom Carbon Copies of the Letter Are to be Sent

EXERCISE 140

Directions. Type the letter on onionskin paper, using the current date. Eight copies are to be mailed, and one copy must be kept for the office files. In determining the placement of the letter, provide for the listing of the names of those to whom carbon copies are to be sent. Use a modification of the block form of letter with a blocked inside address and paragraphs, and with the closing lines indented to the complimentary close position. Use open punctuation. Address an envelope for each letter.

In building the carbon stack, place a piece of paper on the desk and a carbon sheet (glossy side down) on top of it; add paper and carbon until you have eight sheets for carbon copies and one sheet for the original. Place the stack of papers and carbon sheets under the flap of an envelope; depress the paper release slightly; roll the papers into the machine far enough for the feed rolls to grip the stack; depress the paper release again to free the papers from possible creases and to avoid wrinkling the carbon; then twirl the papers into the writing position. The envelope will keep the top of the papers even. When the papers have been inserted, remove the envelope.

Mr. Horton N. Hall Manager Book Readers Association Chicago, Illinois Dear Mr. Hall We are mailing from this office a form letter on the use of memberships in the *Book Readers Association* as gifts to friends or employees. This letter is being sent to a select list of men, women, and business firms in the sales district of this office. You will not want to use this letter, but you may want to write something similar and mail your letter to those whose names appear in the index of your "A" classification. A copy of our letter is enclosed. (P) Here are some things you should stress in all your mail and personal selling: (P) 1. Book dividends 2. Monetary advantage of joining the Association 3. Freedom to choose from the large list of books published each month 4. The news items sent out each month regarding all important new publications 5. The use of the Association membership as insurance against missing the important books of the month (P) You and your salesmen have established a fine record for memberships in your territory. Intensify your drive for members now while you are in the "success mood." Yours very truly (J. L. Tigart) Secretary Enclosure C/c to Mr. A. C. Brownlee, Mr. Mark L. O'Donovan, Mr. C. V. Peterson, Mr. James Richardson, Mr. Leonard E. Winslow, Mr. William O. Wundt, Mr. P. Thomas Young *(Strokes, 1326; words, 180.)*

LESSON 16
FINGER GYMNASTICS
1 minute

Drill 14. Place your hands flat on the desk, palms down, fingers extended. Raise the wrists slightly and draw the fingers toward the palms of the hands until the finger tips are on the desk; then lift the fingers, one at a time, high in the air in a curved typing position. Lightly tap the desk as you bring each finger back toward the palm of the hand. This is a scratching motion.

RECONSTRUCTION PRACTICE
5 minutes

Directions. Use a 60-space line. Set the machine for double spacing.

4f 8k 2s 9l 4f 9l 2s 0; 7j 5f 0; 5f 0; 12 13 18 14 19 20 15 50

4f$f 8k'k Isn't the amount $310?   3d#d Bill #158 is not paid.

What is the sum of 14 and 28 and 30?   Order #59 amounts to $758.

Please pack my box with five dozen jars of liquid gum.

TECHNIQUE PRACTICE 16
10 minutes

Directions. Use each of the first three sentences for two one-minute writings. Set the goal for the second writing one word in advance of the rate of the first writing. Type the last two sentences on the letter level until you feel that you have acceptable control of the letters.

STROKES

Our goal is to learn to type as well and rapidly as possible. 61

We need to learn to type figures quickly; as, 4 and 8 are 12. 61

Can we do each day's work better than that of the day before? 61

Drill
(y) Yesterday was today; use today wisely before it is yesterday. 61

(z) Zeal and zest for work do not characterize the lazy students. 61

EXERCISE 16
12 minutes

Directions. Set a tabulator stop for a 5-space indention. Type the exercise twice. Use a half sheet of paper for each writing. Leave 10 spaces in the top margin. Type on the stroke level.

All letters of the alphabet are used in this exercise.

STROKES

You know that the rules for expressing numbers have not 56

been standardized, but there is some agreement. For example, 118

you must state size and weight in figures; as, The package is 180

not quite 5 feet 10 inches long, but it weighs 37 pounds. We 242

type sums of money in figures; as, Joe owes them $50, but you 304

owe only 75 cents. Even sums of money should be typed without 367

the decimal and ciphers. 391

1. Mr. Frank Martin Osgood
   1169 Orange Road
   South Pasadena, California

2. Mrs. Anna Jean Boswell
   Secretary to the President
   Southern Academy for Girls
   Nashville, Tennessee

3. Miss Ada C. Hatcher
   Griffin, Georgia

4. The Reverend H. M. Carson, D.D.
   First Presbyterian Church
   Louisville, Kentucky

5. Rabbi Levy Rattner
   Congregation Beth Jehuda
   Negley Avenue
   Pittsburgh, Pennsylvania

6. Dr. Oliver C. Chesterton
   Highland Building
   St. Paul, Minnesota

7. Professor Carl H. Michaelson
   School of Education
   University of Indiana
   Bloomington, Indiana

8. The Reverend Paul S. O'Connor
   Rector, St. Peter's Church
   Aberdeen, South Dakota

9. McNary & Griffith
   Attorneys at Law
   State National Bank Bldg.
   Dallas, Texas
   Attention of Mr. J. O. McNary

10. President Franklin D. Wishart
    Methodist Theological Seminary
    New Haven, Connecticut

11. Miss Elfreda Witmer
    807 First Street, North
    St. Petersburg, Florida

12. Mrs. Samuel J. Tomlinson
    1207 St. George Terrace
    Cincinnati, Ohio

13. Mr. Harry Carmichael
    St. Moritz Hotel
    Detroit, Michigan

14. Marshall Bell Company
    384 Market Street
    San Francisco, California

15. J. H. Bund & Company
    Box 1274
    Chicago, Illinois

16. Mrs. T. Morris Hunter
    Box 53
    Bowling Green, Kentucky

17. Mr. Kelly Chamberlayne
    68 Warrington Drive
    Evanston, Indiana

18. Grant, Pierce, and White
    Special Agents
    1421 Spaulding Bldg.
    Denver, Colorado

19. Miss Margaret Hansen
    116 Poplar Street
    Ithaca, New York

20. John May Company
    14 Dearborn Street
    Los Angeles, California

21. Mr. Franklin M. King
    Box 528
    Cedar Falls, Iowa

22. Mr. C. B. Polson
    St. Regis Hotel
    Albuquerque, New Mexico
    Type in lower left corner of the envelope,
    "Please Forward."

23. Mrs. W. Henry Lamson
    128 East 57th Street
    New York, New York

24. Mr. Marvin T. Simpson
    R. D. 7
    Whiteland, Missouri

25. Miss Clara Stanhope
    One Lombard Drive
    Boston, Massachusetts

26. J. H. Rutland Bros.
    Consulting Engineers
    583 Mills Building
    El Paso, Texas

27. Miss Sara Jane Gillispie
    7 Woodlawn Apartments
    Kansas City, Missouri

28. Dr. James Blackburn
    15 Laurel Circle
    Madison, Wisconsin

Reaches to 6-_ (the underscore), the hyphen (-), the asterisk (*), and colon (:)

Illustration No. 44
Reach to 6-_ (underscore)

Illustration No. 45
Reaches to hyphen (-) and asterisk (*)

Illustration No. 46
Reach to backspace key

Stretch the little finger to the key to be controlled; guard against swinging the elbow outward. Move the hand slightly forward by bending the other fingers; but move only the *; finger* from typing position.

```
;p-;  ;-;  ;*;  first-class  ;*;  ;-;  ;*;
```

The colon (:) is the shift of the semicolon key and is controlled by the *; finger*. To type the colon, depress the left shift key with the *a finger* and strike the semicolon key.

To Underscore: Depress the backspace key (No. 1) to the first letter of the word to be underscored and strike the underscore once for each letter in the word. If an entire sentence is to be underscored, type the sentence, move the carriage back to the first letter, depress the shift lock (No. 29), and strike the underscore once for each letter in the words to be underscored. The use of the shift lock makes it unnecessary for you to hold the finger on the shift key. To release the shift lock, depress the shift key. Spell each word as you strike the underscore. Underscore the word but not the space between words or the marks of punctuation.

The figure *6* is above and slightly to the left of *y*; the shift of *6* is the underscore (_). The *j finger* controls this key.

Stretch the controlling finger until it is straight; make the reach with as little change in hand position as possible.

```
jy6j  j6j  j6j  j_j  j6j  j_j  six 6 June 26
```

The hyphen is the last key in the top row and is controlled by the *; finger*. The shift of the hyphen is the asterisk (*).

On some typewriters, the shift of the hyphen is ¾ instead of the asterisk.

LOCATION DRILL

10 minutes

Directions. Type the drill twice. Use shift lock when underscoring in the last sentence.

STROKES

```
jy6j  j6j  j6j  16  26  j6j  j_j  think  j6j  16  36  46  f5f  f%f  6%  $6          59
```

```
The note is for $600.  We pay 6% interest.  It is due April 6.               62
```

```
This is first-class mail.  Use the * for footnote reference.                 60
```

```
NEVER underscore punctuation marks or the space between words.               62
```

CORRECT SALUTATIONS

(Based on "Correct Salutations" by R. R. Aurner)

The following is not a complete list of correct addresses and their accompanying salutations. One correct address is given for each individual listed, and the salutations that may be used with that address are given in order of decreasing formality.

Governmental Officials

President of the United States:

The President	Sir:
The White House	To the President:
Washington, D. C.	Mr. President:
	Dear Mr. President:

Other Governmental Officials:

For all other governmental officials, the address may consist of the name preceded by the words "The Honorable," and followed by the official position, the city, and the state. The salutation is selected according to the degree of formality desired. For example, for a governor of a state the address and salutation would be:

The Honorable Philip M. Small	Sir:
Governor of Wisconsin	My dear Sir:
Madison, Wisconsin	Dear Sir:
	My dear Governor Small:
	Dear Governor Small:
	Dear Governor: (informal)

Educators

President (college or university):

President Frank L. Lang	My dear Sir:
University of Chicago	Dear Sir:
Chicago, Illinois	My dear President Lang:
	Dear President Lang:

Doctor of Philosophy (or Laws, or Medicine):

Dr. Richard L. French	My dear Sir:
4210 Mandan Crescent	Dear Sir:
Madison, Wisconsin	My dear Dr. French:
	Dear Dr. French:

Professor (college or university):

Professor Neville Hughes	My dear Sir:
Department of History	Dear Sir:
University of Wisconsin	My dear Professor Hughes:
Madison, Wisconsin	Dear Professor Hughes:

Churchmen

Clergymen (Protestant):

The Reverend W. B. Sund, D.D.	Reverend Sir: (formal)
2001 Park Avenue	My dear Sir:
Cleveland, Ohio	Dear Sir:
	My dear Dr. Sund:
	Dear Dr. Sund:

Rabbi (Jewish Faith):

Rabbi John S. Wise	Reverend Sir: (formal)
209 Dunlap Street	My dear Sir:
Chicago, Illinois	Dear Sir:
	My dear Rabbi Wise:
	Dear Rabbi Wise:

Priest (Roman Catholic):

Reverend Carl R. Rand	Dear Reverend Father:
164 Lansing Place	
Mobile, Alabama	

Military Service

General

General D. H. Lunt	Sir:
Commanding Officer	My dear Sir:
Army of the United States	Dear Sir:
Washington, D. C.	My dear General Lunt: (informal)
	Dear General Lunt: (informal)

Lieutenant

Mr. W. H. McCall	Dear Sir:
Lieutenant, U. S. A.*	My dear Mr. McCall:
(place address here)	Dear Mr. McCall:

* In case of retired officers, omit U. S. A.

NOTE: For officers below the rank of captain, the salutation should not use any designation of rank or title. Use *Dear Sir:* or *Dear Mr. ———:* or one of the variants.

Naval Service

Admiral

The Admiral of the Navy of the United States	Sir:
(Place address here)	My dear Sir:
	Dear Sir:
	My dear Admiral Wohl: (informal)
	Dear Admiral Wohl: (informal)

Captain

Captain H. R. Hunt, U. S. N.	My dear Sir:
(Place address here)	Dear Sir:
	My dear Captain Hunt:
	Dear Captain Hunt:

NOTE: For officers below the rank of captain, the salutation should not use any designation of rank or title. Use *Dear Sir:* or *Dear Mr. ———:* or one of the variants.

Familiar Salutations

For Men

Sir:	Dear White:
My dear Sir:	My dear John:
Dear Sir:	Dear John:
My dear Mr. White:	
Dear Mr. White:	*Plural*
My dear White:	Gentlemen:

For Women

Madam:	My dear Miss White:
My dear Madam:	Dear Miss White:
Dear Madam:	
My dear Mrs. White:	*Plural*
Dear Mrs. White:	Mesdames (or) Ladies:

LESSON 17

RECONSTRUCTION PRACTICE

Directions. Use a 60-space line. Set the machine for double spacing.

6j 16 2s 8k 3d 91 4f 0; 5f -; 2s 6j "s _j 2s 6j 3d #d 7j &j

1 3 13 4 7 47 2 1 21 3 6 36 5 9 59 3 0 30 2 9 29 1 6 16 6 3

Does their bill come to $650?   Is the rate 6%?   Pay them $39.

You should think.   You should WORK.   He said, "Work hard."

TECHNIQUE PRACTICE 17

Directions. 1. Type each of the first four sentences once; use the last sentence for two one-minute timed writings.
2. When two groups of unrelated figures come together, separate them with a comma.
3. Be sure to space twice after the colon in line 3.

	STROKES
The due date is March 30, 1946. The account pays 2% interest.	62
In 1938, 27 of these 65 companies reported a very big loss.	59
SHIFT LOCK: To be used in typing a succession of capitals.	59
There are four 16-room apartments for rent in this building.	60
Most of us are willing to work hard for the thing we want.	58

EXERCISE 17

Directions. Set a tabulator stop for a 5-space indention. Type the exercise twice. Use a half sheet of paper for each writing. Leave 10 spaces in the top margin. Type on the stroke level.

All letters of the alphabet are used in this exercise.

	STROKES
You can't expect to learn to type by the trial-and-error	57
method. There is a right way to learn to type just as there	118
is a right way to do everything else. Right typing calls for	180
the use of a quick stroke, the eyes held on the copy, and the	242
carriage kept moving continuously. If you want to be skillful	305
in typing, seize every chance to improve the way in which you	367
work as well as to increase the quantity of work you do.	423

6. If the stenciled material is too high, turn the adjusting knob toward the left; if it is too low, turn the knob toward the right.

7. If the side margins are not even, adjust the guides for the paper feedboard and move the paper to the right or the left.

8. If the paper clings to the stencil, dust a thin coat of talcum on a sheet of mimeograph paper and run the sheet slowly through the mimeograph.

9. If sheets of bond or other nonabsorbent paper are used, interleave the sheets with used mimeograph paper unless your mimeograph has interleaving equipment.

EXERCISE 137

Directions. Use the block form of letter with open punctuation. In setting up the letter, leave ample space for the insertion of the date, the inside address, and the salutation. Prepare a stencil and run off twenty-eight copies of the letter from the stencil.

For some time we have been aware that frequently book readers intend to join the Book Readers Association and then neglect to do so. To overcome this tendency, we have concluded to make it very much worth while for such persons *not* to delay. (P) If you will join the Book Readers Association within the next thirty days, we shall give you a copy of the book selected by patrons of the Association as the outstanding publication of the month. (P) We hope you will decide now to join the Association. If you do, all that is necessary is to write your check for $12.50 and mail it in the enclosed postage-free return envelope. Membership in the Association will make an excellent gift for friends or employees. We shall be glad to have prospective members recommended by you. Sincerely yours BOOK READERS ASSOCIATION J. L. Tigart, Secretary Enclosure *(Strokes, 853; words, 140.)*

POSTAGE-FREE RETURN ENVELOPE

A postage-free return envelope is a business reply envelope on which is printed the guaranty that the postage will be paid by the addressee. It is necessary to get a permit for the use of a business reply envelope or card. The use of this kind of envelope is quite common among businesses sending out numerous requests for information or solicitations of orders. Instead of sending a stamped and addressed return envelope when there is no assurance that the communication will be answered, a business considers it better practice to use a postage-free card or envelope (although it costs more) and to pay the postage when the card or the envelope is returned.

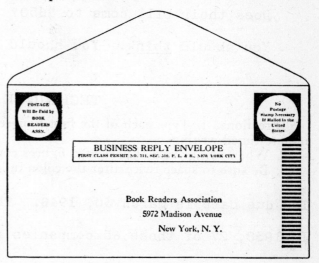

Illustration No. 67 — Business Reply Envelope

EXERCISE 138

Directions. The mimeographed copies of the letter given in Exercise 137 are to be mailed to the addresses listed on page 202. On each copy fill in the current date, the inside address, and the proper salutation. In filling in the date, the inside address, and the salutation, try to match the type in the rest of the letter. If the typing is too dark to match the mimeographed copy, strike the letters more lightly; if the typing is not dark enough, put a new ribbon in your typewriter. Address an envelope for each letter; place the letter under the envelope flap, add a pencil or typewritten note that a business reply envelope must be enclosed, and present the letters for the signature of your teacher. When the letters have been approved, fold them for mailing.

Letter shops that make a business of preparing form letters for business houses have established for their typists an envelope-addressing standard of 150 envelopes an hour. To hold their positions, workers MUST produce this minimum number of addressed envelopes. The typists "chain-feed" the envelopes.

To "chain feed," insert into the machine the next envelope to be typed before removing the first. As you turn the cylinder to remove one envelope, you automatically turn the next into position to be typed. In the case of envelopes, prepare a chain of three before typing the first.

Reaches to ½-¼, ¢-@, / (diagonal)

Illustration No. 47
Reach to ½-¼

Illustration No. 48
Reach to ¢-@

Illustration No. 49
Reach to / (diagonal)

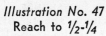

Make the reach by moving the ; *finger* to the right. Hold the other fingers in typing position.

These special keys are used infrequently in ordinary typing; but they are used in statements, invoices, and market quotations.

;¢; ;¢; ;@; Order 4½ doz. @ 38¼¢ each.

The diagonal (/) is below the semicolon and is controlled by the ; *finger*. You have already learned that on most typewriters the shift of the / is ? (or the fraction ¾).

Make the reach with a direct movement of the ; *finger* and without changing the hand position or moving the other fingers from typing position.

;/; The fraction is 2/3. Use ½ or 1/2.

In typing "made" fractions (fractions for which there are no special keys) use the /. In typing ½ or ¼ with other fractions that must be made, such as ⅔, type all fractions in a uniform manner.

The ½ is to the right of the letter *p*; the shift of the ½ is the ¼. This key is controlled by the ; *finger*.

Make the reach direct from the ; position without going through the position for the letter *p*.

;½; ;¼; ;½; ;¼; The ¼ is the shift of ½.

The ¢ (cent or cents) is to the right of the ; key. The shift of the ¢ is @ (at). This key is controlled by the ; *finger*.

LOCATION DRILL

10 minutes

Directions. Type the drill twice.

STROKES

This is first-class mail. I had 26 three-cent stamps for you. 62

When typing many carbons, use 1/2 and 1/4 instead of ½ and ¼. 61

Space between whole numbers and "made" fractions; as, 7 1/3. 60

Use the ¢ and the @ symbols when typing market quotations. 58

Use the * for footnotes and the hyphen (-) for compounds. 57

6. Take this combination of **backing sheet,** cushion sheet, and stencil sheet, and place it in the typewriter with the backing sheet next to the cylinder. Use a normal typing stroke, striking with equal force all letters and characters except marks of punctuation, which should be struck lightly.

7. **Precaution:** When the cylinder has to be rolled back to bring the stencil to the starting point, or to make an insertion or a correction, the loose ends of the stencil and backing sheets must be held together firmly to avoid wrinkling the cushion sheet or the stencil sheet. An alternative method is to remove the stencil from the typewriter and to reinsert it.

8. **Making Corrections:** Correct any error in the typing by the use of a correction fluid.

   a. Roll the stencil forward so that the line on which the error has been made is clear of interference; rub the smooth rounded end of the brush handle gently over the place where the error was made. This closes the perforations of the stencil and prevents the fluid from running through to the backing sheet.

   b. Spread a small quantity of the correction fluid as a thin coating over the error.

   c. Allow the fluid to set for a few seconds; then type the correction, using a normal stroke.

9. **The Printing Operation:** When you are ready to run the stencil, remove the cushion sheet and attach the stencil to the cylinder of the mimeograph. Hook the buttonholes over the buttons and draw the narrow part of the buttonholes snugly against the button shanks, by holding both the lower corners of the stencil sheet with the hands; then fasten the lower end of the stencil clamp.

10. Care must be used in spreading the stencil smoothly over the surface of the ink pad. If the stencil sheet becomes overlapped or wrinkled, it can be raised and respread on the ink pad without risk of injury. Do not pull this sheet, however, as an uneven strain might tend to distort the alignment of the typewritten matter. Vertical wrinkles can be removed by pulling the finger tips across the extreme side margins of the sheet.

11. When using stencil paper that does not extend to the stencil clamp, lay on the inking pad a piece of blank paper of sufficient length to extend from under the bottom of the stencil sheet. This will permit clamping, as described above.

12. The stencil should be cleaned as soon as it is used and filed for future use. To clean a stencil, lay it between two sheets of absorbent paper (regular stencil paper or newspaper) and rub gently. Dip the stencil in a shallow pan of benzine or brush the stencil lightly with a soft brush dipped in benzine; then dry the stencil between pages of a newspaper. File the stencil between clean sheets of paper that will not cling to the stencil. Have oiled paper between the folds of the stencil. Better still, file the stencil in the regular folders prepared for this purpose.

Complete information about the mimeograph machine that you are to use will be furnished by the nearest office handling the equipment. Booklets containing such information are for free distribution. Study the instructions carefully and learn how to operate the mimeograph quickly, accurately, and without waste effort.

Hints on Running a Stencil

1. To remove horizontal wrinkles in a stencil, lift the stencil and replace it so that it will be smooth.

2. To remove vertical wrinkles in a stencil, gently pull the tips of the thumbs across the extreme side margins of the sheet.

3. If you are using a short stencil, cover the exposed portion of the pad with a piece of paper. Place one edge of the paper under the end of the stencil; place the other under the clamp.

4. Take approximately a hundred sheets of mimeograph paper in your hand and separate them by quickly flicking them with your thumb. If the papers stick to one another, blow into the stack as you flick the sheets.

5. Run a few trial copies slowly to distribute the ink evenly. Inspect these to see that the copy is clean. Look at the back of the sheet to make certain that it is free from ink smudges. If the stencil needs to be inked, follow the directions given in the booklet that is furnished with the machine.

LESSON 18

You have now initiated all keyboard reaches. You should feel a definite command of the reaches to the letters; and you will continue your special drill practice until you are certain that you can command your fingers in the control of the figures and special symbols. Let each day's work show measurable improvement. There will be lessons or portions of lessons that must be typed with special emphasis upon absolute accuracy of stroking. There will be other drill periods when the goal will be increased stroking rate. Know the purpose of the materials and the practice procedures used; then work intelligently to achieve the established goal.

TECHNIQUE CHECKUP   *2 minutes*

1. Do you keep the carriage moving without jerks and without pauses? It is not how fast you type, but how smoothly and continuously you type, that will give you good typing power.
2. Check your posture.
    a. Is your chair correctly placed?
    b. Are your feet on the floor?
    c. Are your elbows held in toward your body?
    d. Do you have the "curve of typewriting" in your fingers?
    e. Are your wrists held low without resting on the frame of the typewriter?
    f. Are your thumbs curved, the right one held over the space bar and the left one kept out of the way of the fingers and the right thumb?
3. Maintain an alert, well-controlled typing position.

RECONSTRUCTION PRACTICE   *4 minutes*

Directions. 1. Use a 60-space line.
             2. Set machine for double spacing.
             3. All letters of the alphabet are used in the first two lines.

```
mix fix six for vow how now can cad cut big but bog joy aim

quick check amaze poise excel quick amaze check excel poise

4f 8k 48 48 5f 7j 57 57 2s 91 29 29 3d 6j 36 36 5f 0; 50 50

2s"s 8k'k I said, "Can't we pay bill #48 for $275 on April 3?"
```

TECHNIQUE PRACTICE 18   *10 minutes*

Directions. Use each of the first three sentences for two one-minute writings. Set the goal for the second writing one word in advance of the rate of the first writing. Type the last two sentences on the letter level.

	STROKES
It is due each man that he find one thing he can do very well.	62
Nothing is more true than that men must control their thoughts.	63
You think there is never time enough to do all you want to do.	62
We pay 2½% interest. Hall & Moss 1956 (Series B) bonds pay 3%.	63
Joe packed my sledge with five dozen boxes of frozen quail.	59

[43]

Article		Fine Composition		
Firm		Address	Cat. No.	
Superior Cork Co.		Cleveland, Ohio	690-Z	
Walker & Williams		Pittsburgh, Pa.	598-5	
Weaton-McKee & Co.		Youngstown, Ohio	392-1	

Illustration No. 66 — Index Card for an Article

TYPING ON CARDS

Postal cards are used frequently to send routine acknowledgments, announcements of meetings, or other impersonal messages. The spacing used is determined by the length of the message. The style of address on the front of the card is the same as that used on envelopes.

Government postal cards are 5½ by 3¼ inches. Fifty-five horizontal spaces and twenty vertical lines represent the total space available. After allowing for the necessary margins, not more than fifty horizontal spaces and seventeen vertical lines are left for use.

Before typing an exercise, estimate the length of the message and adjust the margin stops so that there will be no danger of writing beyond the margins of the card. To produce neat work, place the edges of the card under the paper clamps or the envelope guide.

The return address and the current date should be typed in the upper right corner on the message side of the card. Omit from this side of the card the address of the person or the business to which you are writing. The salutation and the complimentary close may be omitted if it is necessary to save these lines for the message itself. Use single spacing on postal cards except when the message is very short. Double-space between paragraphs.

EXERCISE 136

Directions. The following is a postal card message received by the Elder Light Manufacturers, Inc. Type the name and the address of this company (1249 Woodford Street, Chattanooga, Tennessee) on a card according to the directions for addressing envelopes. Use single spacing and a forty-space line. Leave three spaces between the date and the salutation. Use the same spacing between the major divisions of the message as that used in typing letters.

Cleveland, Ohio (current date) Gentlemen: We acknowledge the receipt of your order #629-Y for 75,000 Part #470-4, our #2030 Fine Composition. (P) We appreciate your business. Shipment will be made promptly. Yours truly, SUPERIOR CORK COMPANY

BUDGET XV

STENCILS

Through the use of a stencil, several hundred copies of a letter may be made available in a comparatively short time. The typing and the running of a stencil necessitate a familiarity with the materials and equipment used in this office procedure.

1. **Stencilizing:** Type the material to be stenciled. Check for accuracy of form and typing.

2. Clean the typewriter type thoroughly.

3. Adjust the ribbon lever for stenciling.

4. Insert the porous cushion sheet between the stencil sheet and the backing of the stencil sheet. In typewritten work the **cushion sheet, or a substitute,** should never be omitted. Its use is required to prevent the cutting out of letters.

If you will substitute a sheet of plain paper for the cushion sheet, you will be able to proofread from the imprints on the paper. This is easier than proofreading from the stencil. Another device is to substitute a carbon sheet.

5. Place the top edge of the model copy at the corner marks indicated on the stencil sheet, and determine how far down on the stencil the first line of the copy should be typed. The numbers at the sides are intended to serve as a guide to the proper placement. Note the number opposite the desired starting point. Register this number mentally because it marks the place at which the stencil should begin.

EXERCISE 18

16 minutes

Directions. 1. Set a tabulator stop for a 5-space indention.

2. Use each paragraph for two three-minute writings. Type the first writing with the ribbon lever set for ribbon typing; type the second writing with the lever set for stenciling and try to increase the number of words typed.

In the second writing, you should type at least one word more than you typed in the first writing.

STROKES

In learning to type, you must tell your fingers what you   57

want them to do. No one can do this work for you. The steps   119

that lead to skill are definite and there is no royal road   178

that you can take to avoid them. Think the letter or the word   241

you want to type, and your fingers will do their work without   303

error.   309

Pay attention to what you are to do. Know when your own   57

work is right or wrong. You can do this if you give thought   118

to how you work as well as to what work you do. Let yourself   180

write with a feeling of ease and of sureness. If you work in   242

the right way and keep at it, fine typing power will be yours   304

without fail.   317

SPEED EMPHASIS

10 minutes

STROKES

us am he of is to go an do am or us so so it it am he me me   59

or for for he the the an and and and for the and for the the   60

did did sir aid aid rug fur pan pan fit wit sob fob tub rob   59

make such make sick wish with paid them they both such both   59

I can work. I can work with them. I can work well with them.   62

They paid for both of them. They make more than he makes.   58

It is our duty to do all we can to have the work done right.   60

[44]

(Outgoing Letter)

superior cork company armstrong building cleveland ohio attention mr f e stevens gentlemen upon receipt of your telegram quoting a price of $7 a thousand on part #470-4 a strip of #2030 we compared your quotation with others and found that you were about $1 a thousand too high we therefore wired you to that effect as is shown by the enclosed copy of our telegram (P) in reply we received your message that you could not meet the reduction we requested we then had a long-distance telephone conversation with mr stevens about the matter (P) we know that #2030 Fine is a more suitable composition for our particular work than anything we have ever been able to get elsewhere while we should like to take advantage of the lower prices offered by others we are going to stay with #2030 Fine because of the high quality of this composition furthermore you have always taken care of us extremely well on deliveries and we want to continue doing business with you (P) please enter our order for 75,000 part #470-4, #2030 Fine Composition make shipment as quickly as possible yours very truly elder light manufacturers inc r l elder president enclosure (*Strokes, 1185; words, 204.*)

INDEXING AND FILING

Indexing is the process by which a file clerk determines the name, the number, or the subject under which a paper is to be filed. In the simplest filing systems, papers may be filed alphabetically under the names of the businesses or the individuals from whom incoming letters are received or to whom outgoing letters are written. Before papers can be filed, they must be indexed. The usual sequence of activities in connection with filing is:

1. Read.   4. Sort.
2. Index.   5. File.
3. Code.

After a paper has been indexed, it must be placed in a container, usually a folder. The alphabet is used as the basis for filing. The individual folders should be arranged in alphabetic order behind the various guides. Papers are placed in a folder with the headings toward the left and are arranged according to the dates. They are filed so that the paper with the latest date is on top. The use of pins or paper clips should be avoided. Papers should be stapled together, the latest paper being on top.

Cross-reference sheets or cards are used frequently when correspondence that deals with more than one important topic is filed. The numeric system of filing is an indirect method necessitating a card index for filing and reference. Cross-reference sheets or cards are used also with the other methods of filing (alphabetic, geographic, or automatic) when, as the names indicate, there is need for cross reference. The cross-reference sheet is treated exactly as a piece of correspondence, but the cross-reference card is filed in a card tray.

EXERCISE 135

Directions. Type the cross-reference card in Illustration No. 65, which shows a numeric subject. Insert a card, gauging accurately so that the company name will be typed on the ruled line. Typing on ruled lines involves the use of the variable line spacer to reset the line in order that it may conform to the ruled line.

Superior Cork Company	
Armstrong Building	
Cleveland, Ohio	
See also	
Fine Composition	746-1

Illustration No. 65 — Cross-Reference Card with a Numeric Subject

Directions. Catalogues are usually indexed by both the name of the article and the name of the manufacturer or the seller. On the subject card for each article are listed the names of the businesses selling that particular article and the catalogue file number of each business. Type the card in Illustration No. 66.

LESSON 19

FINGER GYMNASTICS   *1 minute*

Drill 13. Place the fingers and the thumb of one hand between two fingers of the other hand. Spread the two fingers. Repeat the drill until all the fingers of each hand have been spread apart in this way.

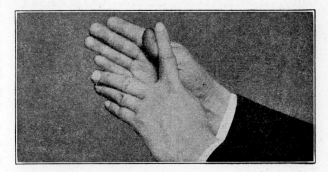

TECHNIQUE EMPHASIS   *1 minute*

1. Strike the center of the key.
2. Use a rhythmic swing in returning the carriage; start typing without pause.
3. Keep the carriage moving continuously.
4. Sit erect with feet on the floor.
5. Use a "hinge" motion for the control of the shift keys; hold the hands near the typing position.

RECONSTRUCTION PRACTICE   *6 minutes*

Directions. 1. Use a 60-space line.
2. Set the machine for double spacing.

```
3d 7j 37 37 4f 8k 48 48 2s 6j 26 26 5f 9l 59 59 5f 0; 50 50

Date the letter May 28.  Wire them on May 30.  Ask for $70.

Think the word.  Buy 6 quarts.  Buy a West & Jones (1956) bond.

He said, "I can sell the farm."  For SALE:  150-acre farm.
```

TECHNIQUE PRACTICE 19   *10 minutes*

Directions. 1. Type the drill through once; then select for special repetition practice, the sentences that help you to increase the facility of stroking on certain of your weak controls. You probably know better than anyone else just which of the five sentences will give you the particular help you need. Practice the sentence until you feel some measurable improvement in the continuity of your stroking.
2. Type on the stroke level.
3. The last sentence contains all the letters of the alphabet.

Drill   STROKES

(e) Equalize the power behind strokes and eliminate the jerks.   58

(h) Humility, hope, faith--all are traits which make men achieve.   61

(w) When do we know what straws show which way a wind will blow?   60

(y) Youth yearn mainly to know that they may do mighty things.   58

Eliza quickly mixed that very big jar of new soap for them.   59

[45]

satisfied with this product. Yours very truly, SUPERIOR CORK COMPANY (F. E. Stevens) Vice-President *(Strokes, 745; words, 123.)*

EXERCISE 131
NIGHT LETTER

Directions. Indicate the class of service desired. Type three copies: one copy for the telegraph company, one copy for the office files, and one copy to be enclosed with Exercise 134.

(Outgoing Night Letter)

Mr. F. E. Stevens, Superior Cork Company, Armstrong Building, Cleveland, Ohio. Your quotation part 470-4 strip dollar a thousand too high. Wire immediately if can quote better price and how soon can begin shipment. Require 75000 ELDER LIGHT MANUFACTURERS, INC.

EXERCISE 132
FAST TELEGRAM

Directions. Indicate the service desired. Type only one copy.

(Telegram from Cleveland, Ohio)

Elder Light Manufacturers, Inc., 1249 Woodford Street, Chattanooga, Tennessee. Cannot quote lower price part 470-4. Can ship initial quantity three days after receipt of order SUPERIOR CORK COMPANY

EXERCISE 133
LETTER OF CONFIRMATION

Directions. Type the following two-page letter in the modified block form used in Style Letter No. 13, page 178. Use mixed punctuation. Single-space and indent the quoted telegrams.

(Letter from Cleveland, Ohio)

Elder Light Manufacturers, Inc., 1249 Woodford Street Chattanooga, Tennessee Gentlemen: We have received your telegram of yesterday, which reads as follows: (P) "Your quotation part 470-4 strip dollar a thousand too high. Wire im-

mediately if can quote better price and how soon can begin shipment. Require 75000." (P) In our quotation on Part #470-4, we made a slight reduction in the price of the strip. This gave you the benefit of such saving as we felt was warranted by the size of your order. We are aware that other manufacturers of strips are making lower prices than the price we are naming. As we have had an opportunity to examine this competitive material, we know it is of a quality inferior to ours. We do not feel, therefore, that we should try to meet the lower prices quoted. (P) Our #2030 Fine Composition was developed for this particular trade. At first we supplied #240 Fine Composition; but we found that, as it did not have the necessary softness for use in head lamps, it caused the breakage of glass. Research and experimentation finally produced the #2030 material, which represents the best composition that has been offered the trade up to this time. We do not make this statement on the basis of our own findings alone, but on the basis of information received from many customers. We recently received a report from one manufacturer of lights who informed us that our composition was thoroughly tested along with various other types of material and was found to be the only composition that could meet all the necessary requirements satisfactorily. (P) As much as we regretted our inability to offer you a lower price, we felt it necessary to telegraph you as follows: (P) "Cannot quote lower price part 470-4. Can ship initial quantity three days after receipt of order." (P) This telegram we now confirm. Yours very truly, SUPERIOR CORK COMPANY (F. E. Stevens) Vice-President *(Strokes, 1910; words, 324.)*

EXERCISE 134

Directions. Use the block form with open punctuation. Type the dictator's name on a line with the official title. Make one carbon copy.

Directions. Set a tabulator stop for a 5-space indention. Use each paragraph for two three-minute writings. Type the first writing with the lever set for ribbon typing; the second writing with the lever set for stenciling. In the second writing, you should type at least two words more than you typed in the first writing.

	STROKES
For a few lessons you have been working for speed. Soon	57
you are to begin work for control even though this may mean	117
some loss of speed for the time being. You know at just about	180
what speed you type. For the next timed writing, then, deduct	243
five words from your rate per minute and let this lower speed	305
be your goal when typing this slow, controlled timed writing.	366

It is often helpful to check the point at which you want	57
to be typing at the end of each half minute. This is a good	118
plan to use when working for speed; but it is just as good a	179
plan to use when working for control. Type stroke by stroke	240
and let your main effort be to keep the carriage moving with-	300
out pause. In the end, you will have speed with control.	357

CENTERING
4 minutes

Explanation. Horizontal centering is not new to you. The directions for each drill and exercise that you have typed called for correct horizontal centering of the material on the page. You will be expected to center your exercises both horizontally and vertically in all subsequent lessons. You will recall

Paper 8½ by 11 inches has 66 writing lines of 85 pica spaces or 102 elite spaces.

Half sheets have 33 writing lines.

Use 40 as the point at which the center of the paper is placed when you operate a pica-type machine; use 50 as the center point for an elite-type machine.

Vertical Centering. 1. Count the lines required to type the exercise.

In double-spaced material, count the typed line and the space that follows. The count for the last typed line is not to include a following space as the space becomes a part of the bottom margin.

2. Subtract total lines required from available writing lines (66 lines for a full sheet; 33 lines for a half sheet).

3. Divide by 2 to get the width of the top and bottom margins. If the result contains a fraction, let the extra line appear at the bottom.

Horizontal Centering. 1. Move the carriage so the carriage-position indicator is at the centering point.

2. Backspace once for each two letters or spaces in the line to be centered.

3. Begin writing at the point where the backspacing is completed. Disregard fractions.

Another rule which can be used if you are operating an Underwood typewriter is:

Set the carriage-position indicator at 0; strike the space bar once for each letter and space in the line to be centered. The figure on the front *red scale* that is indicated by the carriage-position indicator will be the point on the *white scale* at which you should begin typing.

BUDGET XIV

You are working for the ELDER LIGHT MANUFACTURERS, INC., of Chattanooga, Tennessee. Carbon copies of all outgoing mail from your office should be made. Do not type carbon copies for incoming mail.

EXERCISE 128

FAST TELEGRAM

Directions. Indicate in the upper left corner of the telegraph blank the service desired. Type three copies of the telegram by the use of carbon paper. In an office three copies of an outgoing telegram are usually made, unless the message is to be delivered to the telegraph company by telephone; then two copies are typed. One copy is filed; another is sent with a letter of confirmation or is sent to the addressee in place of a letter of confirmation. The original copy of this telegram will be sent to the telegraph office; one carbon copy will be filed; and the other copy will be sent as a confirmation.

(Outgoing Telegram)

Superior Cork Company, Armstrong Building, Cleveland, Ohio. Wire best price quantity order part 470-4 strip 2030. ELDER LIGHT MANUFACTURERS, INC.

EXERCISE 129

FAST TELEGRAM

Directions. Indicate in the upper left corner of the telegraph blank the service desired. As this is an incoming telegram, type only one copy.

(Telegram from Cleveland, Ohio)

Elder Light Manufacturers, Inc., 1249 Woodford Street, Chattanooga, Tennessee. Can furnish part 470-4 at $7 per thousand f.o.b. Cleveland. Letter follows. SUPERIOR CORK COMPANY

LETTERS OF CONFIRMATION

It is customary to confirm a business telegram. This is done by mailing a copy of the telegram to the addressee or by writing a letter of confirmation that quotes the message in full.

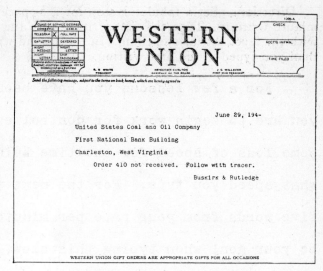

Illustration No. 64 — A Telegram

The importance of the letter of confirmation is not alone in providing a check on the telegram: businessmen frequently use the letter of confirmation to present additional information that could not be given easily in the telegram.

EXERCISE 130

LETTER OF CONFIRMATION FOR A TELEGRAM

Directions. Type the letter in the modified block form that was used in Style Letter No. 13, page 178. Use mixed punctuation. Single-space and indent the quoted telegram.

(Letter from Cleveland, Ohio)

Elder Light Manufacturers, Inc. 1249 Woodford Street Chattanooga, Tennessee Gentlemen: In answer to your telegram asking for our price on a quantity order of Part #470-4, a strip of #2030 Fine Composition, we wired you as follows: (P) "Can furnish part 470-4 at $7 per thousand f.o.b. Cleveland. Letter follows." (P) We are glad to confirm this telegram and to say that we can make shipment of a reasonable quantity within two or three days after the receipt of your order. Our terms are 2% on the fifteenth of the month following the date of shipment, or 60 days net. (P) We hope you will give us your order, as we are certain that you will be

CENTERING DRILL

6 minutes

Directions. Use a half sheet of paper. Center the drill vertically. Center each line of the drill horizontally. Use double spacing.

UNIVERSITY SCHOOL OF BUSINESS ADMINISTRATION

Department of Secretarial Science

Second Term Registration from January 16 to February 3

Room 236 Administration Building

9:30 a.m. to 4:30 p.m.

ANALYSIS OF VERTICAL CENTERING			
	Lines on half sheet, 8½ x 5½ inches	33	$24 \div 2 = 12$
	Lines to be used in typing the drill	9	Top margin, 12 lines
	Lines to be divided between top and bottom margins	24	Bottom margin, 12 lines
			Proof: $12 + 12 + 9 = 33$

LESSON 20

RECONSTRUCTION PRACTICE

6 minutes

Directions. 1. Use a 60-space line and double spacing.
2. Move the carriage to the center point and then backspace once for each two letters and space in the heading, **LESSON 20.** Type the heading.
3. Space up three times; type the drill on the letter level.

The check is for $591.20. Don't ship that car on Bill #483.

The interest rate is 6½%. He does first-class work, I think.

decade descend murmur barbarous preparation excessive question

quizzical nineteen nunnery Mississippi labyrinth encircled

TECHNIQUE PRACTICE 20

10 minutes

Directions. 1. Center the heading, **TECHNIQUE PRACTICE 20.** Remember to release the shift lock before typing the figures.
2. Have three spaces between the heading and the first line of the drill.
3. Type each sentence once; then use each of the last two sentences for a one-minute writing.

STROKES

When will workers know how to work well without waste of time? 62

Type all fractions in the same form; for example, 2/3 and 1/4. 62

Check the way you type as well as the quantity of work you do. 62

It is just as easy to form a good habit as it is a bad one. 59

If we try and fail, it is finer than if we did not try at all. 62

[47]

The word "Stop" and words designating punctuation marks, such as "comma," "period," etc., will be counted and charged for. As the marks of punctuation are transmitted, it is unnecessary to use words to indicate punctuation.

Type the signature. The sender's telephone number or address, or both, may be typed in the lower left-hand corner of the telegram for the convenience of the telegraph company in transmitting an answer.

Messages may be filed by telephone or sent by messenger to the telegraph office. When messages are filed by the telephone, the charges are included in the subscriber's telephone bill (in most cities). The original copies of messages telephoned should be kept in the files along with the carbon copies of all telegrams sent by messenger. This plan will save time in checking the monthly bill and will provide exact copies for reference.

METHODS OF COUNTING CHARGEABLE WORDS

All words, figures, and letters in the text of domestic messages are counted and charged for. All groups of letters, when the letters are not dictionary words or combinations of dictionary words, are counted at the rate of five letters to a word. A hyphen or bar of division (/) appearing in a group of letters will be counted as one character in the group. Other characters appearing in a group of letters are counted as one word each. Examples:

Ababa	1 word
Egadol (6 letters)	2 words
BD-AC	1 word
BX:BXL	3 words

Groups of figures, when used in their natural sense, are counted at the rate of five characters for one word. A fraction bar, period, or decimal point, comma, colon, dash or hyphen, appearing in a group of figures will be counted as a figure. For example, the following are counted as one word each: 12345, ¾, 22½. Marks such as $ & are counted as one word each. In combinations of letters and figures, each unbroken sequence of five or fewer letters or figures (a fraction bar, period, or decimal point, apostrophe, comma, colon, dash or hyphen being counted as one character associated with the immediately preceding sequence of letters or figures) is counted as one word. For example, $180 is counted as two words; AB123, as two words; and A3C, as three words; A-B34 as three words. Ordinal numbers are counted at the rate of five characters to a word. Examples: 101st, as one word; 1002nd, as two words.

The following signatures are carried free:
1. One signature
2. Two or more members of the same family
3. Any two combinations of: firm name, one individual name, title, department, branch, division.

Example of extra words: Standard Canning Co., John Smith *and John Brown* (extra words in italics).

Illustration of the Methods of Counting Chargeable Words

Counted as one word:

All political subdivisions (states, counties, townships, cities, boroughs, etc.); as, New Jersey, New York, Salt Lake City.

Geographic names are counted as written:

San Francisco Bay	3 words
Great Salt Lake	3 words
California Valley	2 words

Special abbreviations common to business transactions, such as a.m., p.m., f.o.b., C. O. D., O. K., S. S.

Dictionary words are counted as one word. The hyphen is rarely used in the words *tomorrow, today, tonight.*

Counted as more than one word:

Initials and names such as G. W. Brown (three words).

Abbreviations for the names of railroads and such names: as, B&O (three words because of the combination of characters). It is common practice to use the following words to indicate railroads:

Bando (B&O RR)	1 word, five letters
Pandle (P&LE RR)	2 words, six letters
Cando (C&O RR)	1 word

Miscellaneous words such as all right, post office, air mail, parcel post, New Year.

To guard against mistakes or delays, the sender of a message can order it repeated, that is, telegraphed back to the originating office for comparison. For this, one half the unrepeated message rate is charged in addition.

The telegraph company is liable for mistakes or delays in transmission of an unrepeated message to the extent of $500 only; in the transmission of a repeated message to the extent of $5,000.

Directions. 1. Center the heading, **EXERCISE 20**, horizontally and the exercise **vertically.** Triple-space between the heading and the first line of the paragraph.
2. Use a 60-space line.

VERTICAL CENTERING

Available lines		33
Heading	1	
Extra spaces between heading and paragraph	2	
Used lines: $(8 \times 2 - 1 = 15)$	15	18
Lines for top and bottom margins		15
$15 \div 2 = 7$ spaces for top margin; 8 spaces for bottom margin		

3. After the exercise has been typed once, insert another sheet of paper and type the exercise for three minutes. Determine the gross words per minute.

All the letters of the alphabet are used in this exercise.

STROKES

The world needs each of us. This may sound queer to some 58

who have felt that there is no place where they are wanted and 121

no work for them to do. When you can do some work well, you 182

can be very sure that the call will come just when you least 242

expect it, perhaps. You must be a good worker, though; and 302

you must be ready to do whatever work comes. It is not the 362

kind of work or the size of the first pay that counts; get 421

started and you can go on to higher things and higher pay. 479

SPEED EMPHASIS
10 minutes

Directions. Type each sentence for one minute. Contrast your rate of typing on the first and second sentences.

You must learn to handle difficult letter combinations with the same sureness that you now type the small and frequently practiced words. The typing of these sentences should show you the importance of knowing how to type material of varying degrees of difficulty. This typing should also indicate to you the necessity of building strength in handling the infrequently used letters.

If time permits, retype the first, the third, and the fifth sentences for one minute each. Note improvement in speed and in control.

STROKES

It is a lot of fun to be able to write with ease and speed. 59

A haze blew crazily across the horizon to daze the amazed man. 62

He is in demand who tries to do a little more than he must. 59

In the overture, the oboe overdoes the harmonic overtones. 58

It is the way you stick to a thing that makes you a success. 60

TELEGRAMS

Telegraph, cablegram, and wireless service offers a means of quick communication that business employs daily. The kind of service to be used is determined by the urgency and the length of the message.

SERVICES AVAILABLE	CHARACTERISTICS	DELIVERY	BASIS OF CHARGE
Telegram, or Fast Telegram.	Given precedence over all other messages.	Immediate.	Minimum charge based on ten words. Charge for each additional word.
Day Letter.	Deferred service that may be used at any time of the day or the night. Transmitted at reduced rates after the fast telegrams have been sent.	Usually within an hour or two after it has been sent.	Fifty words sent at one and a half times the rate for a ten-word fast telegram. Extra charge for an additional ten words or fewer than ten words.
Night Telegram, Overnight Telegram, or Night Letter.	Accepted up to 2 a.m.	During following morning.	Minimum charge made for a twenty-five word message. This charge varies from about four fifths to about one half of the cost of a ten-word telegram between the same two points. The amount of the relative saving increases as the cost of the ten-word telegram increases. For more than twenty-five words, a small additional charge is made for each group of five words or less.
Timed Wire Service.	Sent by a telegraph typewriter installed in the office of the business.	Same as that for other telegrams.	Rate based on time used by the typist or operator in transmitting the message.
Serial Service.	Useful when several messages are sent on the same day to the same person or business at the same address.	Same as that for other telegrams.	Number of words in the messages is totaled at end of the day, and charge is made as if for one message.

Illustration No. 63 — Chart Showing Telegraphic Services

PREPARATION OF TELEGRAM

Type telegrams with double spacing. Use ruled blanks for handwritten copies of message, which are usually prepared in the telegraph office. Type a small *x* in the space provided for indicating the kind of service desired. Type the date below the printed heading and the address one double space below the date. The title in the address, the salutation, and the complimentary close, which are used in a letter, are omitted in telegraph messages. The following punctuation marks when employed as such by the sender in the text of a message will be transmitted as written by the sender, but will not be counted or charged for: comma, period, colon, semicolon, dash, hyphen, quotation marks, parentheses, question mark, apostrophe.

UNIT II — *MAKING TYPING HABITS PERMANENT*

3 minutes

The purpose of Unit II is to make permanent the correct habits that have been initiated. Repetition with interest and attention is one of the most effective ways of establishing these correct habits. The repetition drills given in this unit are, therefore, for the purpose of establishing typing technique that will call for only the correct responses in all your work.

GENERAL DIRECTIONS FOR TYPING THE DRILLS AND EXERCISES

Paper to Use. 1. Reconstruction Practice and Speed Emphasis. These drills are not to be handed in for correction. Therefore you can use drill paper—paper that may have some writing on one side.

2. Technique Practice and Exercise. Use a half sheet for each typing.

Form. 1. Type your name in the upper left-hand corner on the first line.

2. Type the date on the line with your name, but in the right-hand corner of the page.

3. Determine the exact top and bottom margins to be used for the correct placement of the typed material on the page. When determining these margins, you must take into account the heading of the drill or the exercise that is to be typed.

4. Center the heading horizontally.

5. Always triple-space between the heading and the first line of the drill or the exercise. Triple spacing between the heading and the first line of a drill or an exercise leaves two extra spaces only. The typing begins on the third line.

Timed Writings. 1. If your teacher cannot time you, use a watch with a secondhand and time yourself on the sentences and paragraphs marked for timed writings. Determine the gross words per minute. (See the footnote on page 26.) Encircle the errors if any have been made. Note the frequently recurring misstrokes and be on guard against continuing them.

2. Record the results of the timed writings on the form included in the workbook. If you do not have the workbook, rule a sheet of paper in the form shown below:

RECORD OF TIMED WRITINGS

DATE	LESSON	GROSS WORDS PER MINUTE		NUMBER OF ERRORS	
		ONE-MIN.	FIVE-MIN.	ONE-MIN.	FIVE-MIN.
Sept. 12	21	25		2	
Sept. 13	22	27		3	
Sept. 14	23	25		0	

LESSON 21

RECONSTRUCTION PRACTICE

5 minutes

Directions. 1. Use a 60-space line.

2. Set the machine for single spacing.

3. Type each line twice. Double-space after the second typing of the line.

Drill

(b)   big bar bug beg buy bag fob rob rub tub fob rib tab tub fib

(c)   checks decade chance scarce cocoa click clench clerical accede

(e)   ever deed edge need cede made deck read else head been seed

(h)   hardly highly hunch thanks hyphen health handle rhythm height

[49]

Through the exercises you are required to type and through the chart of the kinds of services you may use, you can learn what you need to know about telegrams. Cablegrams and radiograms are much the same in their use; but the cost is more, of course, than that of a telegram, and the means of sending a message is different. A cablegram is sent by telegraph wires to a cable office just as a telegram is sent. From there it is sent through lines laid on the ocean floor. From the foreign office it is sent over telegraph wires to the place of delivery. A radiogram is sent by a telegraph company and not by a radio station such as those that send out programs. It is sent by telegraph wires to a station and from there it goes out through the air. It is then picked up by sets on the same wave length as that used in sending it. It may have to be sent over telegraph wires from the place at which it is received, but it is not sent solely by wire. A person can file a message at a telegraph office by means of the telephone, a messenger (who may be called by means of the telephone or a buzzer), or the teletype.

A charge is made for the address and the signature in a cablegram or a radiogram. A firm doing business abroad may use a code word for its cable address. This code word is listed with the cablegram companies, and it may be used on all messages except those that require delivery by mail. There are special rates for slow messages, which cost much less than full-rate messages. A slow message must be written in the language of the country in which it is filed, in the language of the country to which it is going, or in French. This condition must be met in order that the deferred rate may be obtained. The charge for a night cable letter is based on a minimum number of words; and the message, just as other slow messages, must be in plain language.

You can send money to any place where there is a cable or telegraph office. To do this, you pay the sum of money to be sent plus a sending charge. This service is quite expensive and is not used unless other means of sending funds are not feasible. Some safeguards are set up to protect the person who sends money by telegraph, just as there is protection for the drawer of checks. The one who is to receive the funds may need a third person to identify him. This type of identification is not always required, but the one who is to receive the money is likely to be quizzed and made to establish his identity. It is not always possible for the one to whom money is thus sent to find a person who knows him and who is known to the agent; but if he must be identified, the money will be held until all the required conditions have been met. Funds that are sent on a caution order will be paid when a proper amount of caution has been taken.

STROKES

908
981
1055
1134
1216
1299
1381
1460
1542
1623
1701
1782
1859
1928
1955

2026
2101
2177
2246
2326
2403
2483
2559
2634
2704

2781
2858
2937
3015
3094
3173
3254
3331
3407
3482
3562
3639
3650

TECHNIQUE PRACTICE 21

10 minutes

Directions. Center the drill vertically. Type the heading, **TECHNIQUE PRACTICE 21**, centered horizontally. Triple-space after typing the heading. Type each line twice. Double-space after the second typing of the line. Remember to release the shift lock before typing the figure 21.

Sentence 1. Use figures to express time with a.m. or p.m. Separate the figure for the hour from the figures for the minutes by a colon. Do not space after a period used within an abbreviation written in small letters.

Sentence 2. Separate hundreds from thousands with a comma except in a number designating a page, an insurance policy, a room, a telephone, a house, or a year.

Sentence 3. Express even sums of money without the decimal and ciphers.

Sentence 4. The comma and period are always typed before the quotation.

Sentence 5. Use the sentence for a one-minute timed writing. You should type a minimum of a line and a half in the minute.

STROKES

Dr. Decker will be in his office from 9:30 a.m. until 3:45 p.m.   63

Joe's policy is No. 290516. It will expire July 10, 1958.   58

The Baxter & Lowe order #182, dated April 17, amounts to $360.   62

"Know thyself," he said, "and all else will be added to you."   61

Any man can do anything that he makes up his mind he can do.   60

EXERCISE 21

15 minutes

Directions. 1. Use double spacing. Set a tabulator stop for a 5-space indention.

2. Center the exercise vertically; the heading, horizontally. Triple-space after the heading.

3. Repeat the exercise on a second sheet of paper.

The quotation mark is typed *before* the semicolon but always *after* the comma or the period.

All the letters of the alphabet are used in this exercise.

EXERCISE 21

STROKES

Do not grow careless in your work. That habit is quite   56

as bad as the drug habit, and it is formed in very much the   116

same way. Take a little dose of "don't care" and mix it with   178

a small part of "it doesn't matter"; then put in "I realize I   240

can get by." The dose is certain to be habit-forming. Just   301

keep it up for a time and you will be down and out.   352

ANALYSIS OF VERTICAL CENTERING

Line for heading	1	Available lines	33	$19 \div 2 = 9\frac{1}{2}$ Therefore:	
Extra spaces	2	Lines used	14	Top margin	9
Lines in paragraph	11			Bottom margin	10
Total lines used	14	Lines in top and bottom		Lines used	14
		margins	19		33

SENTENCE PRACTICE

Directions. Use a 70-space line. Use the sentences for one-minute writings and for drill in calling the throw.

	STROKES
If I cannot do great things, I can do small things in a great way.	66
What we call luck is simply pluck and doing things over and over.	65
Do not hesitate to undertake the task because it is big; grow with it.	70
Motto: Two ears, but only one mouth—hear twice as much as you tell.	69
No honest effort can be utterly lost; strength grows through effort.	68

CORRECTIVE DRILL PARAGRAPH

Directions. Use a 70-space line; a 5-space indention; single spacing.

(Emphasizing letters *q, u*)

	STROKES
The parents of Victor Johnston formerly lived at Quaker-	55
town, Pennsylvania. Victor's father showed great mission-	112
ary zeal and assisted the Indians by barter in their quillwork.	177
Victor's mother made quilts and canned quarts of quinces,	235
which she sold in Quebec. Victor was reared a Quaker; but	294
he can no longer meet the requirements of his Quaker re-	349
ligion because, after he grew up, he quickly renounced the	408
teachings of Fox, the early leader of the Quaker church.	466
Now he likes to read books like *Quentin Durward* and *Quo*	522
Vadis. Quite recently he took a trip to a place some miles	582
north of Guayaquil, in Ecuador. He does not want to be	638
quoted, but he said recently that he does not expect to quit	699
traveling until he has visited the Quirinal.	743

TIMED WRITING

Directions. Use a 70-space line; a 5-space indention; double spacing. If you complete the test before time is called, start at the beginning and continue typing. After time has been called, check the writing carefully.

	STROKES
It was not many years ago that the receipt of a telegram was a cause for	73
great fear in a home. Telegraph service was used to report deaths, to ask for	152
a last-minute change in plans, and for other types of messages that called for	231
more rapid delivery than that which would be obtained by using the mail.	305
Today business makes daily use of the telegram. This service speeds up the	381
wheels of business and is thought of as a saving rather than an expense to a	458
firm. Even in the home, the receipt of a telegram no longer makes one turn	534
pale, as was once true. The social use of telegrams, cablegrams, and radio-	609
grams is now quite common. Telegraph service is no longer costly. You	681
should know how to use all its forms. By all means, you should know when to	758
use fast messages and just when to economize by sending deferred messages.	832

TEST EXERCISE 21

10 minutes

Directions. Type the test exercise with the same directions used for the preceding exercise except that you will type it only once.

The quotation mark precedes the question mark if the quoted matter is not a question.

All the letters of the alphabet are used in this exercise.

STROKES

Have you made up your mind just what you want to do, or 56

are you, without knowing where you are going, "on your way"? 117

In the business world the need is for workers who can live up 179

to an exact aim, who analyze facts in terms of their effect 239

upon the life of the business, and who know without question 300

that service is the key that unlocks the door to success. 357

LESSON 22

RECONSTRUCTION PRACTICE

5 minutes

Directions. 1. Use a 60-space line.
2. Set the machine for single spacing.
3. Type each line twice. Double-space after the second typing of the line.

Drill
(i)   icing king rink idiot owing impious indistinct Indiana sticking

(j)   June July just join jars joke jobs jump joys junk judge joint

(k)   kick kept lack sack rack lake kink deck pack wink think kodak

(l)   label local would lilac lodge could legal labor libel loyalty

(m)   may map mud sum rum hum aim ham gum him bump lamp hump much

MANIPULATION DRILL: THE EXCLAMATION POINT

3 minutes

The exclamation point is made by the use of two regular keyboard characters, the apostrophe (') and the period(.).

Directions. 1. Shift with the left hand, hold the space bar down with the left thumb, and strike the apostrophe and the period *before releasing either the space bar or the shift key.*
2. Most typewriters make a half carriage movement when the space bar is depressed but some typewriters complete the movement on the down motion of the space bar. If your typewriter makes the complete movement when you depress the space bar, strike the period, backspace, and then strike the apostrophe.

I can! I can think!

OUTGOING MAIL

1. Make a carbon copy of each letter.
2. Before removing the typed letter from the typewriter, read it carefully for errors. Make any necessary corrections.
3. Address an envelope for each outgoing letter.
4. Place the letter under the flap of the envelope, with the address side of the envelope and the letter toward you. Stack the completed letters in the order typed, with the faces down.
5. Check carefully to see that enclosures, when necessary, are included with the letters.
6. When the dictator is ready to sign the letters, present them to him with the faces up.
7. As you fold the letters, check the enclosures again.
8. Insert the letters and the enclosures into the envelopes; lay to one side letters that will have to be weighed for additional postage. (Never send a letter with insufficient postage. A letter with insufficient postage may irritate the recipient, and it may result in loss of business.)
9. When you are sure that the letters are ready, seal, stamp, and place them in the basket for outgoing mail.

Illustration No. 61 — Stamping Letters by Hand

Illustration No. 62 — Sealing and Stamping Machine

BUDGET XIII

TECHNIQUE PRACTICE 91

Emphasizing Abbreviations

Directions. Use a 70-space line; single spacing. Type each line twice. Double-space after the second typing of each line.

	STROKES
After Max received his C. P. A. degree, he worked for McNary & Bros.	68
Please send the material to her by C. O. D. express before June 26.	67
Herman earned three degrees by 1926; viz., B. S., M. A., and Ph.D.	66
Louis Dodson Vanderburg, Jr. purchased two racing cars f.o.b. Detroit.	68
Mr. Van Horn paid his son's I. O. U.'s, which amounted to $1,389.75.	70

TECHNIQUE PRACTICE 22

10 minutes

Directions. Center the drill vertically; center the heading horizontally. Triple-space after typing the heading. Type each line twice. Double-space after the second typing of the line.

Sentence 1. Space twice after the exclamation point when it is used at the end of a sentence.
Sentence 2. Space once after an exclamation point used within a sentence.
Sentence 3. Express dimensions and weight in figures and spell *by* in full. (In specifications *x* is used for *by*.)
Sentence 4. When the quotation is a question, type the question mark before the quotation marks.
Sentence 5. Use the sentence for a one-minute timed writing. Goal: two lines in the minute.

STROKES

Work right! Think right! Do right! Be right! Live right! 60

Work right! and think right! and then you will live right! 58

My box is 4 by 6 feet in size and it will weigh 185 pounds. 59

He said, "Is each day's work done as well as you can do it?" 60

You can help yourself by making a fine art of all your work. 60

EXERCISE 22

13 minutes

Directions. 1. Use double spacing. Set a tabulator stop for a 5-space indention.
2. Center the exercise vertically; the heading, horizontally. Triple-space after the heading.
3. Repeat the exercise on a second sheet of paper.

All the letters of the alphabet are used in this exercise.

STROKES

Men have always had to face the problem of just how to 55

earn a living. Once every family was quite independent of any 118

other because the members of a family could produce enough to 180

meet all their needs. Life is more complex now. Our work is 242

specialized. We do that which we can do well and depend upon 304

others for what we need and do not produce. 347

TEST EXERCISE 22

7 minutes

Directions. Unless otherwise directed, use the directions for the preceding exercise when typing the test exercise except that you will type it only once.

All the letters of the alphabet are used in this exercise.

STROKES

What is business? To most of us the term means a place 56

where trade is carried on and where money is exchanged. Busi- 117

ness is much more than just a place of trade. It is a social 179

institution, equal in some respects to the other institutions 241

that we have, such as home, school, church, and organized 209

recreation. Business is the blood of our national life. 355

PART III
OFFICE TYPING PROJECTS

If you can type well, you have one skill that will be an asset in most kinds of office work. Copy skill alone is not enough, of course; you must be able to use good judgment in setting up problems to be typed and in meeting unexpected office situations. You can develop good judgment along with excellent typing power if you will appraise your work habits as well as the product of your effort.

Much of the work in Part III will give a complete picture of an office transaction. The complete file pertaining to a single transaction may include letters, telegrams, orders, shipping forms, invoices, index cards, and other forms common to office work. The exercises, therefore, present integrated problems in office work that will help you to learn to use your developed skill. Establish correct office habits now. The practice materials are provided, but you must evaluate your learning procedures and improve your work habits.

UNIT XI — *TYPING OFFICE FORMS*

Use the following list as a checkup on the procedure involved in the correspondence work of an office:

INCOMING MAIL

1. When you receive the incoming mail, slit each envelope, remove the letter, use the time stamp to show the date and the hour of the receipt of the letter, and stack the opened mail in orderly manner. See that all enclosures are clipped to the proper letters.
   a. Read the letters. It may be necessary for you to get from the files other papers referred to in the letters.

   Place on the dictator's desk the incoming mail together with all papers from the files that will be needed by the dictator in answering the letters.
   b. If your dictator does not wish you to read the incoming mail, place all the letters on his desk. He will then indicate the material he wishes from the files.
2. A telegram should be delivered unopened to the individual addressed. When a telegram is addressed to the company, open it, time-stamp it, and send it directly to the department or the individual concerned, together with related material from the files.

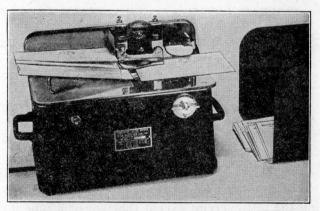
Illustration No. 59 — Letter-Opening Machine

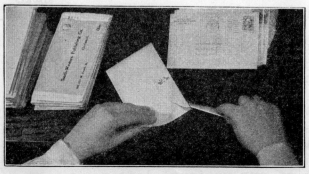
Illustration No. 58 — Opening Mail by Hand

Illustration No. 60 — Stamping Letters for Time

TYPING FROM PROBLEM SITUATIONS

Explanation. Column 1 has directions for typing the sentences given in Column 2. Column 2 contains sentences that are incorrect or incomplete as they stand. The correction is to be made at the point of the word set in bold-faced type. Study the example and the solution of the problem.

Example:

COLUMN 1—DIRECTIONS	COLUMN 2—TYPING PROBLEMS
1. Express the singular possessive.	1. **Jims** mother is here.

Solution:

```
1. Jim's mother is here.
```

General Directions for Typing from the Problem Situations. 1. Type the sentence once only. Do not strike over, cross out, or erase any typing.

2. Know what you are to type before beginning the sentence; then type on the stroke level.

3. This exercise is not to be handed in; therefore it may be typed on drill paper.

4. The solutions need not be centered on the page. Double-space and put each sentence on a line by itself.

COLUMN 1—DIRECTIONS	COLUMN 2—TYPING PROBLEMS
1. Type the quotation and the period in correct order.	1. He said, "He can who thinks he **can**
2. Type the quotation and the comma in correct order; after the last word, type the quotation and the period in correct order.	2. "I **believe** he said, "this is good **typing**
3. Type the colon.	3. A success **recipe** study, think, and work.

LESSON 23

RECONSTRUCTION PRACTICE

Directions. 1. Use a 60-space line.

2. Set the machine for single spacing.

3. Type each line twice. Double-space after the second typing of the line. These directions are to be followed in all succeeding reconstruction practices in this unit.

Drill

(n) not run sun fun gun hand sunk bunk junk rung null next hunt

(o) old bold sold fold told cold gold look room wool fool pool

(p) pack past soap play plan pity plus pick paper prepare pause

(q) quit quick quiet quite quits queen quote queer quart quantity

(r) rear regard robber regular reprove rifler reform remark revere

TABLE OF CONTENTS

CHAPTER I

INTRODUCTION

I. IMPORTANCE OF LETTER TRANSCRIPTION

In 1890 there were 33,418[1] stenographers and typists in the United States; in 1930, there were 811,190.[2] Thus, in the past 40 years the number of stenographers and typists has increased 24 times, while the general population has increased from approximately 63 million in 1890 to approximately 123 million in 1930, an increase of less than twice. These figures confirm the generally accepted importance of stenographic work in the efficient functioning of the business office and indicate the timeliness of this present study which deals with transcription techniques and production standards.

Three recent studies dealing with the duties of the secretary reveal the relative importance of letter transcription to all office duties. Charters and Whitley[1] discovered that letter transcription ranks third in a list of 871 secretarial and stenographic duties. Only typewriting letters and answering the telephone outrank it in a frequency distribution of duties. Nichols[2] found by combining the judgments of secretaries and employers that taking dictation and transcribing ranked first and second respectively in a list of 35 secretarial duties. Kyker[3] found by combining the judgments of stenographers and employers of stenographers that transcription appeared in the first ten ratings assigned to stenographic duties.

A table prepared by Evans shows that transcription consumes more of the stenographer's working time than any other duty.[4] Slightly less than one third of her working day is devoted to this work. Parkhurst writes:

"According to motion studies which have been made, we learn that in a large office the average stenographer who is rated as 'fairly competent' spends twenty-five hours during the week in transcribing notes, the remainder of the time being devoted to taking dictation and to details of office routine. If the stenographer is to transcribe one hundred and fifty letters in the course of a week, and she has twenty-five hours of transcribing time, she must turn out an average of six letters each hour and keep up that pace hour after hour. . . ."[5]

---

1. "Occupations," *Twelfth Census of the United States,* Washington, Government Printing Office, p. 40 (1904).
2. "General Report on Occupations," *Fifteenth Census of the United States,* Washington, Bureau of the Census, Vol. 5, p. 49 (1930).

1. Charters, W. W., and Whitley, I. B., *Analysis of Secretarial Duties and Traits,* Baltimore, Williams and Wilkins (1924).
2. Nichols, F. G., *The Personal Secretary,* Cambridge, Massachusetts, Harvard University Press (1934).
3. Kyker, F. B., *The Commercial Curriculum,* New York, Gregg Publishing Company (1930).
4. Evans, R. B., "Dictating Machines Reduce Office Costs," *Annual Proceedings,* New York, National Office Management Association, pp. 15-18 (1929).
5. Parkhurst, E. N., "Improvement of Classroom Teaching of Transcription Second-Year Shorthand," *Twelfth Yearbook,* Philadelphia, Eastern Commercial Teachers Association, p. 515 (1939).

OPTIONAL UNIT: SPEED EMPHASIS

You can probably afford to take a few periods for the specific purpose of practicing for the improvement of your stroking power. Use the practice materials of Unit III, but hold yourself to a stroking rate of double the speed called for in the instructions for practice. For example, in the speed emphasis paragraphs of Lesson 32, page 71, you are to type each paragraph in one minute; at this time, you are to type each paragraph in a half minute.

MANIPULATION DRILL: CARRIAGE-RETURN AND
TABULATOR-KEY CONTROL

2 minutes

Directions. Repeat the drill given on page 19, Lesson 6. It is important that you learn to control the machine parts by touch. Remember that the control of the tabulator key calls for a "hold stroke" rather than a quick release of the key.

If your words are not correctly aligned in columns, you probably are releasing the tabulator key too quickly. Hold this key down until the carriage stops.

TECHNIQUE PRACTICE 23

10 minutes

Directions. 1. In this and subsequent technique practice drills, center the material vertically and the heading horizontally. Triple-space after typing the heading.

2. Type each line twice. Double-space after the second typing of the line.

3. These directions will not be repeated until a change in the form is desired.

Sentence 1.   Review of use of exclamation point.
Sentence 2.   In stating exact age in years, months, and days, use figures.
Sentence 3.   In stating approximate age in years, use words.
Sentence 4.   Sums of money, whether dollars or cents, should be typed in figures.
Sentence 5.   Use the sentence for a one-minute timed writing. Goal: two lines in the minute.

STROKES

Keep your chin up! Nothing is impossible! You can achieve!   60

Bob is 15 years 9 months and 7 days old and weighs 128 pounds.   62

I think Mary will be nineteen or twenty years old in January.   61

Ralph won the prize of $20, but Charles won only 90 cents.   58

Time that is given to work that is worth doing is never lost.   61

EXERCISE 23

13 minutes

Directions. 1. Use double spacing. Set a tabulator stop for a 5-space indention.

2. Center the exercise vertically and the heading horizontally. Triple-space after typing the heading.

3. Type the exercise twice on separate sheets of paper.

4. These directions are to be followed for subsequent exercises and test exercises unless other directions are given.

All the letters of the alphabet are used in this exercise.

STROKES

The freedom to own things and to run a business is quite   57

often subject to regulation by city or state. For the most   117

part, though, a man may exercise his right to start a business 180

if he observes the laws that have been laid down to keep one   241

man from infringing on the rights of another. The theory of   302

laissez faire, "Let one do as he pleases," is not now thought   364

to be best always for society as a whole.   405

page should be retyped. Separate the footnotes from the text by a line extending approximately 1½ to 2 inches from the left margin. Type footnotes with single spacing, but double-space between them.

The footnotes may be numbered consecutively throughout an article or a chapter of a book, or they may be numbered consecutively on each page, the first footnote on each page being "1." You must be uniform in the numbering of footnote references. For an article, consecutive numbering throughout the manuscript is preferred by many writers; for a thesis, consecutive numbering on each page has its advantages. In the latter case, an omission or an addition may be made by changing only the particular page affected by the change. If the footnotes are numbered consecutively throughout a manuscript, an addition or an omission of one reference necessitates the changing of all subsequent footnotes.

When two footnotes contain references to the same work and one follows the other without any intervening footnote, use *Ibid.*, the abbreviation for *ibidem* (in the same place), and the exact page number for the second footnote.

Place quotation marks and other marks of punctuation as follows:

1. A period or a comma at the end of a quotation should be placed within the quotation mark.
2. A semicolon or a colon should follow the quotation mark unless it belongs only to the quotation.
3. If a question or an exclamation mark applies to the entire sentence, it is written outside the quotation mark; if it belongs to the quotation, it is written inside the quotation mark.

EXERCISE 127

Directions. This exercise has (1) a title page, (2) a table of contents, and (3) part of the introduction to a thesis. The report will be bound at the left side. Have a left margin of 1½ inches and a right margin of 1 inch. In centering lines, center between the margins and not according to the entire width of the paper. The lines on the title page are to be centered as you would center columnar headings.

In the table of contents, leaders (lines of periods) may be used to direct the eye from the title of a division to the page number. In making leaders, alternate the period and the space stroke. In general, the use of lines of periods should be avoided, for the period key, when struck vigorously, makes an indentation in the cylinder that may later cause an uneven impression of letters.

In typing the introduction, use a 60-space line, double spacing, and a 5-space indention. Center the heading 2 inches from the top of the page. Type the quoted paragraph with single spacing and indent it 10 spaces from the left and 5 spaces from the right margin. Place the footnotes on the same pages as the reference figures. Leave approximately an inch for each footnote, in addition to the bottom margin of 1 inch. Number the second page of the introduction in the upper right-hand corner. Type the Arabic 2 approximately an inch from the top and an inch from the right edge of the paper.

TRANSCRIPTION STANDARDS IN BUSINESS CORRESPONDENCE

By

S. J. Wanous

B. Ed., State Teachers College, Whitewater, Wisconsin, 1929

M. A., State University of Iowa, 1930

Submitted to the Graduate School

of the University of Pittsburgh in partial

fulfillment of the requirements for the degree of

Doctor of Philosophy

Pittsburgh, Pennsylvania

1940

All the letters of the alphabet are used in this exercise.

	STROKES
You acquire money with which to buy things through the	55
exchange of service for a wage. This is how specialization	115
has come. The people in the West raise fruit and ship to the	177
markets of the East; those in the East make hats and shoes to	239
sell in the West. Money is the medium of exchange. We have	300
adjusted ourselves to this condition and our American culture	362
has its roots in this specialized business life.	410

TYPING FROM PROBLEM SITUATIONS

5 minutes

Directions. Column 1 has directions for typing the sentences given in column 2. The correction is to be made when typing the expression set in bold-faced type. Type the sentence once only.

Column 1—Directions	Column 2—Typing Problems
1. Type in figures.	1. The check is for **five hundred dollars**
2. Type the exclamation point.	2. We must **think** and **work** and **achieve**
3. Type in figures.	3. The show begins at **eight-thirty** p.m.
4. Type the quotation and the question mark in correct order.	4. He said, "Did you talk with **them**

LESSON 24

RECONSTRUCTION PRACTICE

6 minutes

Directions. Use a 60-space line.

Drill

(s) samples satisfy sarcasm serious season special strange session

(t) tube that fact tuft lift waft lost both fight tight twist twixt

(u) unsound unjust unqualified unconscious unusual humorous unsuited

(v) valve velvet reverse furtive verve quiver never fugitive vapor

(w) would whirl widow window westward well-known wormwood weather

HOW TO ERASE

Erasing is permitted in most business offices. The demand for maximum production is a demand for maximum efficiency in correcting inaccuracies. Retyping a letter wastes time and supplies. The efficient office worker strives for usable first production. When errors are made, skill in making corrections will help to offset the loss of time in making the corrections.

The steps in erasing are as follows:

1. Move the carriage to the right or the left to prevent erasure waste from falling into the typewriter mechanism.

2. Use an eraser shield to protect the letters or characters not to be erased.

3. Turn the cylinder forward if the erasure is to be made on the upper two thirds of the page. If the erasure is to be made on the lower third of the paper, turn the paper backward so that the correct alignment of the type will not be disturbed. (This "back-feeding" is used in making corrections on manuscripts that are bound at the top.)

4. Place a small card or a heavy piece of paper between the ribbon copy (the letterhead) and the carbon sheet. This will protect the carbon sheet and will prevent smudging the carbon copy.

5. Use a soft or pencil eraser for the carbon copy. Use a hard or ink eraser for the original or ribbon copy.

6. Erase lightly with one-way motions. The use of the shield will protect the adjacent typed lines. Make a clean erasure.

7. Remove the card or the piece of paper used to protect the carbon sheet, and roll the cylinder to the correct writing position.

8. Type the erased word or portion of a word, striking the keys with a normal or slightly lighter than normal touch. If the retyped letters are lighter than the other portion of the word, retype the letters with a light stroke. Match the weight of the type by skillfully using the right amount of power in striking the keys.

9. If a correction is to be made after the papers have been removed from the typewriter, separate the sheets and correct the error on the carbon copy and the original copy according to the directions given above. Make the correction on the carbon copy first. This will provide a test of your skill. Insert the sheet, gauge the line and the letter, and type without the use of the carbon sheet. Similarly, insert the original copy and make the correction.

EXERCISE 126

Directions. Set the margin stops for a 65-space line. Adjust a tabulator stop for a 5-space indention. Use double spacing. Type the heading in capital letters 2 inches from the top of the paper. Triple-space after typing the heading. Have a bottom margin of 1 inch. Number the second page by typing the Arabic *2* in the center, approximately an inch from the top of the page. Triple-space after the figure and continue your typing. Single-space and indent the numbered paragraphs ten spaces from the left margin and five spaces from the right margin.

The material in this exercise presents no special difficulty in arrangement other than the placement of the heading and the numbered paragraphs at the end of the exercise. As the pages are not to be bound, uniform margins should be maintained at the left, right, and foot of the page.

TYPING MANUSCRIPTS

In referring to footnotes, use superior figures in the text. Place the figure after the punctuation mark, if any, but without any space between the punctuation mark and the figure. If a reference figure is used with a quoted excerpt, it should stand at the end of the quotation or immediately after the author's name when the name is used to introduce the quotation. Either form is acceptable if used uniformly. Footnotes must appear on the same page as that on which the reference figures appear. When typing an unpaged manuscript, allow one inch for each footnote. If adequate space has not been left at the foot of a page for all footnotes, the

TECHNIQUE PRACTICE 24

Sentence 1. Underscore, or type in all capitals, the title of a book. Do not underscore the space between words.
Sentence 2. You may type the title of books in capitals. When this form is used, do not underscore the title.
Sentence 3. When common possession is to be shown, use the apostrophe with the last name only. The hyphen is a part of the spelling of the compound term and must, therefore, be underscored.
Sentence 4. Place in quotation marks the title of an article.
Sentence 5. Use the sentence for a one-minute timed writing. Goal: two lines in the minute.

STROKES

You can develop good typing power by using <u>College Typewriting</u>. —— 63

You can develop good typing power by using COLLEGE TYPEWRITING. 63

We have read Shields and Wilson's <u>Business-Economic Problems</u>. 61

He wrote an article entitled "Typing Power." Have you read it? 63

Nothing worth having ever comes without a lot of hard work. —— 59

EXERCISE 24

13 minutes

All the letters of the alphabet are used in this exercise.

STROKES

If a nation is to be well off, wealth must be shared so 56

that a majority of its citizens will have an adequate income 117

with which to take care of their needs. When only a few are 178

very rich and the many are very poor, how to share the wealth 240

is a problem that is not easy to solve. One scheme calls for 302

high tax rates on what is earned and on what is inherited. 362

Out of the income from such taxes, we provide for the old and 424

for the poor. 437

TEST EXERCISE 24

8 minutes

All the letters of the alphabet are used in this exercise.

STROKES

Do you realize that more than 60 per cent of those who 55

enter business either fail or quit? Two of the major causes 116

of failure are accepting and extending credit. The basis of 177

business is credit, of course; and good management takes care 239

of credit obligations through wise buying and quick turnovers. 303

Failure to keep the proper books is another cause of failure. 365

It is necessary that at all times a business have records to 426

show just what its condition is. 458

EXERCISE 124

Directions. Set the margin stops for a 65-space line. Adjust a tabulator stop for a 5-space indention. Use double spacing. Type the heading in capital letters 2½ inches from the top of the paper. Triple-space after typing the heading. Have a bottom margin of 1 inch. Number the second page by typing the Arabic *2* in the center, approximately an inch from the top of the page. Triple-space after the figure and continue your typing.

MANUSCRIPT TYPING

Manuscripts should be typed on paper of uniform size, preferably 8½ by 11 inches. Use double spacing. Quotations of more than four lines may be single-spaced and indented; outlines and tabulated material also may be single-spaced and indented. Type on one side of the paper only.

The first page should have a top margin of 2½ inches. Type the title, or heading, in capital letters, centering it horizontally. It is unnecessary to underscore the title, for the use of capital letters gives sufficient emphasis. A period should not be placed after the title. If the title is a quotation or an exclamation, use the proper mark of punctuation. Triple-space between the title and the first line of the copy. Have an inch margin at the left, right, and bottom of each page.

Number each page except the first. Use Arabic numerals. If the manuscript is not to be bound at the top, type the number in the center of the paper, approximately an inch from the top of the page. Triple-space between the number and the first line of the typing.

If the manuscript is to be bound at the top, leave a top margin of 2 inches on each page after the first. Number the pages at the bottom, beginning with the second page. Place the figure in the center, approximately an inch from the foot of the page.

If the manuscript is to be bound at the side, have a left margin of 2 inches and a right margin of 1 inch. Each page except the first should be numbered at the top, the figure to be typed approximately an inch from the top of the page and an inch from the right edge of the paper.

Underscored words will be set in italic type by the printer. If you are typing from print and find an italicized word in the copy, underscore the word. Titles of books, periodicals, and theses are usually underscored when they are typewritten. It is correct, but not the best practice, to quote the title of a book. In typing the work of this unit, underscore the titles of books and place within quotation marks the titles of chapters and articles.

Do not end a page with a hyphenated word. If possible, avoid having more than two consecutive lines end with a hyphenated word. *Never* leave just one line of a paragraph on a page. The bottom margin may be one line narrower or wider to avoid carrying the last line of a paragraph to the following page, or to avoid leaving a hyphenated word at the end of the page.

EXERCISE 125

Directions. Set the margin stops for a 65-space line. Adjust a tabulator stop for a 5-space indention. Use double spacing. Type the heading in capital letters 2½ inches from the top of the paper. Triple-space after typing the heading. The numbered paragraphs are to be single-spaced, double spacing being used between the paragraphs. When you come to these paragraphs, reset the margin stops for a 55-space line with uniform indentions of 5 spaces on the left and the right. Have a bottom margin of 1 inch. Number the second page by typing the Arabic *2* in the center, approximately an inch from the top of the page. Triple-space after the figure and continue your typing.

TECHNIQUE EMPHASIS: SHIFTING FOR CAPITALS   *7 minutes*

Directions. All capitals must be correctly aligned. If your typing has capital letters out of alignment, hold the shift key down firmly and use a little more deliberate, even slow, movement in striking the capital and releasing the shift key.

Speed up the return of the controlling finger from the shift key. Type the following sentences at a slow enough speed so you can strike the second letter of each capitalized word without a perceptible pause between it and the capital letter.

I am. I can. I will. I shall. I believe. I am sure I can.

We shall go in April. We shall go to Spokane in April.

I know Jack, Henry, and Mary will stay in Maryland until May.

Thomas Spaulding was in Spain in April before going to Algiers.

He said, "He and I met Joe and Frank in Spain last April."

LESSON 25
RECONSTRUCTION PRACTICE   *5 minutes*

Directions. Use a 60-space line.

Drill

(x)   box fox six tax mix six lax mix wax six fix box six lax six

(y)   you yes day may say hay lay may ray jay joy boy may buy joy

(z)   zeal zero zest zinc quiz hazy lazy maze haze quiz size quiz

(-)   self-conquest well-known tie-up son-in-law daughters-in-law

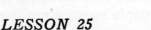

MANIPULATION DRILL: REMOVING THE PAPER, REINSERTING IT, AND TYPING OVER THE COPY   *8 minutes*

It is often necessary to remove the paper from the typewriter before you have completed the work. You must learn to reinsert the paper and gauge the line and letter skillfully to continue the typing.

Directions. 1. Type the word *this*. Before you return the carriage, locate the alignment scale (No. 15). Note the relation of the top of the scale to the bottom of the letters. Move the carriage to have one of the white lines on the scale point to the center of the letter *i* in the word *this*. For most typewriters, the letter *i* can be used best to gauge the letter spacing, but typewriters vary slightly and you will want to know the machine you are using.

2. Remove the paper from the typewriter; then reinsert it. Gauge the line horizontally; and, through the use of the variable line spacer (No. 38), set the line so the top of the line scale is in the right relation to the bottom of the letters in the word.

3. Operate the paper release (No. 23) and move the paper to the left or the right, as necessary, and gauge the correct letter spacing by centering with letter *i*.

4. Retype the word over the first writing. The second writing should print exactly over the first. Strike the keys lightly.

You will improve in the exactness with which you are able to control the machine parts as you repeat this drill from time to time.

Each paragraph has a syllable intensity of 1.30 and includes all letters of the alphabet.

A manuscript is an author's copy of his own material. Many famous authors | 75
have written their first drafts on the typewriter rather than by hand. The | 151
typed word is quickly read, the meaning easily grasped, and the speed with | 226
which the thoughts may be put on paper adds clearness to the expression. | 300
Even authors who must use the "hunt-and-peck" system—those who have not | 373
been trained as touch writers—often find their work done with more ease at | 449
the typewriter than by hand. Work habits of writers differ, of course, just as | 529
work habits of students differ. The best way to do a thing is the way in which | 609
you can do the work in the least time and with the best results. The best way | 688
for you to write may not be the same as the best way for me to do my writing. | 767
Still, there are some rules that must be followed when a manuscript is typed | 844
for publication. Most of these rules come to us from writers and publishers, | 922
who realize the relation between the first impression a manuscript makes and | 999
the final judgment of the critic. | 1034

When you write the first draft of a theme, a speech, or a paper for a maga- | 1108
zine, set the typewriter for triple space so that there will be plenty of space | 1188
for corrections. Some writers carefully check and correct the manuscript as | 1265
they write; but others prefer to complete the first draft in rough form, even | 1343
though such a form means that a great deal of rewriting will have to be done. | 1422
This practice seems to be the sounder because there is no danger of losing the | 1501
big thought in the details of expression. Once the whole picture has been put | 1580
on paper, details of form and of expression must be taken care of. If one writes | 1662
a first draft carefully, corrections may be reduced to a minimum. If this is the | 1744
aim, one should be certain he is not guilty of failing "to see the forest for the | 1826
trees." In your own composition at the typewriter, use the technique you find | 1905
best suited to your way of working. Just as the form in which a thought is | 1981
clothed is of less importance than the thought itself, so the way you work is | 2059
of less importance than what you accomplish. | 2105

When you type any matter that is to be published, use a good grade of paper | 2181
of the regular size, and type on one side only. All manuscripts should be | 2256
double-spaced. Quoted material may be single-spaced if it has more than three | 2335
or four lines. Quotation marks may be used; but it is good form to indent the | 2414
quoted matter and to write with single spacing, double spacing being used | 2488
between the paragraphs. If the marks are used, place one at the first of each | 2567
quoted paragraph and one at the end of the last paragraph. Number each page | 2644
except the first. Use Arabic numbers for all the pages in the major division of | 2725
the manuscript. Some writers use small Roman numbers for the pages that | 2798
precede the first chapter. Read each page and check for errors that may have | 2876
been made in the last typing. Set a high standard for your work so that when | 2954
the work is done, you will know that you have done your best. Let the skill | 3031
of your typing equal the beauty of your diction. Perfection is a high goal, but | 3112
it is one that is worth while. | 3142

TECHNIQUE PRACTICE 25

10 minutes

Sentence 1. Note method of expressing title of article and the placement of quotation before the semicolon. Underscore or type in capitals the titles of books.

Sentence 2. Space between a whole number and "made" fraction.

Sentences 3, 4, and 5. Use each sentence for a one-minute timed writing. Goal: two lines and two words.

	STROKES
The title of the article is "War Debts"; of the book, Taxes.	60
In writing fractions with whole numbers, use 5½ or 5 1/2.	57
If we want to do so, we can do much more work than we now do.	61
We need a lot of pluck to get ahead rather than a lot of luck.	62
No one is too poor to help to enrich the lives of other men.	60

EXERCISE 25

15 minutes

Directions. 1. Use a full-sized sheet of paper for this paragraph.

2. Use the paragraph for two five-minute timed writings. The goal for the first writing should be the completion of the entire paragraph. This goal can be achieved if you will type a line each half minute. For the second writing, set your goal for eight lines. This lower goal will tend to give you a sense of control that should make for fine accuracy and ease in typing.

All the letters of the alphabet are used in this exercise.

	STROKES
You want to win just as I do. When we go into a game,	55
only one of us can be first. This is not the way things work	117
out in learning, though. Each can expect to win just as much	179
as he is capable of winning through the thoughts he thinks and	242
the work he does. Do not let yourself ever think that you	301
need to have someone give you the breaks. All you need is a	362
lot of pluck and the willingness to stick to your work until	423
it is done as you know it should be done. You can win, all	483
right; but realize that how much you win depends on you and	543
not on anyone else. Make up your mind to do your work as well	606
as you can at all times.	630

SPEED EMPHASIS

5 minutes

	STROKES
did for and the can but pay vow big bit bud rug rub rob fob	59
(Say the word.) wish with such down when work work then them they hand hand	59
turn make both sick such half half kept kept form land held	59

[58]

TECHNIQUE PRACTICE 90

Emphasizing Syllabication

Directions. Set the margin stops for a 65-space line. Set a tabulator stop for a 5-space indention. Use single spacing. Type each sentence twice. Double-space after the second typing of each sentence. Study the following explanatory notes before typing any of the sentences:

Sentence 1. When an added syllable doubles the consonant, divide the word between the consonants.

Sentence 2. The suffix *sion* or *tion* is separated from the rest of a word as one syllable.

Sentence 3. When a word is to be divided at a vowel, write the vowel with the first part of the word, placing the hyphen after it (except in such words as *gradu-ation*).

Sentence 4. Words pronounced as one syllable are not divided, even when a consonant has been doubled to form a past tense.

Sentence 5. You will notice that this hyphened word comes under the exception mentioned above in connection with the third sentence.

I left at 10 a.m. in an automobile with the intention of stopping for a week at 2957 Crescent Drive, Long Beach, California.

The pastor was presented with an expensive radio as an expression of devotion on the part of his congregation.

Dr. Walter Reed sacrificed his valuable life for the experiment that isolated the carrier of the germ of yellow fever.

Madam Curie worked against odds, but her interest never flagged in the work that led to the discovery of radium.

In his long career, Robert took many degrees, but his graduation from high school was the event he remembered best.

CORRECTIVE DRILL PARAGRAPH

Directions. Use a 70-space line; 5-space indention; double spacing.

	STROKES
(Emphasizing letters *c, i, k, o*) There are chronic kickers just as there are chronic knockers.	63
Of the two, give me the kicker in preference to the knocker. The	129
knocker is apt to expect you to agree with him, thus making you	193
a partner to his knocking; the kicker likewise may expect you	255
to back him up in his kicking. When you realize what this silent	321
partnership in knocking and kicking is doing to you, the damage	385
to your own thinking has probably been done already. It is well	450
enough to say, "Each kick and each knock is a boost"; but the	512
world's happiness is lessened because there are so many knock-	573
ers who knock the motives as well as the acts of others, and be-	636
cause there are so many kickers who kick just for the sake of	698
making others squirm. Kick against injustice, of course; then	761
work to make conditions better. The only knocking you should	823
do is the knocking at the portals of today's opportunities, in	886
order that the doors may swing wide open for an honest, knock-	947
erless, and kickerless worker.	977

TIMED WRITING

Directions. Use a 70-space line; 5-space paragraph indention; double spacing.

LESSON 26

RECONSTRUCTION PRACTICE

5 minutes

Directions. Use a 60-space line.

Drill
(sw) swim swore switch swear swoon swell swain swamp swarm sweep

(br) broke bride bring break bread brick bribe breezy brazen brief

(ce) cedar cement ceramic certificate ceremony descend centered

(str) string struck streak strong strange straight strategy stream

TECHNIQUE PRACTICE 26

10 minutes

Sentence 1. Check on the shift-key control.
Sentence 2. Units of measure must be typed in figures.
Sentence 3. The quotation mark precedes the question mark if the quoted matter is not a question.
Sentence 4. Alphabetic sentence to be typed on the stroke level.
Sentence 5. One-minute writing. Goal: two and a half lines.

	STROKES
Larry and Robert will go to the Appalachian Club on April 1.	60
We have to buy 9 gallons of gas and 6 quarts of oil tomorrow.	61
Didn't he win a lot of fame and fortune as "The Lone Eagle"?	60
Couldn't Liza mix the big jars of soapy water very quickly?	59
No one knows what he can do until he has done all he can.	57

Remove the paper; reinsert it; gauge the line and the letter spacing; and type over the last line.

EXERCISE 26

13 minutes

Directions. Type the paragraph twice on separate half sheets. Use double spacing. Center the heading horizontally and the entire problem vertically.

All the letters of the alphabet are used in this exercise.

	STROKES
America is not a nation that can get along without the	55
rest of the world, no matter how much we boast of our amazing	117
wealth. We are a dependent nation. In Mexico is grown a sisal	181
hemp called "henequen." This is the only known fiber that is	243
sufficiently strong to be used in self-binding reapers which	304
will contract when wet and not expand, as is true of most of	365
the other fibers. We have need of Mexico just as we have need	428
of all the rest of the world.	457

UNIT X — *PROBLEMS IN MANUSCRIPT TYPING*

In the typing of manuscripts, there are many problems that have no direct connection with one's ability to type at a fast or a slow rate of speed, but that have a great bearing on the accuracy of the completed manuscript. Some of the specific details upon which there is agreement are given in the practice materials of this unit. With respect to some details, usage sanctions more than one form. Uniformity must be maintained, however, throughout a particular manuscript.

BUDGET XII

SYLLABICATION CHECKUP

Directions. Assume that each word comes at the end of the line of writing and that the division should be made at the proper place after the bell rings. Indicate the correct division of the words by writing the word with the hyphen at the point where the division should be made.

Bell Rings on the Typing of the Third Letter		Bell Rings on the Typing of the Fifth Letter	
1. material	6. desirable	11. persuasive	16. impression
2. manuscript	7. knowledge	12. application	17. followed
3. business	8. physical	13. importance	18. direction
4. separately	9. famous	14. quotation	19. illustrate
5. reached	10. preparation	15. correction	20. regretting

SENTENCE PRACTICE

	STROKES
If you add to the happiness of others today, you increase your own.	67
A man is the superior being of the earth, no matter what happens.	65
Will you drift, or will you make the fight? It's up to you to decide.	70
Through zeal, knowledge is gained; through lack of zeal, it is lost.	68
Live so that you will not be too much affected by the attitude of others.	73

MANIPULATION DRILL

Squeezing letters. If a letter has been omitted from the end or the beginning of a word, you can make the correction without erasing the entire word. If a letter has been omitted from the end of a word, and if your typewriter has the half-space mechanism, move the carriage to the last letter typed; depress and hold down the space bar as you type the omitted letter. If your typewriter does not have the half-space mechanism, move the carriage to the space following the word; depress the backspace key halfway and hold it in that position as you type the omitted letter. If a letter has been omitted from the beginning of a word, and if your typewriter has the half-space mechanism, move the carriage to the space between this word and the preceding one; depress and hold down the space bar as you type the omitted letter. If your typewriter does not have the half-space mechanism, move the carriage to the first typed letter of the word to which the correction is to be added; depress the backspace key halfway and hold it in that position as you type the omitted letter.

Directions. Type the following sentence just as it is shown here. Then move the carriage to the correct position for adding the letter *s* to the word *this*. The letter *s* will occupy half of the space between the words.

He thought thi report a very good piece of work.

The corrected sentence should look like this:

He thought this report a very good piece of work.

TEST EXERCISE 26

8 minutes

All the letters of the alphabet are used in this exercise.

	STROKES
Do you realize just how much America needs the rest of	55
the world? An example of the need for the products of other	116
countries can be found in our daily newspapers. We could not	178
have our quick service and well-printed papers if we did not	239
buy from the rest of the world. Every week more than 52,500	300
tons of paper pulp and paper must be brought to us from other	362
countries. We cannot isolate ourselves, for we need the	419
products of the world.	441

TYPING FOR CONTROL

7 minutes

Directions. Use each sentence for a one-minute timed writing. Your goal is to type at a controlled rate rather than at your fastest rate. You should have not more than an average of one error for each two lines.

	STROKES
When you play, play hard; when you work, don't play at all.	59
The man does things who knows what he wants and works for it.	61
Make up your mind to do better work now than ever before.	57
It is what we think and do that makes us what we want to be.	60

LESSON 27

RECONSTRUCTION PRACTICE

5 minutes

Directions. Use a 60-space line.

4f7j 1471 3d8k 4738 2s91 1291 5f6j 1561 ;0;- 1940 5f6j 2561

(Figure review.)   1 4 7 147 3 8 2 382 5 6 1 561 4 9 3 493 5 0 1 501 5 0 7 507

4f$f 7j&j 3d#d 8k'k 2s"s 91(1 0;); -;*; 5f%f 6j_j 2s"s 91(1

Frank & Moss owe $150. The note is for 6%. Type this right.

BUSINESS STATISTICS COMPANY

200 WALL STREET

NEW YORK CITY

June 27, 194-

Mr. C. O. Kendall, President
Valve Foundry and Construction Company
Johnstown, Pennsylvania

l.c

My Dear Mr. Kendall:

~~Unfortunately~~ we shall not be privileged to call ~~personally~~ *make a personal* on you before going to press with our current issue of <u>Business Statistics</u>. ~~We make it a regular practice~~ before revising our *business* analysis, to call upon as many of the leading executives ~~in busi- ness~~ as possible. *(1 we try)*

Perhaps you will ~~bear with us this time and~~ accept this *to give* letter as an invitation to contribute ~~a word~~ about your company *business* and your forecast of the valve and casting business for the re- *(statistics)* mainder of the year.

~~Were this a personal call,~~ we ~~would suggest~~ *want* a frank expression from you regarding your present earnings and sales, your plans for expansion or development of new methods - in fact, any per- tinent details that ~~would lead~~ us to *make* a fair appraisal of your company and your industry. *(will help)*

~~With the hope that you will accept this "letter visit" from us in the spirit in which it is sent and that you will favor us with your reply as soon as you can, we are~~

We are eager to gather data that are accurate. We take pride in our reputation for reliable business forecasting; and we shall,

Yours Very Truly, *l.c*

Business Statistics Co. *sp. in full*

F. D. Marshall, Manager *all caps*

3 spaces

JPH

P. S. Enclosed is a copy of the section of <u>Business Statistics</u> that is scheduled for revision on July 5, together with our present description of your Company. *l.c.*

Enclosure

therefore, appreciate your help in our effort to continue our effective service to business.

(*Strokes, 1274; words, 152.*)

TECHNIQUE PRACTICE 27

Sentence 1. A trade name or trade-mark may be indicated by quotation marks.
Sentence 2. Indicate a quotation within a quotation by the single quotation mark (the apostrophe).
Sentence 3. The plural form of letters and figures may be expressed with the apostrophe and *s*.
Sentence 4. In market quotations, express the plural of figures by adding the *s* without the apostrophe.
Sentence 5. One-minute writing. Goal: two and a half lines.

	STROKES
Our new "Wearever" tires are on sale now at a 3½% reduction. —	60
We wrote, "We want you to read the article, 'Nothing to Do.'"	61
I could not read what Joe wrote for he made his 2's like z's.	61
General Transport 4s are due in 1957 and are selling at 93½.	60
It is only in action that you will have the power to grow.	58

EXERCISE 27

13 minutes

All the letters of the alphabet are used in this exercise.

	STROKES
Because you want to learn to type with maximum skill as	56
soon as possible, just train your mind to tell your fingers	116
what to do. The gaining of skill gets down to fundamentals.	178
It forces you to study the best ways of setting up right ways	240
to work. You have to take stock of yourself, of how well you	302
can command your mind as well as your muscles. This is your	363
task. No one can do the work for you. The more quickly you	424
realize the fact, the better work you will do.	470

TEST EXERCISE 27

8 minutes

All the letters of the alphabet are used in this exercise.

	STROKES
Your school asks you to obey certain rules and to live up	58
to certain customs while in the classroom. Your teacher will	120
mark papers, observe you at work, and tell you how to get rid	182
of the wrong ways of typing. This textbook gives you drills	243
to improve your technique and projects to help you realize	302
sustained typing power. The development of typing power is	362
your task, though, and no one else can do the work for you.	423
Make these helps a part of your own way of doing your work.	482

recently analyzed, 235 of the 622 combinations of incorrectly made strokes have fewer than 20 errors to a letter. Let me illustrate: The letter *b* was struck for the letter *q* once. On the most casual inspection, this error would be discarded as of no significance. I am reasonably certain that out of 63,000 errors, if we eliminate those having fewer than 20 misstrokes, we are not eliminating any types of errors that need to be studied. (P) With the *a finger*, the *; finger*, and the *j finger*, I find that errors are caused frequently by a failure to keep the fingers curved. I believe that this is the explanation for such errors as striking *y* for *h* and *j* for *m*. This faulty technique often occurs in using the *t finger*, too. I frequently find that a student misstrikes *t* for *g* many times. (P) Transposition errors are traceable directly to imperfect controlling of the letter-making impulses. Usually the corrective drill for this type of error is a slow, well-sustained rhythmic drill written on the letter level. Transposition errors occur particularly when the student is making the transition from letter-by-letter typing to typing on the word level. (P) In the beginning work, the student sees a letter, thinks that letter, and strikes the letter. Just as soon as possible, he should be led to group letters into their natural sequences. Instead of typing *i-t* as separate letters, he should learn to type the word *it*. I have found that this transition is made most effectively through typing from dictation. The remedy for the transposition error, then, is to go back to using copy on the letter-recognition level. This should be done only until there is an apparent smoothness in the manner of typing copy. It would be fatal for the student to stay on the letter-recognition level for a very long time. (P) One error shown is that which has to be called imperfect shifting. Al-though this is not technically an error, as the entire letter is discernible, it does show poor technique. The remedy for this is fairly simple: The student must give a lengthened one-count to the shift-key control. A little more time must elapse between the movement to the shift key and the striking of the letter. Use such a drill as the following: (P) I am I can I will I shall I believe (P) The omission of letters or words seems to be directly traceable to reading too far in advance of the typing or to lifting the eyes from the copy. The addition of letters seems to be caused by a failure to think the ending of the syllable vigorously. Usually a letter is added that completes a familiar suffix ending or that is seen in the succeeding word. (P) One experiment I have been trying recently may interest you. I have been having the students type as they pronounce the word or the syllable. Immediately after this, I ask the students to type as they pronounce the word or the syllable with the lips closed. Of course, what I am trying to get is a vigorous typing impulse. I do not want the lips to move, nor do I want the students to set up the habit of spelling all words. (P) I suggest that you have your students list and analyze their errors over a period of one, two, or three weeks; then send some of the error-analysis charts to me. Perhaps I shall be able to suggest specific corrective drills for the students. At any rate, I shall be interested in continuing our correspondence on how to correct typing errors. Sincerely yours (L. B. Ross) Enclosure (*Strokes, 4976; words, 846.*)

EXERCISE 123

Directions. Type the letter on page 181 in a modified block style with all lines blocked at the left margin except the closing lines, which should be blocked in the position for the complimentary close. Use a 60-space line and mixed punctuation. Make all the corrections indicated.

TYPING FOR CONTROL

Directions. Use each sentence for a one-minute timed writing. Type at a controlled rate rather than at your fastest speed. Goal: two lines without error.

	STROKES
Before you can work to some purpose, you must have a purpose.	61
There is no price too dear to pay for perfection in our work.	61
If you are willing to work, you need never doubt your success.	62
Use all of your time just as well as you would use one hour.	60

LESSON 28

RECONSTRUCTION PRACTICE
5 minutes

Directions. Use a 60-space line.

8 3 1 831 2 9 5 295 5 1 7 517 5 1 7 517 4 0 1 401 2 6 1 261

3d#d 7j&j James & Young ordered #16 rings. We sent them #17.

4f$f 8k'k 2s"s He asked, "Won't the check be for $374.50?" —

5f%f 9l(1 0;); The interest rate is 8% (on the note for $150).

TECHNIQUE PRACTICE 28
9 minutes

Sentence 1. Form the singular possessive by adding apostrophe and *s*. Type the title of an article within quotation marks. If the quoted matter is not a question and the sentence is, type the quotation before the question mark.

Sentence 2. The symbol may be used with figures in place of *No.*

Sentence 3. It is preferable to type the expression *per cent* as two words, although it is acceptable to type it as one word.

Sentence 4. Use for a one-minute timed writing.

Sentence 5. Use for a one-minute timed writing.

	STROKES
Have you seen James Maxwell's article, "Our Social Heritage"?	61
The # (number) is the shift of 3; underscore, the shift of 6.	61
Per cent may be typed as two words; % is used in tabulations.	61
What is the use of having a fine plan if you do not use it?	59
Fit yourself for work and then find the work that fits you.	59

Remove the paper; then reinsert it and type over the last line of the drill.

The inverted paragraph may be used in other styles of letters when several paragraphs in a letter have subjects. This method of typing the paragraphs makes reference to them convenient. The subjects may be typed in capital letters, or they may be typed in small letters and then underscored.

Directions. Type Style Letter No. 12, using a 60-space line for the first line of each paragraph. Also use open punctuation. Block the complimentary close and the company name so that the name will end at the right margin. Leave two spaces between the company name and the word *By*. This word indicates the position for the penwritten signature. It is better practice to type an official title or to leave the space below the company name blank, rather than to indicate the position for the penwritten signature by typing the word *By* or a line. Type the notation at the left margin, two spaces below the reference initials.

The customary form for typing the dash is two hyphens without a space before or after the hyphens. In this letter the dash is one hyphen with a space before and after it (paragraph 1).

EXERCISE 121

Directions. Type the letter in the modification of the block form shown as Style Letter No. 13. Use mixed punctuation. The quoted paragraph should be indented ten spaces from the left margin and five spaces from the right margin. Block the closing lines so that they will end at the right margin of the letter.

EXERCISE 122

LETTERS OF MORE THAN ONE PAGE

Letters of more than 275 words should be written on two or more pages. The last paragraph of the first page should contain at least two lines, and the first paragraph of the second page should have at least two lines. Avoid ending a page with a hyphened word. The margin at the bottom of the first page should be as wide as the left margin, unless it is necessary to avoid carrying a single line to the next page.

The heading for the second page should begin two inches from the top of the page and should contain the name of the person or the business to which the letter is being written, the page number, and the date. The second-page heading should be typed, beginning at the left margin, in one of the two following styles:

(a)

Miss Dodson   2   July 31, 194—

(b)

Miss Dodson
Page 2
July 31, 194—

Leave four spaces between the second-page heading and the first line of the body of the letter. Complete the typing of the letter as you would if you were finishing it on the first page.

Directions. This is a three-page letter. Type the letter in the block form. Use open punctuation. Type an appropriate heading on each page after the first.

Miss Mildred L. Dodson Head, Typewriting Department School for Secretaries Philadelphia, Pennsylvania My dear Miss Dodson Your letter enclosing samples of typing errors made by your students reached me Monday. Analyzing errors apart from the students at work is difficult and somewhat dangerous. The error in the typing tells but half the story—and it is usually the less significant part of the problem. Still, I am glad to try to help you in determining some of the causes of the errors. (P) The outstanding weakness as shown by the errors you sent is the difficulty with adjacent-key controls. I think the difficulty is caused psychologically by an indefinite, or at least a relatively weak, impulse to type. The association between the controlling finger and the key to be controlled evidently is weak because so many errors appear in adjacent-key controls. For corrective practice, I have been using the word drills on adjacent-key controls given on the enclosed sheet. Corrective drills must be typed at a well-sustained rhythm if they are to be of value. For that reason, three-letter and four-letter words are of little value after the student has set up the habit of continuous typing. (P) There are, of course, some accidental errors that can never be interpreted. For instance, I can see no cause for striking the letter *s* for *n*. Out of a total of slightly more than 63,000 errors

All the letters of the alphabet are used in this exercise.

	STROKES
Pay attention to what you are doing. Know when your work	58
is right or wrong. Do not depend upon your teacher to check	119
your papers, but check each paper so that you will know how	179
well you can type. Analyze your errors and try to find the	239
weakness in technique that causes them. You can do much for	300
your progress in typing just by finding out how you can best	361
learn to type. It is up to you to see that your work is right.	425
Know that it is exactly right before it leaves your desk.	482

TEST EXERCISE 28   *8 minutes*

All the letters of the alphabet are used in this exercise.

	STROKES
The way in which you learn to type will influence your	55
habits of typing for a long time. Just as important is the	115
organized follow-up that will improve and make those first	174
habits exact. Each day of practice should bring you more	232
skill. How you work is equal in importance to how much you	292
work. Measure the work of each day in terms of how much	349
better you typed at the close of the day than you typed at	408
the beginning.	422

TYPING FOR CONTROL   *7 minutes*

Directions. Type each sentence for one minute without error. Type on the stroke level.

	STROKES
I must conquer my weaknesses, or they will surely conquer me.	61
The first element of success is the determination to succeed.	61
Force yourself to type at a speed well within your control.	59

FOREIGN TRAVEL SERVICE

MUNSON BUILDING

BOSTON, MASSACHUSETTS

March 3, 194-

February 1, 1949

14

Miss Margaret Closson Frazier 44
1749 Ridgeway Drive 64
Lansing, Michigan 82

My dear Miss Frazier: 105

    Our New York office has forwarded to us your letter of 160
inquiry about the trip you expect to take to the Scandina- 217
vian countries this summer. 246

    We are sure you could not plan any trip that would give 302
you more to see or more latitude in your movements in get- 359
ting from place to place than the trip you have in mind. We 420
quote below a statement from one of our clients of last year, 482
in order that you may understand more clearly the detailed 541
care we endeavor to give: 568

> "Although this was my sixth trip to Europe, 612
> I can truthfully say I never had so many 653
> details taken care of and so much done to 695
> make me comfortable while with a conducted 738
> party. The director arranged a month's 778
> independent trip for a friend and me that 820
> was a marvel in every way." 849

    Some pamphlets are being mailed to you today under sepa- 904
rate cover. We should like to send one of our representa- 961
tives to your home to discuss the matter in detail with you. 1023
We know we can be of service to you. 1061

                    Yours very truly, 1079

                    FOREIGN TRAVEL SERVICE 1102

Block

Henri Maurice Le Bouf

                    Henri Maurice LeBouf 1123

hbf 1127

Mailing References: 1148
    Pamphlet 25-C, Sweden 1170
    Pamphlet 30-1, Norway 1191

(Strokes, 1191; words, 181.)

Style Letter No. 13 — Modification of the Block Form of Letter with a Quoted
Paragraph and Mailing References

LESSON 29

RECONSTRUCTION PRACTICE

Directions. Use a 60-space line.

	STROKES
Did the quick fox jump over Robert Johnson's lazy brown dog?	60
If there were no hard things to do, there would be no growth.✗	61
Was bezique the card game that they played just to vex Jake?	60
The world makes way for the man who knows he can make good.✗	59

Remove the paper; reinsert it, and type over the last line.

TECHNIQUE PRACTICE 29

Sentence 1. Use the apostrophe in contractions.
Sentence 2. Reconstruct the correct way to type the exclamation point.
Sentence 3. Check on the shift-key control.
Sentence 4. In the tabulated reports, orders, and bills, you may use ' to express feet and " to express inches; as 6' 10" (six feet 10 inches). Note the placement of the period after the symbol for inches.
Sentence 5. Type the period before the quotation mark. Contrast the placement of the quotation and period in this sentence with the placement of the symbol and period in sentence 4.

	STROKES
It's a good plan to try to do far more work than is expected.	61
Do noble things! Do not just dream about them all day long! ✦	60
Mary Appleton will go with Janice Spaulding to Atlantic City.	61
Six feet ten inches may be written 6 ft. 10 in. or 6' 10".	58
He said, "Success is learning to walk right past failures."	59

EXERCISE 29

All the letters of the alphabet are used in this exercise.

	STROKES
You can get an average of your typing rate to use as the	57
basis for your goal for the next major section of the work to	119
be done. Type a paragraph under time. See how many strokes	180
you type; then set as the goal the strokes that you type plus	242
fifty. As we count five strokes to a word, this is equivalent	305
to saying that you will add a word each day for the next ten	366
days of practice. Set your goal in gross strokes. You will	427
learn later how much you will be penalized for each error made.	490

Lakeside Estates, Inc.

Buffalo, New York

February 18, 194-

Mr. Robert J. Penner   39
728 West 58th Street   60
Albany, New York   77

Dear Mr. Penner   93

YOU CAN LAUGH AT MONEY WORRIES - just as many others are now   154
     doing - by following the same kind of business that has   210
     built some of the country's largest fortunes.   257

About $12,000,000,000 is invested in the business to which we   319
     refer. It is twice as large as the steel industry.   372

We are dealing exclusively in the ONE BRANCH of this business   434
     in which, you will agree, there is little element of chance   494
     or speculation. We are not selling stocks, bonds, or any   552
     other type of so-called securities.   589

We can show you a plan of investment that is today bringing   649
     a return of approximately 15 per cent per annum.   699

You will receive a check EACH MONTH from the Investment Oil   759
     Company, the Hill Petroleum Company, or one of the other   816
     major oil companies, as you prefer.   853

If you wish to know how you may participate in this unusual   913
     proposition, full details will be sent you. Just write   969
     your initials on the line marked and mail this letter in   1026
     the enclosed envelope. (No stamp is necessary.)   1076

                Yours very truly   1093

                LAKESIDE ESTATES, INC.   1116

           By *E. B. Marsh*   1119

EBM/hbf   1127

O. K. _____   1134

(Strokes, 1135; words, 176.)

Style Letter No. 12 — Inverted-Paragraph Style of Letter

[177]

All the letters of the alphabet are used in this exercise.

STROKES

If I were to select one trait that must be emphasized   54

above all others in beginning workers, it would be that trait   116

or quality that leads men to follow through on work until it   177

is completed. When the work is not completed one day, the   236

worker must see that it is done the next day. It is lack of   297

judgment, rather than lack of willingness to work, that is   356

usually the difficulty. Most beginners in business want to   416

do well; they fail because they do not follow through.   470

TYPING FROM PROBLEM SITUATIONS   *7 minutes*

Directions. Column 1 has directions for typing the sentences given in Column 2. The correction is to be made when typing the expression set in bold-faced type. Type the sentence once only.

COLUMN 1—DIRECTIONS	COLUMN 2—TYPING PROBLEMS
1. Indicate the title of the article.	1. He wrote the article **More Power to You.**
2. Indicate the title of the article and place the quotation and question marks in correct order.	2. Did you read Smith's article **More Power**
3. Indicate the possessive form for the authors of the book.	3. We read **Smith and Hall** LEARNING TO FLY.
4. Punctuate with the colon. Express fraction in figures.	4. This is the way to type a whole number and **fraction seven and two-thirds**
5. Make needed corrections.	5. Policy **149,361** is for $1,500.00.
6. Make needed corrections.	6. The box is **eight by twelve feet.**

LESSON 30

RECONSTRUCTION PRACTICE   *5 minutes*

Directions. Use a 70-space line.

STROKES

I wish that you would pack Mary's box with five dozen jugs of liquid.   69

Rate yourself on the whole of your work and not on just one phase of it.   72

Hugh saw a brown fox jump quickly over that lazy old black dog of mine.   71

Get typing speed, by all means, but get it through right habits of work.   72

McNEIL-DOBSON Reports, Inc.

FINANCIAL REPORTS AND FORECASTS ★ ★ ★ COLUMBUS, OHIO

January 10, 194-

Mr. T. W. Baird | 33
842 Highland Park | 51
Seattle, Washington | 71

Dear Sir | 80

Prosperity always returns--it always has! Are you | 131
ready for it? Are you ready to capitalize current | 182
and forthcoming opportunities as business continues | 234
its sharp upward rise during the winter months? DO | 286
YOU KNOW WHICH STOCK GROUPS LOOK BEST? | 326

So that every investor, not a regular subscriber | 375
to McNeil-Dobson Reports, may have our opinion on | 425
certain market groups and business prospects, we | 474
have prepared a special report on market conditions. | 528
We should like to send this to you gratis; but to | 578
avoid hundreds of "curiosity" requests, we have to | 629
make a nominal charge of $3 to cover cost. | 673

We believe we can be of service to you in helping | 723
you to capitalize on the present market. A $3 in- | 773
vestment now will pay you rich dividends. | 816

Yours very truly | 833

McNEIL-DOBSON REPORTS, INC. | 861

N. B. Dobson

N. B. Dobson, Vice-President | 890

mcb | 893

(Strokes, 893; words, 128.)

Style Letter No. 11 — Full Block Style of Letter

Summary of Spacing Instructions.

1. Space once after the
   a. comma
   b. semicolon
   c. period used with an abbreviation
   d. exclamation point when it is used *in the body of a sentence*
   e. question mark when it is used *in the body of a sentence*
   f. whole number when used with a "made" fraction
2. Space twice after
   a. punctuation at the end of sentences
   b. the colon
3. The dash is made with two hyphens, without spacing before or after
4. At the end of a quotation, type
   a. a period before the quotation mark
   b. a comma before the quotation mark
   c. a semicolon after the quotation
   d. a colon after the quotation mark
   e. an interrogation point *before* the quotation if the quoted matter *is* a question; *after* the quotation if the quoted matter *is not* a question
   f. an exclamation point *before* the quotation if the quoted matter is an exclamation; *after* the quotation if matter *is not* an exclamation.
5. A quotation within a quotation is typed in single quotation marks ('). The quotation marks are placed with relation to other punctuation marks according to the rules given in item 4 above.
6. Type in quotations the titles of articles; underscore or type in capitals the titles of books.

	STROKES
I said, "Has he done good work?" Did he say, "He has done good work"?	70
They sent the book *Middletown,* but not the article "Peace with Honor."	70
He has not read "Speed Typing"; he, however, has read "Tips to Students."	73
Joe asked, "Has he read 'Speed Typing'?" He said, "I read 'Is It Speed?'"	74
Joe said, "He has read 'Speed Typing.'" I said, "I read 'It Is Speed.'"	72

EXERCISE 30

Directions. Use the paragraph for a five-minute writing.   *7 minutes*

All the letters of the alphabet are used in this exercise.

	STROKES
It was an old belief that the one who ate the heart of a brave man	67
would come into the possession of that man's bravery. Down through the	139
years, men have been trying to find short cuts that would lead to quick	211
achievement of one kind or another. The Tartars carried the idea to its	284
extreme conclusion. They ate their books in order to get facts that were	358
in them. This seems queer to us; yet it is no more lazy a way of trying	431
to get facts than that of some now in school who try to learn by sleep-	500
ing on their books. Perhaps this modern way of trying to learn is not	571
very much of an improvement over the way the Tartars had; hard work is	642
just about the finest method yet evolved for getting ahead. Try it.	711

MARSHALL INSURANCE COMPANY
HOME OFFICE:
NASHVILLE, TENNESSEE

STROKES

Date:	November 25, 194-	18
From:	Agency 42, L. G. Mason, General Agent	56
To:	S. O. Tabor, Clarksville, Tennessee	92
Subject:	Policies Nos. 219816-7-8--McAllister	129

We have your letter requesting information with regard 184
to handling the McAllister matter. We are glad to have the 244
change in premium date made. We are enclosing proper forms 304
for Policies Nos. 219816-7-8. You understand, of course, 362
that these forms are to be signed by the insured and to be 421
witnessed properly. 442

As there is a loan under Policy No. 219816, it will be 497
necessary to execute a new loan agreement containing the new 558
premium date in its terms. We are enclosing such an agree- 617
ment to be signed by both Henry W. McAllister and Susan H. 676
McAllister. You will please have this agreement signed and 736
witnessed, and will return it with the other papers. 790

The installment of $14.52 on Policy No. 219816 and the 845
installment of $12.35 on each of the other two policies, 902
with interest of $11.57 on the loan of September 2--a total 962
of $50.79, are to be paid; and the check is to be forwarded 1022
with the request for modification. 1058

This will give you the information you requested. If 1112
there is any further help that we can give you, let us know. 1172

(Strokes, 1172; words, 221.)

Style Letter No. 10 — Interoffice Style of Letter Without a Salutation or a Complimentary Close

TEST EXERCISE 30

Directions. Use the paragraph for a five-minute writing.

All the letters of the alphabet are used in this exercise.

STROKES

Just what is it that educates? I am quite certain it is not one type | 70

of study as opposed to another, for what we study seems to have little | 141

to do with what we become. We must learn to think, to be sure; but we | 212

learn to think through solving problems and problems abound in all our | 283

work. We must learn to do some things well, too; for if we know how to | 355

do some things very well, we can always take care of ourselves and help | 427

to carry our share of the world's work. It does not seem to make much | 498

difference what is studied so long as one gains the power to think and | 569

the power to do things well. These are two outcomes of education that | 640

must be the common possession of all of us if we expect to succeed. | 707

MANIPULATION DRILL: GAUGING THE LINE AND THE LETTER   *4 minutes*

In this drill you are to fill in letters that have been omitted from a sentence. Use the same machine parts as those used in the previous drill for gauging the line and the letter and for typing over a completed sentence. (See page 57.)

Directions. 1. Type the following line exactly as it is given.

```
Capi al is not what a man has, but what a m n is.
```

2. Remove the paper. Reinsert it. Gauge the line and the letter spacing, and fill in the letter *t* omitted from "Capital" and the letter *"a"* omitted from "man."
3. Repeat the drill to add to the ease with which the machine is controlled.

TYPING FOR CONTROL   *6 minutes*

Directions. Type the paragraph until you type it with facility and without error.

All letters of the alphabet are used, but the paragraph emphasizes the control of the letter t.

STROKES

Attention to a subject generally results from interest in the work. | 68

Pick out an exciting story and you will be amazed to see to what extent | 139

you shut out the rest of the world. The truth of the matter is that if | 210

you become interested in what you do, you will quite likely be attentive | 282

to it and do it with ease. | 308

2975 Benton Drive   18
Zanesville, Ohio   35
October 26, 194-   52

Dear Dr. Norton   68

      I thank you most sincerely for sending to me   113
a copy of your book, <u>The</u> <u>Principal</u> <u>and</u> <u>His</u> <u>Work</u>.   163
I know that a closer reading will give me a great   213
deal of help in meeting the problems of my school.   265

      Let me take this opportunity to say that, of   310
all the classes I had, my work with you at the Uni-   361
versity was the most stimulating, enriching, and   410
permanent in its contribution to my preparation for   462
teaching. I like to pay tribute where tribute is   512
due, and I owe a great deal of my present success   562
to the work I had under you.   592

      When I finish studying <u>The</u> <u>Principal</u> <u>and</u> <u>His</u>   637
<u>Work</u>, I shall write you again. In the meantime,   686
please accept my thanks for this further evidence   736
of your goodness to me.   761

            Sincerely yours   777

            George W. Allen

Dr. James Fisher Norton   801
Columbia University   821
New York, New York   839

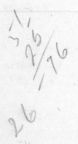

(Strokes, 839; words, 132.)

Style Letter No. 9 — Personal or Formal Style of Single-Spaced and Indented Letter

UNIT III — *IMPROVEMENT PRACTICE*

Skill in typewriting calls for endurance, speed, and accuracy—factors that result in typing power. It is not enough that you have mastered the fundamentals of typewriting as they are given in Units I and II; you must now force yourself to higher levels of typing skill. This drive for greater speed must be followed immediately by a drive for definite control on the higher level of skill. Speed without accuracy is of little use. Develop speed, yes; but, above all, develop speed with accuracy.

Paper to Use. Use drill paper for the special drills, such as word-recognition drills; use a half sheet of paper for the technique practice; and use a full sheet for the exercises.

LESSON 31

WORD-RECOGNITION DRILL   *7 minutes*

Words of the same length are arranged in line drills so that the rhythm of words may be emphasized. The short lines of words in the drills require fewer eye fixations than longer lines, and will thus add to the ease with which you type. As you type, *think the word*. Let the entire word become the stimulating factor so your typing response will be on the word level.

Directions. 1. Use a 70-space line.
2. Set the machine for single spacing.
3. Type each drill twice; then double-space. You will type the two short lines in one line, similar to the following example:

>   if he he is to go if it or or he an of us an or am do he me he so by by
>   if he he is to go if it or or he an of us an or am do he me he so by by

1. if he he is to go if it or or he an
   of us an or am do he me he so by by

2. for for the for the due for due she
   bit did and may did may big for big

3. them when them they when turn turn
   lake make down wish name with such

4. form than when they sick such sick
   torn down with both both land work

5. firm such firm such paid laid they
   make lake hand hang duck pale male

6. worm sown clam jamb cozy mane yams
   owns lamb dial goal pant kale hale

TECHNIQUE PRACTICE 31   *6 minutes*

Directions. 1. Use a 70-space line and single spacing.
2. Use each sentence for a one-minute writing.
3. Double-space between writings.

STROKES

If you want to make progress, do all you are told to do—and some more.   71

If we want to do something well, we must keep ourselves out of the rut.   71

Very few of us work up to the limit of what we can do if we really try.   71

Lost time is never found again, but time wisely used pays rich dividends.   73

All of us need a lot of pushing and guiding if we are to do fine work.   70

ing a strange place. He has an office of his own with a big staff of helpers. A   1407

fine spirit is shown there, for all his workers know exactly how to meet people   1487

and how to be helpful to them. This is the outgrowth of his desire to give   1563

what he needs when he is in a strange place. Students should give thought to   1641

meeting people. It is a good thing to put oneself in the place of the other per-   1721

son. From that point of view, it is easy to see what one should do in most cases.   1805

Young workers may not give much thought to their part in caring for the   1877

supplies in an office. They may not realize that waste of paper, envelopes, and   1958

stamps increases the cost of running an office. If they did, they would use   2035

more judgment and quit some of their careless habits. They would try to see   2112

the facts through the eyes of the employer, who has to keep close tab on the   2189

overhead expense. Workers often take supplies for their own use. If the owner   2269

does not object, it may be all right; but there should be a clear understanding   2349

on that point. Saving time and avoiding waste are two chief duties of the   2424

employee.   2433

EXERCISE 117

Directions. Type Style Letter No. 9 in the single-spaced and indented style. Use a 50-space line and open punctuation.

When typing formal or personal letters, place the inside address at the left margin six to eight spaces below the complimentary close. This style of letter is used for official communications, formal social invitations and acceptances, or purely personal letters.

EXERCISE 118

INTEROFFICE CORRESPONDENCE

The interoffice or interdepartment letter-head is used, as the name implies, for correspondence between offices or departments of the same company. It is customary to omit the usual salutation, complimentary close, and pen-written signature, although it is the rule of some offices that each interoffice letter must show the penwritten signature or the initials of the dictator.

Directions. Use a 60-space line. Type Style Letter No. 10 with single spacing and 5-space paragraph indentions. Leave four spaces between the subject line and the first line of the letter.

In policy, bulletin, and room numbers, the figures are written without a comma separating the hundreds from the thousands.

EXERCISE 119

The full block style of letter is seldom used in ordinary business correspondence, but it is unusual and thus striking. If the letter is not long and the letterhead is carefully designed to give a neat, off-centered appearance, the full block style may be used effectively.

Directions. Type Style Letter No. 11 in the full block style. Use a 50-space line and open punctuation.

EXERCISE 120
THE INVERTED-PARAGRAPH STYLE OF LETTER

The inverted-paragraph style of letter is a semiblock form usually typed with single spacing. Its chief claim to distinction is its unusual appearance, which claims the attention of the reader. It is not a good style for use in routine office correspondence, but it may be used to advantage for special sales or advertising letters. In this form the first line of each paragraph is written flush with the left margin, and all succeeding lines of the paragraph are indented a uniform number of spaces, usually five.

After typing the inside address, the salutation, and the first line of the paragraph, reset the left margin stop for a 5-space indention. When it is necessary to begin a new paragraph at the left margin, depress the margin release and backspace to the left margin.

Directions. 1. Use a 70-space line, a 5-space paragraph indention, and double spacing.

2. Move the stop for the right margin to the end of the scale so you can type each line as it is printed. Type a line each half minute. This rate will give you a stroking speed of approximately 26 words a minute. After you have typed the paragraph, practice the words, phrases, or sentences that were "speed traps" for you.

3. Retype the paragraph to demonstrate the added ease and accuracy with which you can type the material under the same conditions.

Note to Instructor: Call the throw.

	STROKES
Take it in your stride. Do not pause when you come to a new word;	67
just think the word if it is a short one, or think the letters if you do	139
not feel you can type on the word level, and the fingers will make the	209
right movements. If you have done your work well up to this point, you	280
can now take the next step in building speed. Relax your shoulder and	350
arm muscles, but tense the fingers and hold them poised lightly above	419
the keys ready for rapid stroking. Do your work in the right way and	488
your skill will increase from day to day. Hold the hands quiet; keep	557
your eyes on the copy; work for the skill that will keep the carriage	626
moving. You will be amazed at the power this practice will give you.	695

ACHIEVEMENT RECORD FOR ONE-MINUTE WRITINGS *2 minutes*

The chart given below shows the record of one student's progress in the one-minute sentence writings. Record your progress on a similar chart. The column headed wpm/e is for recording the gross words per minute and the errors made.

NAME_____CLASS_____INSTRUCTOR_____

SENTENCE	SPEED EMPHASIS 31	TECHNIQUE PRACTICE 32	TECHNIQUE PRACTICE 33	TECHNIQUE PRACTICE 34	TECHNIQUE PRACTICE 35	TECHNIQUE PRACTICE 36	TECHNIQUE PRACTICE 37	EXERCISE 40 5-MINUTE WRITING
	wpm/e	wpm/e	wpm/e	wpm/e	wpm/e	wpm/e	wpm/e	wpm/e
1	32/3	30/0	29/2	37/4	40/2	53/5	2	50/0 = 1 min.
2	28/1	32/1	28/0	35/1	39/3	50/0	0	45/3 = 5 min.
3	30/2	33/0	28/0	35/3	41/1	56/3	1	43/1 = 5 min.
4	31/0	30/1	28/0	37/1	40/0	56/5	0	
5	33/1	28/0	28/0	35/0	42/0	56/1	1	

(Technique Practice 37 column: Not timed)

SPEED EMPHASIS *12 minutes*

Directions. Use each sentence for two one-minute writings. Record the better of the two writings.

Speed Hints. Hold the hands as motionless as possible. Release the keys quickly. Keep your eyes on the copy. Pay attention to what you are typing. Try to type a line each twenty seconds. Work with a sense of quiet control; a feeling of hurry will upset you.

	STROKES
If you want to be a success, do all your work just as well as you can.	70
What we think and what we do molds us into the kind of men we become.	69
Many men owe what they are now to the problems they overcame yesterday.	71
We need to educate ourselves to think and to guard our daily thoughts.	70
If you have to buy a friendship, it will not be worth the price you pay.	72

CORRECTIVE DRILL PARAGRAPHS

STROKES

(Emphasizing letters *a, e, i, l, p, s*)

A pleasant personality may be the pride and the joy of any- 58
one. One quality of personality may be explained as the impres- 121
sion that one person produces on another person. Personality is 186
a prize that all people should attempt to possess. A person may 251
possess a pleasing personality if he will persistently develop his 318
social attitudes to the fullest possible extent. Personal appear- 383
ance is of prime importance in making a pleasing first impres- 444
sion. A proper regard for dress, a friendly approach to stranger 510
and friend alike, and a perfectly sincere desire to help others 574
will do much to aid one in developing a pleasing personality. 635

(Emphasizing letters *o, u, z*)

Zeal and zest in the pursuit of his lifework will lead a man to 64
the zenith of his achievement. Some people take a zigzag course 129
in life and expect just as much success as if the lazy course had 195
not been followed. It does not require a great deal of intelli- 258
gence for one to realize that he who works hard at his task is 321
better able to succeed than the one who theorizes about what 382
should be done but puts off until the zero hour the actual doing 447
of the work. Zeal and zest for work may be acquired even if they 513
do not seem to be inherent. 540

TIMED WRITING

Directions. Seventy-space line; five-space indention; double spacing.

Each paragraph has a syllable intensity of 1.30 and includes all letters of the alphabet.

STROKES

When you begin a business course, you have little idea of the opportunities 76
that the training will open up to you. You are quite engrossed from day to 152
day with the routine of your studies, and do not realize that you are laying the 233
foundation of knowledge that will form a wellspring from which you will draw 310
during all your business life. You are learning how to handle matters that may 390
arise when you have settled down to the real work of holding a job. Your 464
teachers will try to teach the general things that may come up, but they can- 540
not expect to foresee them all. It is in the unusual happenings that your judg- 619
ment will be called upon, and it is in the handling of these that you can best 698
prove your worth. You may not think meeting people and handling supplies 772
important, but they are. No detail is too small to receive from you due thought. 854

The ability to meet people properly is important in the business world. This 932
calls for judgment and courtesy based on kindness. The courtesy used in an 1008
office is of the same essence as that used in social life. There is not the same 1090
personal element, of course; but there should be the same desire to put people 1169
at their ease and to create the right atmosphere of kindliness. A college presi- 1249
dent once said that he had never quite conquered an amazing shyness on enter- 1325

LESSON 32

WORD-RECOGNITION DRILL

5 minutes

Directions. 1. Use a 70-space line. Set the machine for single spacing.
2. Type each drill twice; then double-space. You will type the two short lines in one line.

Practice Procedure. Each drill calls for a slightly different approach to the typing of the word. Type each word as rapidly as you can type with correct sequence of strokes; then pause slightly to get the right mind-set for typing the following word. Practice the words until you feel a flowing stroking that indicates the absence of shoulder and forearm tenseness. You should be able to develop facile stroking of these words in a short time, but you are to be the judge of the difficulties you need to overcome and of the number of repetitions that are necessary.

1. who can yet his way job men old use
   yes why may its fur got box end let

2. this what some give same live find
   file most said list sign word told

3. each does come four note glad road
   stop take file fine club coat band

4. blue boys held kept mail once name
   much most near wife wire used with

TECHNIQUE PRACTICE 32

13 minutes

Directions. 1. Use a 70-space line and single spacing. Double-space between line groups.
2. Set the ribbon lever for stenciling.
3. Use each sentence for a one-minute writing. You should type a line each twenty seconds, or three lines in the minute of writing.
4. Set the lever for ribbon typing. Type each sentence for one minute. Your goal is to type the sentence once in thirty seconds.

	STROKES
When you make a mistake, do not keep looking back at it for a long time.	72
If what we think is clear and true, what we do will be sure to be right.	72
We must put more into the world than we take, and give more than we get.	72
It takes time to do anything well, but to do a thing well is worth much.	72
It is wise for all of us to do the very finest work we can at all times.	72

EXERCISE 32

12 minutes

Directions. 1. Use a 70-space line, a 5-space paragraph indention, and double spacing.
2. Move the stop for the right margin to the end of the scale so you can type each line as it is printed.
3. Type a line each half minute. This rate will be approximately 28 words a minute.
4. Retype the paragraph under the same conditions. Type with control.

	STROKES
Not all words can be typed in just the same way. Some words, for	66
example, can be typed as wholes; other words have to be thought of in	136
parts or even in terms of single letters. The good student will try to	208
learn how to type words on the different levels of skill. Those words	279
that can be typed as wholes will speed up the stroking and add to the	349
total production for the period. Those words that must be typed on the	421
stroke level need not cause a loss of smoothness in typing if they are	492
quickly recognized and the right way to handle them is used. One good	563
way to speed up your typing is to learn to pass from a word to the next	635
word without pause. Do this, if you want to increase your speed.	700

UNIT IX — *PROBLEMS IN THE ARRANGEMENT OF LETTERS*

You have learned the commonly used forms of business letters. In this unit of practice material, you will study the special adaptations of letter forms that are made in many offices. There is no merit in following an exact style of letter unless the style fits the needs of a particular office; but all adaptations must be founded on the general principles of a common-sense interpretation of what is good form in letters and on the ease with which a letter may be typed. Production speed must be maintained, but many special arrangements of letters may be used without reducing production.

In order to get some measure of your ability to type problem letters of usable quality, the different portions of the material in this and subsequent budgets of work will not be timed nor will the material be organized in lessons. You are to follow, in general, the outline for practice given below but you are to make adaptations as your own analysis of your writing needs suggests:

1. Reconstruction practice   3 minutes
2. Selected sentence practice   5 minutes
3. Paragraph writing for control or to measure timed-writing power   5 to 10 minutes
4. Exercise typing for remainder of period

Select your own reconstruction and sentence practice material. You can refer to the index for page numbers of special drill material such as drills for shift key control, calling the throw, corrective drills, and speed emphasis material. Special drill material is given with each lesson in the preceding units of work. You should select your practice materials and practice procedures to help you to achieve a particular goal, whether that goal is the improvement of technique or the increase in speed or control.

BUDGET XI

Machine Adjustments for Drill Practice:
1. Full sheet of paper; 70-space line; 5-space paragraph indention.
2. Each portion of drill material should be typed until you feel you have made measurable improvement in typing.

SENTENCES FOR TECHNIQUE PRACTICE

	STROKES
Up! and face the future! Whatever the past has been, you have TODAY!	69
You say you deserve success—then prove it! Don't rest with words!	67
Your order No. 132 (our File 173-Y) will be shipped early next week.	68
"Call the word 'impossible' that 'blockhead word,' " said Mirabeau.	66
The ordinary envelope used in business measures 3 5/8 by 6 1/2 inches.	70
Bank clearings increased 13% in 22 cities in 1935 (Dun & Bradstreet).	69
In technical reports, you may use ' for minutes and " for seconds.	66

SENTENCES FOR CALLING THE THROW

	STROKES
We show proper pride when we insist on doing what we know is right.	67
Imperfect knowledge is the parent of doubt; thoroughness dispels doubt.	71
When we express a lovely thought, we are giving as the angels give.	67
No reason for doing a thing is a good reason for letting it alone.	66
All is possible to him who believes; easy to him who will persevere.	68
If you make use of small opportunities, greater ones will come to you.	70
Minutes are to hours what pennies are to dollars—save both to win.	67
We think highly of a man who is wiser today than he was yesterday.	66

SPEED EMPHASIS

Directions. Each paragraph is to be typed in one minute. The purpose of this practice is to increase your stroking rate. You are to type as accurately as you can, of course; but you are to speed up your stroking until you can type each paragraph in a minute. For the first typing of the paragraph, set the ribbon lever for stenciling.

After you get your expected gross stroking rate, set the lever for ribbon typing and type each paragraph at a slower speed. Try to type each paragraph without error. This typing for control need not be timed.

32-word rate

STROKES

If our work is worth doing at all, it is worth doing as well as we	67
can do it. Good work always brings a rich return because it gives the	138
power to keep growing.	160

37-word rate

Do your work without fear. If you have normal use of your fingers	67
and if you will set up right habits, you can learn to type well. You	137
can prove this by doing good work right now.	181

40-word rate

We learn most when we know that we can learn. Doubt and fear are	66
almost sure to keep us from doing as well as we can. When we know	133
there is nothing to fear if we work right, our work will be joyful.	200

LESSON 33

WORD-RECOGNITION DRILL

Directions. 1. Use a 70-space line and single spacing.
2. Type each drill twice; then double-space. Type the two short lines in one line.
3. Follow these directions for all succeeding word- and phrase-recognition drills.

1. for end big and box cut did fit due
fur got man sir may own the men she

2. both down form girl hair make half
hand land name town turn when with

3. work wish paid sick sign such than
them bush they city torn form sown

4. look good book poor soon feel been
call fill fall bill full miss less

TECHNIQUE CHECKUP ON POSTURE

You have initiated the correct habits of typing, but it is necessary for you to check these at frequent intervals to make certain that you are not relaxing your effort to make the right technique permanent.

1. In getting ready to type, do you place your chair so that, when you are seated, the front of your body is 8 to 10 inches from the base of the typewriter?

2. While typing, do you lean slightly forward from the hips?

3. While typing, do you keep your fingers poised *lightly* in their typing positions?

4. While typing, do you hold your shoulders erect, but not rigid?

5. While typing, do you hold your right thumb above, not on, the space bar?

6. While typing, do you keep your left thumb curved and held out of the way of the fingers and the right thumb?

7. While typing, do you keep your eyes on the copy and do you maintain an alert body position?

8. While typing, do you keep your feet on the floor in front of the chair?

9. While throwing the carriage, do you keep your eyes on the copy?

10. After throwing the carriage, do you start typing without hesitation and without moving your eyes from the copy?

LESSON 89

RECONSTRUCTION PRACTICE

Directions. 1. Use a 70-space line; single spacing.
2. Type Technique Practice 88 as a series of five one-minute tests.

TECHNIQUE PRACTICE 89

Directions. 1. Use a 70-space line; single spacing.
2. Type each line three times. Double-space after the third typing of each line.

	STROKES
In 1920, 518,493 cars were shipped f.o.b. Detroit to the Canal Zone.	68
Mr. Thomas worked 925 men on a project that was planned to employ 600.	70
"Form No. 194," he explained, "will tell you of the new route to Zero."	71
An explanation of Schedule B is in Vol. VIII, Chap. XI (see Fig. 1).	68
On February 28 he reported the sale of 36,582 copies of the brochure.	69

EXERCISE 116

This exercise gives a summary of advertising and sales promotion costs of the Longwood-Slocum Company for the past four years.

Directions. Type the heading in all capital letters. Make the horizontal rulings with the underscore. Double-space between the heading and the double lines. Double-space between the double lines and the column headings. Single-space between the column headings and the single horizontal line. Double-space after the horizontal line before typing the problem. Total the four columns and insert the correct figures. Have 3 spaces between columns.

SUMMARY OF ADVERTISING COSTS

Item	(1)	(2)	(3)	(4)
Circulars	$10,294.76	$ 7,723.75	$ 7,397.86	$ 8,755.98
BUSINESS DIGEST	22,677.79	23,425.28	25,330.18	23,772.43
Automatic Letters	977.87	1,131.26	840.59	1,280.77
Samples	13,735.29	12,606.58	11,369.07	14,219.28
Magazine Advertising	1,942.56	1,146.09	1,466.94	827.30
Donations	154.70	35.00	51.00	50.00
Direct Mail	3,925.45	4,586.25	6,298.64	5,187.24
Awards to Salesmen	597.83	604.46	950.70	52.78
Christmas Presents	6,740.08	8,796.47	4,579.01	4,364.46
Exhibits and Dues	997.87	1,278.25	875.98	1,059.06
Prizes	327.94	1,691.19	1,198.65	651.66
Miscellaneous Costs	160.48	72.48	298.15	119.68
TOTAL				

TECHNIQUE PRACTICE 33

12 minutes

Directions. 1. Use a 70-space line and single spacing. Double-space between line groups.

2. Set the ribbon lever for stenciling. Use each sentence for a one-minute writing. Type a line each twenty seconds. These sentences are slightly more difficult than those of preceding lessons.

3. Set the lever for ribbon typing. Type each sentence for one minute. Your goal is to type the sentence once each thirty seconds. This will be a much slower stroking rate and you can pay attention to the sequence of strokes so that your writing will be with good control.

	STROKES
A man's fortune is in his own hands, and he can shape it as he wills.	69
Start each day with a fixed plan to do more than you have done before.	70
Success is doing what you can do well and doing well whatever you do.	69
It is the way you stick to a thing that makes you a success or failure.	71
Many a man has done well at the last hour because he would not let go.	70

EXERCISE 33

13 minutes

The paragraph is marked to guide you to type at the rate of 32 words a minute. The dot above the word indicates the half-minute goal; and the figure indicates the minute goal. Be guided in your typing rate by these marks. If you reach the half-minute goal before time is called, reduce your rate slightly and give attention to typing with smooth and flowing stroking; if you are not typing rapidly enough when the half-minute time is called, increase the speed of your stroking.

Directions. Use a 5-space paragraph indention, and double spacing. Type the exercise for two five-minute writings and check the writings for accuracy.

Note to Instructor: Call the half-minute and minute goals. Say, "Half," "One," and so on for five minutes.

	STROKES
The men who make their living driving trucks on long hauls say that	68
they go at a fairly low speed until they get adjusted to the feel of the	141
wheel and to their position. They tire quickly if they are not relaxed	213
and easy. These men say they make speed if they drive slowly at first	284
and work up little by little to a rapid speed. The men should be able	355
to tell others the right mind-set for the long haul, since driving is	425
their daily business. What they say has meaning for the typing student,	498
too. If you want to stand up under the long haul and gain this prize	568
of good typing power, begin slowly and work up to a rapid stroking.	637
Real power depends much on the way you go at the work you have to do	706
and also on just how hard you try to hold yourself to the finest work	776
you can do at all times.	800

[72]

LESSON 88

RECONSTRUCTION PRACTICE

5 minutes

Directions. 1. Use a 70-space line; single spacing.
2. Type each line once; then select for repetition the lines that provide the best practice for you.

dedcd3d kik,k8k frfvf4f jujmj7j ftfbf5f jyjnj6j swsxs2s lol.l9l ;0;-;

The sum of 38 and 49 and 20 and 51 and 63 and 71 and 82 and 30 is 404.

Order #480-B amounts to $1,250. He said, "Isn't this National 4s?"

We must *work!* Hold the hands steady! (Excess movement reduces speed.)

TECHNIQUE PRACTICE 88

8 minutes

Directions. 1. Use a 70-space line; single spacing.
2. Type each sentence for one minute. Goal: 70 words a minute.

STROKES

The world bestows its big prizes upon the ones who do their work well.	70
You have the desire to do the right thing without being told or watched.	72
The past is of no value only as it can make the life of today fuller.	69
Getting ahead is largely a matter of just keeping ahead of the times.	69
It makes a difference whether you go into a thing to win or to drift.	69

EXERCISE 114

15 minutes

Directions. 1. Type Exercise 113 on a half sheet of paper with single spacing.
2. Determine the placement of columns by the use of the judgment placement tabulating steps. Have 7 spaces between columns.

EXERCISE 115

12 minutes

Directions. 1. Type Exercise 112 on a half sheet of paper with double spacing.
2. Determine the placement of columns by the use of the judgment placement tabulating steps. Have 7 spaces between columns.

OPTIONAL WRITINGS

Use the technique practice of this lesson for one-minute writings. Goal: 70 words a minute without error.

SPECIAL FEATURE

If you have difficulty inserting a carbon pack for eight to ten copies, try the following procedure: To insert a dozen or so sheets of carbon and paper evenly into the typewriter, place the top of the assembled sheets into a small folded paper and then feed into the machine. After the carbon pack has been inserted far enough for the feed rolls to grip it, operate the paper release lever to release the pressure and avoid creasing the carbon.

SPEED EMPHASIS

Directions. Each paragraph is to be typed in one minute. The purpose of this practice is to increase your stroking rate. You are to type as accurately as you can, of course; but you are to speed up your stroking until you can type each paragraph in a minute. For the first typing of the paragraph, set the ribbon lever for stenciling.

After you get your expected gross stroking rate, set the lever for ribbon typing and type each paragraph at a slower speed. Try to type the paragraph without error. This typing for control need not be timed.

ONE-MINUTE WRITINGS

37-word rate

	STROKES
See yourself as others see you and do not overlook the defects you	67
find. If you want to do so, you can overcome your faults. Work that	137
is well planned can work the magic spell for you.	186

40-word rate

Why waste time when there is so much to be done and so little time	67
in which to do it all? You have to set up right work habits; you have	138
to learn to type rapidly and with good control; then do it now.	201

45-word rate

Just as soon as I begin to think of myself as a worker, all that I	67
have to do in class will take on a new meaning for me. The daily work	138
is a means for getting me ready for the time when work in the business	209
world will begin.	226

LESSON 34

PHRASE-RECOGNITION DRILL

4 minutes

1. by the in our of you we can is not
   to get we did if you to put he let

2. to say we pay he can on the of his
   do not he had if his to let if one

3. if she of all if the do you at our
   it has to her we may in its go for

4. as you in all to the he did of our
   at all if not of the on our is the

5. to you in the at his to our on his
   we had he has to say to all at the

6. at you we say at all as all to pay
   if his at his by you at its do say

TECHNIQUE PRACTICE 34

12 minutes

Directions. 1. Set the ribbon lever for stenciling. Use each sentence for a one-minute writing. Type a line each fifteen seconds.

2. Set the lever for ribbon typing. Type each sentence for one minute at a controlled rate. Record these one-minute writings.

	STROKES
True worth is in being, not in seeming; in doing, not in dreaming.	66
When you know a thing can and should be done, you can find the way.	67
We are not here to play, to dream, or to drift; we are here to work.	68
Let me never fail to be kind, for I shall never pass this way again.	68
When the wrong thought appears, crowd it out with the right thought.	68

CHECK LIST FOR TABULATING

Judgment Placement

Many of the steps in the judgment-placement plan are the same as the steps you have been using in the mathematical-placement plan. The steps in which the differences occur are those that concern the vertical placement of the tabulation itself and the horizontal placement of the columns.

1. Plan your tabulation with pencil and paper before you attempt to type it.

2. Determine the vertical placement of the material.
   a. Count the number of lines required to type the material. Include all extra lines used between the main heading and the secondary or the columnar headings.
   b. Subtract the total number of lines required from 66, the number of lines available on paper 8½ by 11 inches.
   c. Subtract 3 from the answer found in Step b to make the adjustment for the off-center vertical placement.
   d. Divide the remainder found in Step c by 2. The result is the number of lines to be left in the top margin. (Disregard fractions.)

3. Center the main heading horizontally, and type it at the proper point so that the top margin determined in Step 2 will be of the right depth.

4. Determine the horizontal placement of the columns.
   a. Determine the number of spaces desired between the columns. This number depends upon the nature of the material itself, but it is usually from 3 to 7.
   b. Count the number of spaces required to type the longest line in each column.
   c. Add the number of spaces required for each column to the total number of spaces to be left between the columns, and subtract this sum from the number of spaces available.
   d. Divide this number by 2. If an extra space is left, add it to the left margin.

5. Set the left margin stop and tabulator stops.
   a. Set the left margin stop at the point corresponding to the number of spaces in the left margin.
   b. Add to this the number of spaces in the first column and the number to be left between the first and second columns. Set the first tabulator stop at this point.
   c. Add the number of spaces in the second column and the spaces to be left between the second and third columns. Set the second tabulator stop at this point.
   d. Determine the correct point for each of the remaining tabulator stops.

6. If a secondary heading is used, center it horizontally three spaces below the main heading.

7. Determine the placement of each columnar heading.
   a. Space up the number of lines desired between the main heading or the secondary heading and the columnar headings.
   b. Find the difference between the number of spaces required for each columnar heading and the number of spaces in the longest line in that column.
   c. Divide by 2.
   d. If the columnar heading requires more spaces than there are in the longest line in the column, backspace from the left margin of the column the number of spaces found in Step c; if the columnar heading does not require so many spaces as there are in the longest line in the column, indent the required number of spaces from the left margin of the column.

OPTIONAL EXERCISE

Directions. Determine the machine adjustments for Exercise 113 by judgment placement. Use 7 spaces between columns.

Directions. 1. Use double spacing.

2. You are to complete the typing of each paragraph in two minutes. Gauge your speed to type the first paragraph at the rate of 32 words a minute, the second paragraph at 35 words, and the third paragraph at 40 words a minute.

3. To make the jumps in speed called for in these timings, begin the typing at a rate well within your control. Be sure you are relaxed and that your stroking is controlled—not jerky. Increase your speed after you get *the feel* of the typing. A dot above the word you should be typing at the half minute and the figure 1 or 2 at the word you should be typing at the end of the minute will guide you in the rate you must type.

TWO-MINUTE TIMED WRITINGS

32-word rate

	STROKES
Some words do not flow so smoothly as others when you are typing at	68
a rapid pace, but you must learn how to handle all words on the highest	140
level of skill possible for you to use. Relax, and you will find it is	212
possible to use the flow of typing skill that makes for real power. You	285
must not be tense as you are typing.	321

35-word rate

There are some speed traps in typing just as there are speed traps	67
in driving. We fall into these traps because we do not use sound sense	139
in holding ourselves to the right way of typing a line or a word. Some	211
reaches give more trouble than others; these should be worked on until	282
they can be typed with as good control as the other reaches are typed.	352

40-word rate

If our work is worth doing at all, it is worth doing as well as we	67
can do it. There is no sense in letting ourselves feel that we can get	139
by without half trying. Most of us have as good a chance to do fine	208
work as anyone else if we know how to use our time wisely and if we can	280
learn to love our work. There is a price of hard work that all of us	350
have to pay if we wish to do anything of real worth.	402

SPEED EMPHASIS

Directions. After you have gained your speed goals for the three preceding paragraphs, use the remainder of the period for retyping the technique practice to develop added ease in your work.

Directions. Use double spacing. Follow the tabulating steps on page 155 to determine the proper adjustments.

ACCUMULATED VALUE OF MONTHLY DEPOSITS OF $1

Year	2 Per Cent	3 Per Cent	4 Per Cent
1	$ 12.13	$ 12.20	$ 12.26
2	24.51	24.76	25.02
3	37.13	37.70	38.29
4	50.01	51.04	52.10
5	63.14	64.78	66.46
6	76.54	78.93	81.41
7	90.21	93.51	96.96
8	104.26	108.54	113.14
9	118.49	124.01	129.97
10	133.00	139.96	147.49
11	147.80	156.38	165.70
12	162.90	173.30	184.66
13	178.30	190.74	204.38
14	194.02	208.70	224.90
15	210.05	227.20	246.25

JUDGMENT PLACEMENT OF TABULATED MATERIAL   *13 minutes*

You have learned how to place material with mathematical precision. The experienced office typist frequently places tabulated material by judgment. When judgment placement is used, the method of determining the machine adjustments differs somewhat from that used for mathematical placement. Usually, the typist determines on the number of spaces to be left between columns. This number will be 3, 5, or 7 spaces. In tabulated reports, columns that are placed reasonably close together are read with ease; to insure ease and accuracy in reading, therefore, use no fewer than 3 nor more than 7 spaces between columns.

Study the following check list for tabulating by judgment placement. Note the points of agreement and also the differences between this method of setting up tabulated reports and the method you have been using.

LESSON 35

PHRASE-RECOGNITION DRILL

1. of time it will on that is that
   we take in time as they at that

2. in this we will of this if they
   we feel at this of that we must

3. to take on this we hope to that
   we find at last we want to make

4. at once to find in such to come
   he will of such to this of them

5. of what to keep to look he does
   in your to work on hand to know

6. to such on that we make we wish
   at this of whom in town on them

TECHNIQUE PRACTICE 35

12 minutes

Directions. 1. Set the ribbon lever for stenciling. Use each sentence for a one-minute writing. Type a line each fifteen seconds.

2. Set the lever for ribbon typing. Type each sentence for one minute at a controlled rate. Record these writings.

	STROKES
For most of us, the troubles that never come are the hardest to endure.	71
Turn your face to the sun, and the shadows will ever fall behind you.	69
We can use our hard times and hard problems as means to step upward.	68
If we want to move up front, we must know how to use our time wisely.	69
It does not matter so much where you live as how well you live there.	69

EXERCISE 35

27 minutes

Directions. 1. Use double spacing.

2. You are to complete the typing of each paragraph in three minutes. Gauge your speed to type the first paragraph at the rate of 32 words a minute, the second paragraph at 35 words, and the third paragraph at 40 words a minute.

3. A dot above the word you should be typing at the half minute and the figure 1, 2, or 3 at the word you should be typing at the end of the minute will guide you in the rate you must type.

THREE-MINUTE WRITINGS

32-word rate

	STROKES
Why is it that some students seem to learn with ease while others	66
in the same class have to work so much harder to make even the smallest	138
gain in skill? Not all of us learn at the same rate or in the same way;	211
and it may be that some students who seem to be slow in learning to type	284
are gaining their skill at a natural pace for them. Most of us set up	355
handicaps of our own making just through the use of the wrong way of	424
doing things or through the fear we let take hold of us.	480

Directions. 1. Use a half sheet of paper; double spacing.
2. Triple-space between the main and the secondary headings; double-space between the secondary and the columnar headings and between the columnar headings and the body of the problem.
3. Add the columns and type the totals.

CARPET MANUFACTURED IN THE UNITED STATES
Summary in Square Yards

	1940	1941
Axminster	29,042,147	24,831,411
Wilton	9,766,178	10,266,199
Velvet	21,047,658	16,337,024
Tapestry	4,733,636	6,796,850
Chenille	546,340	329,178
Others	8,090,337	8,632,273
Total	73,226,296	67,192,935

TIMED WRITING   *8 minutes*

Directions. Type the timed writing on page 162, Lesson 85, with a 70-space line, a 5-space paragraph indention, and double spacing. Goal: An average of not more than one error for each four lines. If you meet this goal, you have good control; if you type without error or with not more than one error, you have superior control.

LESSON 87

RECONSTRUCTION PRACTICE   *5 minutes*

Directions. Use a 70-space line; single spacing. Type Technique Practice 86 once; retype any lines that you failed to type with ease and sureness.

TECHNIQUE PRACTICE 87   *8 minutes*

Directions. 1. Use a 70-space line; single spacing.
2. Type each sentence for one minute. You should type these sentences with good control at a minimum rate of 60 words a minute.

	STROKES
Your habits are the raw materials that finally form your character.	67
When a man is master of his own sphere, he has earned his degree.	65
Resolve each day to do much better work than you have done before.	66
Life is quite short, you know. You can't afford to waste any time.	67
Life never held greater opportunities for real men than it does now.	68

[166]

	STROKES
There is such a thing as trying too hard. If you get all hot and	66
bothered about this problem of gaining speed, you are almost certain to	138
tie yourself in mental knots. Turn loose of your fears and let your	207
fingers do their work at their highest rate. If you will do your part	278
and give your fingers a chance, they will move from key to key without	349
loss of time. Keep your eyes on the copy and make the throw without	418
pause and without looking up. Force yourself to do your work in the	487
right way and watch your speed go up.	524

40-word rate

	STROKES
Teach your fingers to strike the keys rapidly. In time you must	65
learn to type without error, but the first goal is to raise your speed	136
through right habits of work. If you have trouble in getting the speed	208
you need, find out what is wrong. It may be that you are fearful of	277
the errors that you make. If you know the purpose of this speed work,	348
you can get rid of your fear. You want to teach your fingers to move	418
rapidly; then you will teach them to slow down and type with control.	489
You must know the speed you want to use and you must see to it that	557
you are in command of the writing all the time.	604

If time permits, retype the paragraphs for control. Your controlled rate of typing should be approximately five words a minute slower than your forced rate.

OPTIONAL PRACTICE: Calling the Throw

Directions. Accuracy is a necessary part of good typing. You are to type a sentence each fifteen seconds, but you are to type without error. Select your rate; that is, select a sentence numbered "40" if you want to type at 40 words a minute. When you have typed this sentence without error, type a sentence at the next higher rate.

		STROKES
40—	1. Strike the center of a key and release it quickly.	50
	2. Curve the fingers; place them lightly on the keys.	50
44—	3. Throw the carriage without pause at the end of the line.	56
	4. Keep the arms still; let the fingers do their work well.	56
48—	5. Too hard a stroke may often cause the machine to skip spaces.	61
	6. Lift the thumb from the space bar and avoid failure to space.	61
52—	7. It will pay to prevent errors rather than to try to correct them.	65
	8. After you throw the carriage, it is foolish to pause and look up.	65
56—	9. Be sure to have the copy placed in the best position for easy reading.	70
	10. When you let your fingers linger on the keys, you hold your rate down.	70

BUDGET X

LESSON 86

RECONSTRUCTION PRACTICE 4 minutes

Directions. 1. Use a 70-space line; single spacing.
2. Type each line once; then select for repetition the lines that offer the practice you need for bringing your control of figures to the level of ease and sureness.

4f7j 3d8k 4f7j 3d8k 2s9l 5f6j 5f6j 2s9l 5f0; 5f0; 1291 3841 5731 4012

The note is for $1,500. The interest rate is 6%. Order #401 is ready.

Miller & Owen's check is for $3,291.50. Read the article "High Wages."

The letter is dated May 29. The check is dated April 30, isn't it?

TECHNIQUE PRACTICE 86 7 minutes

Directions. 1. Use a 70-space line; single spacing.
2. Type each line once; then select for repetition the lines that offer the practice you need for bringing your control of figures to the level of ease and sureness.

	STROKES
If Henry O. K.'s the bill, it is the first he has O. K.'d for a week.	69
Policy #128561 matures when James is 46 years 9 months and 14 days old.	71
His office is at 249-251 Sixth Street; his hours are 10:30 to 11:45 a.m.	72
Albert owes a bill of $12.50 at one store and only 85 cents at another.	71
You should always type fractions uniformly; as, 2/3, 1/2, 1/4, 3/4.	67

EXERCISE 111 12 minutes

Directions. 1. Use a half sheet of paper; double spacing.
2. Triple-space between the main and secondary headings; double-space between secondary and columnar headings.
3. In determining the margins, the vertical and the horizontal placement, and the placement of the columnar headings, follow the tabulating steps given on pages 155 and 156.

YEARLY GROWTH OF MONTHLY DEPOSITS

Interest at 4 Per Cent Per Annum, Compounded Semiannually

Years	$5	$10	$15	$25	$100
1	$ 61.30	$ 122.61	$ 183.92	$ 306.53	$ 1,226.14
2	125.09	250.18	375.27	625.45	2,501.81
3	191.45	382.90	574.35	957.26	3,829.03
4	260.48	520.98	781.48	1,302.46	5,209.85
5	332.32	664.64	996.97	1,661.62	6,646.47
10	737.42	1,474.84	2,212.27	3,687.12	14,748.47

LESSON 36

WORD-RECOGNITION DRILL

4 minutes

1. he the the them them they they them
or for for form form form them form

2. wish work wish with work with work
when they wish work with when turn

3. fight sight right light fight night
sight night right light night right

4. will tell sell well call tall ball
miss pass less loss boss miss miss

TECHNIQUE PRACTICE 36

7 minutes

Directions. Use each sentence for a one-minute writing. Type a line each fifteen seconds, or the sentence four times in each writing.

	STROKES
You can make your dreams and your visions come true through hard work.	70
If we try hard enough, we can just about do anything that we want to do.	72
Wish for what you want, of course; but work for what you want and get it.	73
The plan says that we must keep on working if we want to do big things.	71
It is just as easy to do our work right the first time as to do it over.	72

EXERCISE 36

32 minutes

The paragraph is marked to guide you in typing at the rate you want to set as your goal for this exercise. The superior figures indicate 5-word groups. Determine the rate at which you are to type and then check the figures which you should have reached when the teacher calls out the half minutes and minutes. For example, if you want to type 40 words a minute, place a check mark above "20" for the half minute and a figure "1" above "40" for the minute and so on throughout the paragraph. When the teacher calls the time intervals, you can tell at a glance whether you are reaching your goal or whether you need to increase or decrease your rate.

Directions. 1. Use double spacing and a 5-space indention for the paragraph.

2. Use the same rate for a two-minute writing, a three-minute writing, and a five-minute writing. Each time start typing at the beginning of the paragraph.

3. Advance the rate 5 words; then type a one-, two-, three-, and five-minute writing.

	STROKES
There is an old saying that all is well that ends well, but if we	65
want to be sure that all will end well, we have to do a lot of work to	136
make things come out just as we want them. It is very easy to get in	206
the habit of trusting to luck instead of putting our faith in pluck and	278
hard work; but luck is such a fickle friend it is well never to place	348
too much faith in getting what we want that way. I like to say that	417
he can who thinks he can if he will think he can and work as hard as he	489
can. It does no good to try to win when we have no right to win, for	559
we shall have to pay the price later on. If all of this is true, then	630
it is a lot easier to pay the price each day as we work for the thing	700
we want. If we do this, all will end well for then we will have earned	772
what we win.	785

[77]

Brown's School of Commerce

PHOENIX BUILDING

SAN FRANCISCO, CALIFORNIA

May 28, 194-

13

Miss Charlotte Jane Branson — 41
Principal, Branson's Secretarial School — 81
Stockton, California — 102

My dear Miss Branson — 123

I have been using the Charters and Whitley check list of the — 184
vocational traits for secretaries as a guide for the self- — 242
appraisal of my secretarial students. This check list shows — 303
the frequency ranking of the traits that are conspicuously — 362
present in outstandingly successful secretaries. I am list- — 421
ing below the ranking of ten of these traits, together with — 481
the percentage of employers mentioning each. — 527

Accuracy	1	86	541
Responsibility	2	82	561
Dependability	3	75	580
Intelligence	3	75	598
Courtesy	5	75	612
Initiative	5	71	628
Judgment	5	71	642
Tact	8	68	652
Personal Pleasantness	9	64	679
Personal Appearance	9	64	704

The complete report of this very interesting study of secre- — 763
tarial traits and duties has been published under the title — 823
of _Analysis_ _of_ _Secretarial_ _Traits_ _and_ _Duties_, and is pub- — 879
lished by the Williams and Wilkins Company, of Baltimore, — 937
Maryland. This is the report to which I referred in my talk — 998
with you last week. — 1019

Sincerely yours — 1035

W. K. Moore

W. K. Moore — 1047
Director — 1056

csk — 1059

(_Strokes, 1059; words, 159._)

Style Letter No. 8—Modification of the Block Form of Letter
With a Tabulated Report

LESSON 37

RECONSTRUCTION PRACTICE

5 minutes

Directions. 1. Use a 70-space line and single spacing.
2. Type each line twice. Double-space after typing the second line.
3. Type on the stroke level.

zeal zone quiz size both size part once must quit zeal next quiz next

choice checks scarce cancel clocks concert Celtic decent circle clinic ⸺

murmur hammer museums maximum mysticism mummery mushroom mother-in-law

s"s s"s He said, "Who can do good work?" ;-; ;-; son-in-law first-class

TECHNIQUE PRACTICE 37

5 minutes

Directions. 1. Type each drill twice—and more if you feel the repetition will add to your control.
2. Double-space between the line groups.
3. Type on the stroke level and type at the rate of a line each half minute.

	STROKES
The alert aviators aided their Alma Mater by augmenting the audience.	69
Robert Barbour brought his brother and bride to the bridge breakfast.	69
Charles was accused of cashing a check without a cent in his account.	69
Don did a good deed for his dad and decided he would do so each day.	68
The ecclesiast entered the elevator after the exit of the old editor.	69

EXERCISE 37

30 minutes

Directions. 1. Use a 70-space line, a 5-space paragraph indention, and double spacing.
2. Type each paragraph once. When all paragraphs have been typed, check your work and encircle any errors you have made.
3. In each paragraph divide the total lines typed by the total errors; if you have more than an average of one error for each three lines of typing, retype the paragraphs until you bring your line accuracy to the required average of not more than one error for each three lines.
4. Type on the stroke level.
5. List all errors on the error analysis chart. Be alert to guard against permitting the error to recur.

Beginning with this lesson, the paragraphs are not set in typewriter type. Your line of typing, therefore, may not be the same as the printed line. If you are typing a one-syllable word when the bell rings, complete the word and start the succeeding line. If you are typing a word of more than one syllable when the bell rings, complete the syllable if syllabication can be made at that point, strike the hyphen, and complete the word on the next line.

Margin Release. The margin release (No. 14) is used in writing outside the margin lines without a readjustment of the stops. When the carriage locks at the right margin, depress the margin release and you will have additional spaces for completing the syllable or the word. If it is necessary to begin a line outside the left margin, depress the margin release and backspace to the desired point for typing.

The Underwood typewriter has a special left-margin release (No. A). This machine part is at the right of the carriage thumb piece (No. 36).

On the Woodstock typewriter, the carriage-release lever is used in writing outside the left margin. Depress the carriage-release lever, and bring the carriage back to the desired writing point.

	STROKES
You now have good stroking speed; you must next develop the power to	69
type with accuracy. Specialize in quick but accurate strokes. Just to prove	147
you can type with exactness for a time, type this paragraph without error.	221

	STROKES
¹⁶⁵ When Rex flashed his smile and ¹⁷⁰ turned on the full light of his ¹⁷⁵ charming	890

When Rex flashed his smile and turned on the full light of his charming
personality, old Mr. Dietz quickly offered him a position in his office. Mr.
Dietz thought he had found a helper of great promise. But Rex did not
think he had a position worth much of his time and effort; it was just a
place that he could fill in until his real opportunity came. He was a good
stenographer, so he said; but old Mr. Dietz was puzzled when the first letters
were placed on his desk. It is true the letters were completed in record-
breaking time; but most of them had to be rewritten because, as Rex mum-
bled to himself, "The old crab thinks everything has to be just so."

Rex held that place not quite four months. Then Mr. Dietz let him go to
find something "more suited to his abilities." Rex never has any difficulty in
obtaining a position, but he seems to have trouble in keeping one. He still
flits from one job to another, always looking for the great opportunity and
finding the great failure. He blames conditions for his failure; in fact, he does
not seem to think that he fails. He has a way of convincing himself that he
is right and that the world is "down on him." Yes, Rex is a clever chap, I
know, and he has personality plus; but he isn't finding much success in
business. He just doesn't believe in working his way through a problem if
he can get out of it; and, as he has let himself fail for so long, he may not
have the power now to succeed.

890
968
1239
1112
1188
1267
1340
1412
1482
1555
1635
1712
1788
1871
1948
2024
2096
2171
2249
2279

EXERCISE 110   *14 minutes*

Directions. 1. Type Style Letter No. 8 in the form shown on page 164.
2. Use a 60-space line; open punctuation; current date.
3. To determine the correct placement of the tabulated report, subtract the total number of spaces used in the longest line in the three columns from the length of line used in the letter (60) and divide by 4 (one more than the number of columns). The result will be the number of spaces for the left and right margins and the spaces between the columns.

OPTIONAL WRITING   *9 minutes*

If you think that you can type the letter in Exercise 110 with greater ease and accuracy, re-type the letter; or take another five-minute timed writing to demonstrate improvement in your control.

If the fingers just will not move to the right keys, try the plan of quietly   77
saying the letters. Minimize your chances of making errors through holding   153
yourself to exact techniques. Type without hurry but without waste of time.   231
Keep the carriage moving rhythmically.   269

It was a wise man who wrote, "He can who thinks he can." Very few big   71
things have been realized by men who did not believe a lot in themselves and   148
who did not exact of themselves the best work of which they were capable.   223
The question is, Do you believe you can type well? Just prove it by typing   299
this paragraph without error and with a sense of ease.   353

The business world is in need of well-trained and more capable help. Busi-   74
nessmen say that the need is for workers who have established the habit of   149
doing things right, of turning in work that is the best of which they are   223
capable—not work that will just "get by." This means that employers expect   300
workers to use their heads quite as much as their fingers. In school, as has   378
long been the rule in first-class organizations out of school, each worker must   458
know by his own proof that his work is right.   503

ANALYSIS OF ERRORS

3 minutes

As you type the exercises, you may make errors. The rapidity with which you increase your accuracy will depend upon your success in eliminating these errors. Possibly you have already noticed that you are inclined to repeat the same error again and again. If you elimi- nate the frequently repeated errors, your accuracy will be greatly increased. The first step in eliminating errors is to discover exactly what the errors are. A chart showing the errors made by one student of typewriting is given below.

ERROR-ANALYSIS CHART

Name of Student *Ruth Doyle*   Class *3-3:45* / *11-11:45*   Date Begun *Sept. 20*

Number of Periods a Day *2*   *Miss Richards*   Date Completed _____

		A	B	C	D	E	F	G	H	I	J	K	L	M	N	O	P	Q	R	S	T	U	V	W	X	Y	Z	.	,	-	?	Space
Exercise	38					ι									m					r/r													
Exercise	39				s	i														r													
Exercise	40	z			d	i									n					g/r											p		
Exercise	41													n	m	l																	
Exercise	42	y																															
Exercise	43			v/v						o/o					l		a				r/r									?			
Exercise	44						t													r/y			b										

Illustration No. 50 — Error-Analysis Chart

To record each error, the student entered in the column for the correct letter, on the line for the exercise that was written, the letter struck inaccurately. (The abbreviation *sp.* was used for *space.*) After you complete typing each exercise in remaining lessons of this unit, similarly record each error on a chart.

In addition to the classification of errors provided for on the front of the chart, record the other types of errors on the back of the error-analysis chart. When the chart does not seem to provide space for some types of errors, make a notation on the back of the chart to see whether special drill is needed.

LESSON 85

RECONSTRUCTION PRACTICE
5 minutes

Directions. 1. Use a 70-space line; double spacing.
2. Type each line once; then select for repetition practice the lines that provide the drill you need.

STROKES

Mark has been in Nevada since May. Larry lives in Newton, Massachusetts.   73
Charles will be in Texas in April. Apparently Sam likes California.   68
The check is for $310.50. Marks & Henry shipped order #92-Y May 16.   68
He said, "Isn't the right amount $8,000?" The interest rate is 6%.   67

TECHNIQUE PRACTICE 85
7 minutes

Directions. 1. Use a 70-space line; double spacing.
2. Type each sentence for one minute. Your goal is errorless typing on at least three of the five writings.

STROKES

You can type a good many words in the time it takes to make an erasure.   71
There must be just as little arm and hand motion in typing as possible.   71
Pay attention to what you type, and you will then type with good control.   73
What kind of credentials are you writing for yourself in your daily work?   73
If you want to become a good typist, you must learn to type with control.   73

FIVE-MINUTE TIMED WRITING
8 minutes

Directions. 1. Use a 70-space line; double spacing.
2. Keep the carriage moving continuously, not jerkily. Goal: An average of not more than an error for each four lines typed.

Each paragraph has a syllable intensity of 1.30 and includes all letters of the alphabet.

STROKES

It was failure in little things that brought trouble to Rex Ward, the   70
most likeable boy in my graduating class. Rex never bothered to look ahead   146
to the time when he would have to "face the music" of proving what he could   222
do. Each day to him was just one more chance to go racing through life,   295
quite indifferent to such dull things as plans for the future. Rex was a   369
clever boy, and he had that which people call "personality." In school he   444
traded on his charm of manner, often boasting of getting by without having   519
to work. He didn't believe in working his way through a problem if he could   596
escape it in any way. He thought that he could sow the seeds of pretense and   674
of evasion and still reap something else. Too late he realized that he was to   753
reap in bitterness what he had sown so carelessly in high glee.   818

LESSON 38

RECONSTRUCTION PRACTICE

5 minutes

Directions. 1. Use a 70-space line and single spacing.
2. Type each line twice. Double-space after typing the second line.
3. Type on the stroke level.

> quote quorum request inquiry acquire inquire quickly bequest quietly
>
> examine paroxysm export quixotic fixed exhibit sixty extra pretext box
>
> co-operate twenty-five self-accused self-conceited freeze-out tie-up
>
> bird born grub grab stub stab robe robs rubs knob tubs both barb club

TECHNIQUE PRACTICE 38

7 minutes

Directions. 1. Use a 70-space line, single spacing, 5-space indention, 2-inch top margin.
2. Type each sentence once in paragraph form. Double-space between sentences. Type on the stroke level.

Sentence 1. Divide a word only when it is necessary to do so. A word of four letters must not be divided. If possible, avoid dividing words of five or six letters.

Sentence 2. The division must come between syllables. The addition of the past tense to a word does not necessarily add an extra syllable. Example: stop, stopped.

Sentence 3. When a word containing three or more syllables is to be divided at a one-letter syllable, the one-letter syllable should be typed on the same line rather than the succeeding line. (See the third, fourth, and fifth sentences of the drill for examples of this principle.) A one-letter syllable at the beginning of a word must not be separated from the rest of the word. Example: around.

Pronunciation is generally the most helpful guide to use in determining correct syllabication.

When in doubt as to how to divide a word, you must consult a dictionary for the correct syllabication.

One of the skills that all typists must develop is correct syllabication, for there is no excuse for improperly divided words.

You should never divide words at the ends of more than two consecutive lines of typing if such division can be avoided.

A personal title, such as Miss, Mrs., or Mr., should not be separated from the name to which it belongs.

EXERCISE 38

30 minutes

Directions. 1. Use a 70-space line, a 5-space paragraph indention, and double spacing.
2. Type each paragraph once. When all paragraphs have been typed, check your work and encircle any errors you have made. Divide the total lines typed by the total errors; if you have more than an average of one error for each three lines of typing, retype the paragraphs until you can bring your line accuracy to the required average of not more than one error for each three lines.
3. Type on the stroke level. Keep the carriage moving smoothly and continuously.
4. List any errors you may make. Be alert to guard against permitting the recurrence of such errors.

EXERCISE 108

15 minutes

Directions. 1. Use a half sheet of paper. Type the exercise in four columns with single spacing.

2. Spread the main heading by spacing once between letters and three times between words. To center a heading that is to be spread, backspace once for each letter in the heading and once for the space between words.

P O T A T O   P R O D U C T I O N

Four-Year Average

	Acreage	Production (1,000 bu.)	Per Cent of Total Production
Maine	177,000	43,103	10.9
Minnesota	327,000	30,197	7.6
New York	269,000	28,732	7.2
Pennsylvania	234,000	26,832	6.8
Wisconsin	251,000	23,547	5.9
Michigan	290,000	23,475	5.9

EXERCISE 109

17 minutes

Directions. 1. Use a full sheet of paper; double spacing.

2. Study the arrangement of the columnar headings before you type the problem. Plan for adequate space between the main heading and the first line of the heading for column three.

3. Rule the horizontal lines with pencil or pen and ink after the exercise has been typed.

INCOME IN SELECTED OCCUPATIONS—1920-1936

Occupations	Average Earnings in Dollars per Year	Present Value of Average Earnings for a Working Lifetime—in Dollars
Medicine	$4,850	$108,000
Law	4,730	105,000
Dentistry	4,170	95,400
Engineering	4,410	95,300
Architecture	3,820	82,500
College Teaching	3,050	69,300
Social Work	1,650	51,000
Journalism	2,120	41,500
Ministry	1,980	41,000
Library Work	2,020	35,000
Public School Teaching	1,350	29,700
Skilled Trades	1,430	28,600
Nursing	1,310	23,300
Unskilled Labor	795	15,200
Farming	580	12,500
Farm Labor	485	10,400

	STROKES

In practice for automatization, there are some things that you must try to 75
avoid. Be certain that you have your shoulders relaxed. Do not "jump" at the 154
word; time the strokes well but quickly. The gain in speed will come as you 231
get rid of the pause between strokes. 268

"Haste makes waste" is just as true in typewriting as in anything else. 73
Except for the drives for increase in gross stroking, your typing practice 148
should be with a definite sense of ease and control. You must realize that you 228
should type with a feeling of poise and certainty—and poise and certainty 303
come from typing with correct techniques. 344

Build in your mind and in your spine a definite acceptance of that which is 76
right and a positive rejection of that which is wrong. There must never be 152
any question as to how you will act when the issues are clear-cut. Criticize 230
your motives as well as your acts and see that both are in keeping with the 306
highest type of life you can live. Expect much of yourself and live up to your 386
expectations. 399

If your typing technique is not right, you are making wasteful motions, no 75
matter how many pages you type. The first thing for you to do is to analyze 152
the errors you make; the next, is to work on the drills that will help you to 230
get rid of these errors. Through setting up this habit of studying the errors 309
you make in typewriting, you can learn much about how to get at the heart 383
of the problem. This is a good habit to take with you into your office work. 462
Just try it and see how your work will improve. 509

LESSON 39

SYLLABICATION CHECKUP   *8 minutes*

Directions. 1. Assume that you are writing a timed test and that the bell rings for the end of the line while you are writing each of the words given below. Type the hyphen at the point where you might first divide the word after the bell rings. Example: pro-test

2. If a word cannot be divided, type the word solid. Example: only

3. In addition to the principles of syllabication taught in the preceding lesson, the following principles should be used in determining the correct syllabication of the words listed below:

a. Words ending in such terminations as *able*, *ible*, and *ical* are usually divided between the stem of the word and the termination. Example: econom-ical

b. When two vowels coming together are pronounced separately, they should be divided into separate syllables. Example: continu-ation

Bell Rings on the Typing of the Second Letter of Each Word

1. business
2. seriously
3. difficulty
4. trained
5. reference
6. clerical
7. laudable
8. dividing
9. material
10. graduated

Bell Rings on the Typing of the Sixth Letter of Each Word

1. concerning
2. transcription
3. inquiring
4. dictation
5. possession
6. realization
7. organized
8. arrangement
9. continuous
10. determination

Directions. 1. Use a half sheet of paper; single spacing.

2. Rearrange and type the lines alphabetically. Be uniform in expressing street names—use abbreviations or spell *Street*, *Avenue*, and *Boulevard* in full for all.

3. Determine the spaces between columns by the method explained in the tabulating steps.

POLICYHOLDERS AND ACCUMULATED DIVIDEND

B. J. Young	2095 Andrews Street	139407	$20.15
Alice Crovert	486 Beacon Avenue	98201	7.50
D. L. Parker	2839 Randolf Place	200651	18.37
Joe Decker	28 Marhall Road	290156	37.81
Sue Dowden	505 Duff Ave.	147230	9.12
W. D. Edwards	1260 Wisconsin Street	90562	8.36
Ella Spencer	629 Brandon Drive	204138	14.57
Harry Black	3012 Liberty St.	196390	10.29
M. O. Merritt	401 Park Blvd.	185231	9.26
Robert Elliott	1800 Park View Avenue	201586	7.92
Morris Elliott	1800 Park View Avenue	198491	12.37
A. G. Roberts	401 Dickson Drive	219891	21.73

LESSON 84

RECONSTRUCTION PRACTICE   *4 minutes*

Sometimes it is desirable to give a heading greater emphasis than can be secured by merely setting it all in capitals. In such a case, a spread heading may be used. This type of heading has one space between letters and three spaces between words. To center a heading that is to be spread, move the carriage to the typing center and backspace once for each letter and for each space in the heading.

Directions. Center "Potato Production" in the usual way and then as a spread heading.

TECHNIQUE PRACTICE 84   *7 minutes*

Directions. 1. Use a 70-space line; double spacing.

2. Type each line of Technique Practice 83 once; then select for repetition practice the lines that provide the drill you need.

PLACEMENT OF COLUMNAR HEADINGS (Additional Items of Tabulating Steps)

If the problem has a secondary heading, double-space between the secondary and the columnar headings. If the problem does not have a secondary heading, triple-space between the main and the columnar headings. Double-space between the columnar heading and the first line of the column.

To determine the placement of each columnar heading:

     a. Find the difference between the number of spaces in the columnar heading and the number in the longest line in the column.

     b. Divide by 2.

     c. If the columnar heading is longer than the longest line in the column, backspace the required number of spaces (Step b) from the left margin of the column; if the columnar heading is shorter than the longest line in the column, indent the required number of spaces from the left margin of the column.

TECHNIQUE PRACTICE 39

Directions. 1. Use a 70-space line and single spacing.
2. Type each drill twice—and more if you feel the repetition will add to your control.
3. Double-space between the line groups.
4. Type on the stroke level at the rate of approximately a line each half minute. This slow stroking will permit you to pay attention to the letter sequences and to type with control.

Drill	STROKES
(m) My message to the mayor on the matter must be marked by moderation.	67
(n) Ned Neyland needed no notoriety when negotiating with the Notary.	65
(o) Our officer offered most of his odd collection to our Memorial House.	69
(p) Professor Phelps paused on the platform to propose a meeting in April.	70
(q) Quick responses to quiz questions quite frequently require quick wit.	69

EXERCISE 39

Directions. 1. Use a 70-space line, a 5-space paragraph indention, and double spacing.
2. Type each paragraph once. When all paragraphs have been typed, check your work and encircle any errors made. You are to type with an average of not more than one error for each four lines. Retype selected paragraphs until you meet the line accuracy goal.

3. Type on the stroke level.
4. List errors on the error-analysis chart. If certain errors tend to recur in successive practice periods, check the technique of reading the copy and pay vigorous attention to the sequence of letters.

The dash is made with two hyphens without space before or after the hyphens.

	STROKES
Good key stroking is one of the techniques of typing that you must develop	75
if you want to be an expert in typing. Strike the center of the key and release	156
it quickly—just the opposite to pushing the key with a mashing stroke.	229
Emphasize the use of the right kind of stroke.	275
The excessive emphasis upon slow but sure typing may cause you to stiffen	74
the arm and shoulder muscles and use the shoulder-punch stroke. Relax and	149
lower the shoulders. Emphasize the slight lifting of the finger in making the	228
stroke. Keep the fingers curved. The swift stroke and quick release will bring	309
their just reward in greater skill.	344
When your hands are out of alignment with the keyboard or when you fail	72
to fix your attention on what you are typing, you may develop a glancing	145
stroke that will cause you to strike between the keys or to depress two keys	222
at once. You should realize that indefinite recognition of letter sequence may	302
give just this same faulty glancing stroke. Hold your arms still and your	377
hands in position. Pay attention as you type.	423
Do you ever confuse adjacent key reaches? If so, this difficulty is probably	78
caused by tenseness of muscles that produces a slowing up of motor responses;	156
or you may have incorrect hand position; or you may be using a weak typing	231
impulse caused by slighting individual letter sequences. The corrective work	309
is relatively simple; relax the shoulder and forearm muscles and check to see	387
that there is no in-and-out movement of the elbows. Mentally pronounce the	463
syllable or word as you type.	492

[82]

LESSON 83

RECONSTRUCTION PRACTICE

5 minutes

Directions. Type the reconstruction practice for Lesson 82.

TECHNIQUE PRACTICE 83

7 minutes

Directions. 1. Use a 70-space line; double spacing.
2. Type each line once; then select for repetition practice the lines that provide the drill you feel you need.

Sentence 1. The asterisk is used to call attention to a footnote. When this symbol is not the shift of the hyphen, it can be made by striking capital *A* over small *v*. If, at the end of a sentence, the words enclosed in parentheses belong to the sentence, the period is written outside the parenthesis.

Sentence 2. If the words enclosed in parentheses make a complete sentence, write the period inside the parenthesis.

Sentence 3. Use Roman numerals for numbers of the books of the Bible. Do not space after a colon separating the number of a chapter from the number of a verse.

Sentence 4. Pence is English money and is indicated by *d*.

Sentence 5. The symbol # is used for *No.* in price lists and tabulations.
The period is used after the abbreviation *etc.*, and the question mark punctuates the entire sentence. Had the sentence not been a question, one period would have sufficed to punctuate both the abbreviation and the sentence.

	STROKES
You may call attention to a footnote by the use of * (the asterisk).	68
Please order *Morning Glow* for me. (The latest catalogue lists it.)	67
The first recorded woman letter-writer was Jezebel (I Kings 21:5-10).	69
Post cards of the islands of the British West Indies cost 1d to 6d.	67
Can the symbol for No., #, be used in price lists, tabulations, etc.?	69

EXERCISE 106

12 minutes

Directions. 1. Use a half sheet of paper; single spacing.
2. Double-space between the underscore and the totals for the columns. Check the totals for accuracy.
3. Plan the problem through reference to the list of tabulating steps.

CHIEF RETAIL DISTRIBUTING GROUPS OF MICHIGAN

Groups, Stores, and Sales

Automotive	10,404	$ 505,302,840
Food	17,476	498,684,322
General Merchandise	2,288	302,887,695
Lumber and Building	3,529	204,757,821
Apparel	4,608	184,206,779
Furniture and Household	1,545	94,603,353
All Other Stores	16,440	445,128,050
Total	56,290	$2,235,570,860

LESSON 40

RECONSTRUCTION PRACTICE

5 minutes

Directions. 1. Use a 70-space line and single spacing.

2. Type each sentence twice. Double-space after the second typing of the sentence.

3. Type on the stroke level and demonstrate your control through typing smoothly and accurately.

Drill

(t) **Thomas Staunton wrote a tiresome treatise about that trip into Tibet.**

(v) **Very vivid views on various vocations were fervidly upheld by the voters.**

(w) **Whose wisdom was summarized in these words: "Whither? Whence? Why?"**

(x) **Max fixed the six wax dolls but did not expect to be called an expert.**

(y) **Your youngster yelled to Mrs. Young that you are buying a xylophone.**

(z) **Zona was puzzled that his zeal and zest did not help him seize power.**

TECHNIQUE PRACTICE 40

7 minutes

Directions. 1. Use a 70-space line, a 5-space paragraph indention, and single spacing.

2. Type the drill once. Double-space between paragraphs.

3. Study the explanations to learn the principles of word division.

Sentence 1. In the word *separately,* the bell will ring before the ending *ly.* No division is made in this word because a two-letter syllable at the end of a word should not be divided from the rest of the word. To do so would save one space only, and a complete word is preferable to a divided word.

Sentence 2. Even though the bell will ring after the first *d* in *additional,* it is better to avoid a two-letter division. If the second syllable, *di,* is placed on the first line, the portion of the word on that line is suggestive of the entire word. This is desirable when a word is divided; therefore, do not separate a two-letter syllable from the rest of the word—either at the beginning or the end of the word.

Sentence 3. When a final consonant is doubled before a suffix, the additional consonant should be placed with the suffix.

Sentence 4. When a word containing three or more syllables is to be divided at a one-letter syllable, the one-letter syllable should be typed on the preceding rather than the succeeding line.

Sentence 5. When two vowels coming together are pronounced separately, they should be divided into separate syllables.

	STROKES
If two vowels coming together in a word are pronounced separately,	67
they should be divided into separate syllables.	114
If a final consonant of a word is doubled before a suffix, the addi-	67
tional consonant should be placed with the suffix.	117
Always place the hyphen at the end of the line and not at the begin-	67
ning of the following line.	94
When the root form of a word ends with a double letter, always sepa-	67
rate the suffix from the root word.	102
The abbreviations of the names of societies and the names of associ-	67
ations should not be divided.	96

STATES AND THEIR ABBREVIATIONS

Alabama	Ala.	Montgomery
Arizona	Ariz.	Phoenix
Arkansas	Ark.	Little Rock
California	Calif.	Sacramento
Colorado	Colo.	Denver
Connecticut	Conn.	Hartford
Delaware	Del.	Dover
Florida	Fla.	Tallahassee
Georgia	Ga.	Atlanta
Idaho	Idaho	Boise
Illinois	Ill.	Springfield
Indiana	Ind.	Indianapolis
Iowa	Iowa	Des Moines
Kansas	Kans.	Topeka
Kentucky	Ky.	Frankfort
Louisiana	La.	Baton Rouge
Maine	Maine	Augusta
Maryland	Md.	Annapolis
Massachusetts	Mass.	Boston
Michigan	Mich.	Lansing
Minnesota	Minn.	St. Paul
Mississippi	Miss.	Jackson
Missouri	Mo.	Jefferson City
Montana	Mont.	Helena
Nebraska	Nebr.	Lincoln
Nevada	Nev.	Carson City
New Hampshire	N. H.	Concord
New Jersey	N. J.	Trenton
New Mexico	N. Mex.	Santa Fe
New York	N. Y.	Albany
North Carolina	N. C.	Raleigh
North Dakota	N. Dak.	Bismarck
Ohio	Ohio	Columbus
Oklahoma	Okla.	Oklahoma City
Oregon	Oreg.	Salem
Pennsylvania	Pa.	Harrisburg
Rhode Island	R. I.	Providence
South Carolina	S. C.	Columbia
South Dakota	S. Dak.	Pierre
Tennessee	Tenn.	Nashville
Texas	Texas	Austin
Utah	Utah	Salt Lake City
Vermont	Vt.	Montpelier
Virginia	Va.	Richmond
Washington	Wash.	Olympia
West Virginia	W. Va.	Charleston
Wisconsin	Wis.	Madison
Wyoming	Wyo.	Cheyenne

While it is technically correct to abbreviate *Texas* to *Tex.*, it is better form to spell the word in full.

ANALYSIS OF PROBLEM

1.
   a. 51
   b. $66 - 51 = 15$
   c. $15 \div 2 = 7\frac{1}{2}$ Therefore,
   Top margin 7
   Bottom margin 8

2.
   a.

Col.	
1	14
2	7
3	14
	35

   b. $80 - 35 = 45$
   $100 - 35 = 65$
   c. $45 \div 4 = 11$ with 1 over
   $65 \div 4 = 16$ with 1 over

	Pica	Elite
Therefore,		
Left margin	12	17
Space between columns	11	16
Right margin	11	16

3.

	Pica	Elite
a.	12	17
b.	14	14
	11	16
Tab. stop for Col. 2	37	47
c.	7	7
	11	16
Tab. stop for Col. 3	55	70

Proof:	Left M.	Col. 1	Sp.	Col. 2	Sp.	Col. 3	Right M.	
Pica	12	14	11	7	11	14	11	= 80
Elite	17	14	16	7	16	14	16	= 100

EXERCISE 105 (Optional) *10 minutes*

Directions. 1. Type the words in two columns. There are 36 words to be typed with double spacing. Remember to begin the second column with the nineteenth word.

2. Plan the problem according to the steps used in the preceding exercises. After typing the first word in the first column, tabulate to the position for the second column and type the nineteenth word.

A STUDY OF WORDS

already although altogether anybody anything anyway beforehand downward everybody extraordinary foreclosure furthermore hundredweight inasmuch likewise moreover nevertheless nobody notwithstanding oneself overcome overhead policyholder semiannual semicolon something sometimes somewhat thereupon together underwrite viewpoint waybill whatever whenever whereas

Directions. 1. Use a 5-space paragraph indention, and double spacing.

2. Use the first paragraph for a one-minute writing for control. Set your goal at a rate that is four or five words a minute slower than you type when you are writing for speed. Make yourself type with even stroking and with attention to the letter sequences.

3. You can tell from your one-minute record what goal you should set for the second paragraph that is to be typed for five minutes. Select a rate that is well within your control. The half minute and minute goals should be indicated so you will be guided in the rate you type.

4. Analyze the errors, if any, and select appropriate drills from pages 117 to 119. After you have practiced the drills, you may want to repeat the five-minute writing in order to demonstrate better typing skill.

	STROKES
You should now have all the speed you need for undertaking the next units	74
of work, but you need to give more thought to typing with control. If you	149
type with right techniques, you can be just about certain that you will develop	229
fine typing power. Realize now that it is up to you to do your work in the	305
right way.	315

Most of us do well those things we like to do, and most of us like to do the	77
things we do well. It is not easy to say which should come first, liking our	155
work so we will do it well or doing our work well so that we will like it. It	234
may be we shall have to learn that these are just two ways of saying the same	312
thing. It is said to be good for us to fail now and then so we will not forget	392
that we are not yet on top of the world; but if failure is a part of our daily life,	477
we will soon come to accept it and to expect it; then growth stops. It is not	556
true, of course, that we can learn to do anything we want to do for there are	634
some things that require special abilities we may not have; still, we can learn	714
to do most of the things we want to do because our desires that persist are	790
those that are linked with the things we do now or the way we feel now. All	867
of this sums up to the thought that we can do much more than we are now	939
doing. Most of us need to realize this truth and hold ourselves to higher	1014
standards of thought and work.	1044

LESSON 82

RECONSTRUCTION PRACTICE
5 minutes

Directions. 1. Use a 70-space line; double spacing.
2. Type each line once; then select for repetition practice the lines that provide the drill you feel you need.

f4f j7j s2s k8k d3d l9l f5f ;0; f5f ;-; s2s j6j d3d l9l f5f ;0; s2s j6j

3 1 7 317 2 6 1 261 4 9 1 491 5 8 0 580 3 6 8 368 5 1 2 512 4 6 0 460

4f$f 8k'k Isn't the check for $506.10? 3d#d 6j_j Order #278 is *lost.*

2s"s 7j&j 5f%f 9l(l 5f%f 0;); He said, "The rate (on the note) is 5%."

You want to develop the certainty of stroking when typing the figures and symbols that you have when typing words.

MANIPULATION DRILL—CHARACTERS NOT ON THE KEYBOARD

Use combinations of regular keyboard characters to form symbols not on the keyboard.

Asterisk	*	Capital A and small v
Pound Sterling	£	Capital L and small f
Equal Sign	=	Hyphen—turn cylinder forward slightly
Minus Sign	—	Space before and after the symbol
Ditto	"	Quotation marks

TECHNIQUE PRACTICE 82
8 minutes

Directions. 1. Use a 70-space line; double spacing.
2. Type each sentence once; then select for repetition practice the lines that provide the drill you feel you need.

	STROKES
The letter is dated January 30. The check for Order #581 is for $627.	70
Fractions should be typed in a uniform manner; as, $\frac{1}{2}$, $\frac{1}{4}$, or 1/2, 1/4.	69
He wired, "Ship Hall & Miller's order on March 26." Jones OK'd this.	69
This $1,000 note bears 6% interest. Have you read Robert's *New Taxes*?	70
You have read "Pressure Groups"; but you must read *Slow Up or Blow Up.*	70

What do the quotation marks around "Pressure Groups" tell you about the publication? Is it a book or an article? Check the explanations of Technique Practice 30, page 66.

EXERCISE 104
20 minutes

Directions. 1. Type the following exercise in three columns with single spacing. Triple-space between the main heading and the columns.
2. Use the directions given under Tabulating Steps to determine the correct vertical and horizontal placement of all lines. Before typing the problem, check your placement figures with the analysis given below the problem. If your figures do not agree with those in the analysis of the problem, re-check your figures carefully.

UNIT IV—*INTRODUCTION TO THE BUSINESS LETTER*

2 minutes

You have been developing power to type from straight copy, or paragraph material. You must continue the emphasis upon maintaining and improving your rate and your accuracy in typing. Each week you should demonstrate greater typing ability. Do not neglect your drill practice or your paragraph work. Still, speed in typing straight copy is only one phase of the problem of developing real typing power. You must be able to use this skill in the typing of personal and business papers. The purpose of this unit of work is (1) to give you the drill and the paragraph practice through which you will raise your typing power to higher levels, and (2) to teach simple styles of business letters that will form the basis of your practice in using straight-copy skill to type personal and business papers.

Paper to Use. Use drill paper for the reconstruction practice. If your teacher requests you to hand in the typing of the technique practice, center the typing vertically and horizontally on a half sheet of paper, unless otherwise instructed.

Use letterheads for the exercises. If letterheads are not available, use plain sheets of paper 8½ by 11 inches in size, and leave a 2-inch top margin before typing the date.

BUDGET I

LESSON 41

RECONSTRUCTION PRACTICE

5 minutes

Directions. 1. Use a 70-space line; single spacing.
2. Type each line twice; then double-space.

4f 7j 47 147 3d 8k 38 138 5f 91 59 159 2s 6j 26 261 5f 0; 50 501 2s 6j 26

The letter is dated April 27. Will they ship the goods by January 30?

4f$f 8k'k Isn't the check for $48? 5f%f 1514 The note is for $500 at 3%.

2s"s 91(1 3d#d 0;); He said, "The colon (:) is the shift of the semicolon."

TECHNIQUE PRACTICE 41

6 minutes

Directions. Use a 70-space line; single spacing. Type each sentence twice. Double-space after the second typing of each sentence.

Sentence 1. In stating approximate age, spell the number in full. When an age is stated in years, months, and days, use figures.

Sentence 2. Express dimensions in figures.

Sentence 3. In expressing time, use figures with *p.m.* or *a.m.* (*P. M.* or *A. M.*). Use the colon to divide the hour from the minutes.

Sentence 4. When *o'clock* is used in stating time, spell the hour in full.

Sentence 5. Separate hundreds from thousands with a comma, except in a number designating a page, an insurance policy, a room, a telephone, a house, or a year.

	STROKES
Paul's policy matures when he is 35 years 8 months and 27 days old.	67
The dimensions of this box are 4 by 6 feet; and it weighs 158 pounds.	69
In April my office hours will be 10:00-11:30 a.m. and 2:30-5:00 p.m.	68
With "o'clock," spell the number in full; as, "It is twelve o'clock."	69
Policy No. 38476 for $5,000, issued to Mr. Apple, is listed on page 29.	71

4. *Type the headings.*
   a. Space down to allow for the top margin determined in Step 1-c.
   b. Center the main heading. (Rules for horizontal centering are given on page 46.)
   c. Center the secondary heading.
5. *Type the columns.*
   a. Space down to allow the number of spaces desired between the main or the secondary heading and the body of the tabulation.
   b. Start the columns at the points at which the stop for the left margin and the tabulator stops were set in Step 3.

EXERCISE 103   *10 minutes*

Directions. 1. You are to type the column of words at the right in three columns. Use double spacing.

2. Center the problem vertically and center the longest line of each column horizontally.

3. Before typing, divide the list into three groups of 16 words each. Then type words 1, 17, and 33 in the first line and continue in that manner so that the words will be arranged alphabetically by columns.

You have set your machine satisfactorily for this problem if you followed the exact steps outlined for the trial problem.

WORD STUDY

Words Frequently Misspelled

accommodate	embarrass	miscellaneous
acknowledgment	encouraging	mysterious
addressed	equalization	occasionally
apparatus	exaggerate	occurrence
auxiliary	excellent	personnel
believing	existence	possessor
boundary	governor	preference
carburetor	humorous	privilege
clientele	impromptu	questionnaire
commission	independent	recommendation
comparative	inoculate	repetition
corroborate	insistence	resistance
definite	judgment	superintendent
descend	laboratory	transmissible
discipline	license	unnecessary
distributor	lose	visualized

Illustration No. 57 — Words Tabulated in Three Columns

WORD STUDY
Words Frequently Misspelled

accommodate
acknowledgment
addressed
apparatus
auxiliary
believing
boundary
carburetor
clientele
commission
comparative
corroborate
definite
descend
discipline
distributor
embarrass
encouraging
equalization
exaggerate
excellent
existence
governor
humorous
impromptu
independent
inoculate
insistence
judgment
laboratory
license
lose
miscellaneous
mysterious
occasionally
occurrence
personnel
possessor
preference
privilege
questionnaire
recommendation
repetition
resistance
superintendent
transmissible
unnecessary
visualized

PLACEMENT OF THE LETTER

3 minutes

In your first typing of letters, you will use a placement table to help you to place letters attractively on the page. In the use of the placement table, the following conditions must be kept in mind:

1. Paper with a *2*-inch letterhead is to be used. If the letterhead is not approximately 2 inches deep, increase the space between the date line and the inside address.

2. When plain paper is used as a substitute for a letterhead, type the date approximately 2 inches from the top of the page.

3. Add five spaces to the stop for the right margin to provide for the ringing of the bell at the desired point.

4. Check the placement of the paper guide so that the horizontal centering of the letter will be accurate.

5. Letters having unusual features, such as tabulated material, long quotations, or an unusual number of lines in the inside address or the close, may necessitate modifications in the adjustments called for in the placement table.

Double-Spaced Letters

Classification of Letter	Words in Body of Letter	Length of Line	Spaces between Date and Inside Address
Short	Up to 60	40	8 to 12
Short	61 to 100	50	6 to 8

Single-Spaced Letters

Classification of Letter	Words in Body of Letter	Length of Line	Spaces between Date and Inside Address
Short	61 to 100	40	8 to 12
Medium	101 to 200	45 to 50	6 to 8
Long	201 to 275	55 to 60	4 to 6
Two-page	More than 275	60	4 to 6

If the letter has only a few words more than 275, it is better to crowd the page somewhat in order to avoid using two pages. If elite type is used, a long letter of from 201 to 325 words may be typed on one page by increasing the length of the line to 65 or 70 spaces.

EXERCISE 41

11 minutes

Directions. 1. Type Style Letter No. 1 as it is given in the illustration except for the date and the reference initials. Use the current date and substitute your initials for the second pair in the reference initials.

2. For this length letter, the placement table calls for a 40-space line.

3. Use single spacing and mixed punctuation.

Setting the Tabulator Stops

Use a tabulator stop to save time in indenting to the exact place for the beginning of each line not written flush with the left margin. For the first exercise in this budget, set the tabulator stops as follows:

Stop Used for	Stop Set at	Pica-Type Machine (Centering Point, 40)	Elite-Type Machine (Centering Point, 50)
1. Street address and paragraph indentions	Left margin plus 5	20 + 5 = 25	30 + 5 = 35
2. City and state line	Left margin plus 10	20 + 10 = 30	30 + 10 = 40
3. Date line* and complimentary close	Five spaces to left of the centering point	40 − 5 = 35	50 − 5 = 45
4. Company signature	Complimentary close plus 5	35 + 5 = 40	45 + 5 = 50
5. Official title	Company signature plus 5	40 + 5 = 45	50 + 5 = 55

* The date line is placed two line spaces below the printed names of the city and the state. The date line may be centered under the names of the city and the state, indented five spaces from the beginning of the city and state lines, begun under the first letter in the name of the city, or written so that it will end at the right margin. In the letters in this budget, use the placement given by indenting to the third tabulator position.

TRIAL PROBLEM (Mathematical Placement)

Problem
{
Main heading of 10 spaces
Secondary heading of 27 spaces
Three columns of 16 double-spaced items
    Longest line in Column 1 has 14 spaces
    Longest line in Column 2 has 12 spaces
    Longest line in Column 3 has 14 spaces
}

Instructions

1. *Determine the vertical placement.*
   a. Count the lines required to type the material; include extra lines required between the main and the secondary or columnar headings.

   > Use triple spacing between the main and the secondary headings. Use double spacing between the secondary heading and the first line of the tabulation.

   b. Subtract this number from 66, the number of available lines on paper 8½ by 11 inches.
   c. Divide by 2. This result is the number of lines you must space down from the top of the paper before you type the main heading. Disregard fractions.

2. *Determine the horizontal placement of the columns.*
   a. Count the number of spaces that will be used in typing the longest line in each column.
   b. Add the spaces for all the columns and subtract this sum from 80 for pica (with 40 as centering point) or 100 for elite type (with 50 as centering point).
   c. Divide the result by *one more than* the number of columns in the tabulation. This number represents the number of spaces to be left in each margin and between the columns. If the number is not evenly divisible, add the remaining spaces to the width of the left and right margins.

3. *Set the stop for the left margin and the tabulator stops for the columns.*
   a. Set the stop for the left margin at the point determined by 2-c.
   b. Add to this number the number of spaces to be used in typing the longest line of the first column and the number of spaces to be left between the first and second columns. Set the first tabulator stop at the point that corresponds to this sum.
   c. To the number representing the tabulator stop for the second column, add the number of spaces to be used in typing the longest line in the second column and the number of spaces to be left between the second and third columns. Set the second tabulator stop at the point that corresponds to the sum.

   > Continue in this way until the tabulator stops for all columns in the problem have been set.

Solution

1.
   a.
Main heading	1
Unused lines between main and secondary heading	2
Secondary heading	1
Unused line between secondary heading and first line	1
16 double-spaced items: $16 \times 2 = 32 - 1$ (bottom space) =	31
	36

   b. $66 - 36 = 30$
   c. $30 \div 2 = 15$
   Therefore,
   Top margin   15
   Bottom margin   15

2.
   a.
Column 1	14
Column 2	12
Column 3	14
	40

   b. $80 - 40 = 40$
   $100 - 40 = 60$
   c. $40 \div 4 = 10$
   $60 \div 4 = 15$

Therefore,	Pica	Elite
Left margin	10	15
Space between columns	10	15
Right margin	10	15

3.
	Pica	Elite
a.	10	15
b.	14	14
	10	15
	34	44
c.	12	12
	10	15
	56	71

Proof:

	Left M.	Col. 1	Sp.	Col. 2	Sp.	Col. 3	Right M.	
Pica	10	14	10	12	10	14	10	= 80
Elite	15	14	15	12	15	14	15	= 100

Lippincott Company

OMAHA, NEBRASKA

May 2, 194-

1. Date placed two line spaces below the city and state line.   12

2. Ten line spaces between the date line and the inside address.

First tabulator stop
Second tabulator stop
Third tabulator stop

3. Single-spaced indented inside address.

Mr. J. D. Kenmore   30
713 Jackson Avenue   49
Omaha, Nebraska   65

4. Salutation with colon.

Dear Sir: 76

5. Body of letter with 40-space line and double spacing between the single-spaced paragraphs.

We extend to you a hearty welcome to   113
our city and a cordial invitation to make   155
this store your trading home.   186

We shall be glad to have you use the   223
charge account that has been established   264
for your convenience. We know you realize   307
that a charge account assures you of quick   350
and acceptable service at all times. We   391
hope that you will use this privilege of a   434
charge account freely.   458

6. Complimentary close placed five spaces to the left of center of the paper.

Yours very truly,   476

LIPPINCOTT COMPANY   495

7. Company signature typed in capital letters.

W. T. Powell

Credit Manager

8. Pen signature of dictator.   510

9. Official title typed four line spaces below the company signature.   517

10. Reference initials.

WTP:MOS

Dictator's initials
Stenographer's initials
Third tabulator stop
Fourth tabulator stop
Fifth tabulator stop

(Strokes, 517; words, 70.)

Style Letter No. 1 — Single-Spaced Indented Letter with Mixed Punctuation

UNIT VIII — *TABULATING*

The typist is called upon frequently to arrange statistical or other material in columns. This process is called tabulating. It is important that you develop skill in tabulating, for a great deal of office typing calls for quick and accurate arrangement of material in tabulated form.

BUDGET IX

LESSON 81

RECONSTRUCTION PRACTICE   *6 minutes*

Directions. 1. The basis of an understanding of how to tabulate material is a knowledge of vertical and horizontal centering. You have been centering your typed material since your early lessons. The following practice will recall the exact details for you. Refer to page 46 for specific rules for centering.

2. Use 40 for pica or 50 for elite centering point.

3. Use a full-sized sheet of paper. Center the lines vertically and horizontally.

UNIT VIII—TABULATING

Lesson 81

Reconstruction Practice: 6 minutes

Technique Practice 81: 7 minutes

Tabulating: 20 minutes

Exercise 103: 10 minutes

TECHNIQUE PRACTICE 81   *7 minutes*

Directions. 1. Use a 70-space line; double spacing.

2. Type each line once; then select for repetition practice the sentences that offer the constructive drill that you feel you need. Type each selected sentence until you feel you have made measurable improvement in the control of the material.

	STROKES
The sum of 4 and 8 and 2 and 9 and 3 and 6 and 5 and 7 and 1 is 45.	67
Ship 17 cars of 4/4 C/B (Common and Better) Chestnut on Order #591-Y.	69
On the B & O order, amounting to $568.92, quote terms of 2% 10 days.	68
In tabulated work, 36 feet 8 inches is typed 36′ 8″ or 36 ft. 8 in.	67
Type all fractions in the same way; for example, ¼, ½, or 1/4, 1/2.	67

TABULATING   *20 minutes*

Planning the work is an important feature of tabulating. Clearness and compactness of tabulated work must be maintained. Analyze the facts and figures to be tabulated before you determine the general headings and the columnar headings. The width of the columns and the general layout of the whole problem must then be determined.

You will recall:
  Vertical inch: 6 lines; or 66 lines for full sheet of paper
  Horizontal inch: 10 pica spaces; 12 elite spaces

You must learn:
  With 40 as the centering point for pica machines, you will have a maximum writing line of 80 spaces (not 85). With 50 as the elite centering point, you will have a maximum writing line of 100 spaces (not 102). When 40 or 50 is used as the centering point, the extra spaces are automatically distributed between the left and right margins. If you wish, or if your teacher so instructs you, 43 for pica or 51 for elite type can be used as the exact centering point.

[154]

Now that you have typed Style Letter No. 1, you will better understand the following information on the parts of a business letter:

Letterhead. Most offices use letterheads for correspondence. The standard letterhead size is 8½ by 11 inches.

Date Line. The date line is usually placed in relation to the position of the names of the city and the state printed on the letterhead. Type the date on a separate line two spaces below the names of the city and the state. The date line may be

(1) centered under the names of the city and the state,

(2) indented,

(3) begun under the first letter in the name of the city, or

(4) placed so that it will end at approximately the right margin of the letter. If the letterhead is unusual in its arrangement, the date line may be placed in relation to the position of the body of the letter.

Type the name of a month in the date line in full. When the month, the day, and the year are written on one line, indicate the day by figures only and separate it from the year by a comma. Use *d, st,* or *th* after the day of the month only if the day is typed before the month.

Address. Use the correct title before the name of the person being addressed. This rule applies to the inside address and to the address on the envelope. Never address a letter to an individual without using *Mr.* or whatever other title is correct. The following are the abbreviated forms of personal titles used with names:

Mr.	for a man
Messrs.	for two or more men
Mrs.	for a married woman
Dr.	for a doctor

Messrs. is used with firm names composed of the names of two or more persons.

A period is placed after all abbreviated forms of titles.

Salutation. The correct forms of salutations for business letters are given below.

For a man:

    Dear Sir
    My dear Sir
    My dear Mr. Summers
    My dear Professor Young
    Dear Mr. Hall
    Dear Dr. Long

For a woman:

    Dear Madam
    My dear Madam
    My dear Miss Harrington
    My dear Mrs. Brown
    Dear Miss Harrington
    Dear Mrs. Brown

For a firm of men:

    Gentlemen

For a firm of women:

    Mesdames
        or
    Ladies

When preceded by the word *My, dear* should not be capitalized in the salutation.

The salutation is typed flush with the left margin. When a mark of punctuation is to be used, the colon is placed after the salutation. In single-spaced letters, one extra line space separates the salutation from the last line of the address and from the first line of the opening paragraph.

Body of the Letter. Letters may be spaced with single or double spacing. The length of a letter determines the spacing to be used within the paragraph. There should be two spaces between the paragraphs of a letter. This rule does not call for any extra spacing in the double-spaced form. In typing the single-spaced form, operate the line-space and carriage-return lever one extra time for the correct spacing.

Complimentary Close. The complimentary close of a letter is the courteous ending, such as *Yours truly,* that the writer uses. Only the first word of the complimentary close is capitalized. The colon after the salutation and the comma after the complimentary close are used when close or mixed punctuation has been used in the heading and the address.

Signatures. The firm name should be typed entirely in capital letters two spaces below the complimentary close. A short firm name may be indented five spaces beyond the complimentary close; a long firm name should be blocked under the complimentary close so that it will not extend beyond the right margin of the letter. No punctuation mark is required at the end of the firm name unless an abbreviation is used.

TECHNIQUE PRACTICE 79

8 minutes

Directions. Type Technique Practice 78 as directed. The completed work is important, but more important is the technique you develop through this practice.

EXERCISE 101

30 minutes

Directions. 1. Use a 70-space line; double spacing. Set the machine for a 5-space paragraph indention. Use Exercise 100 for this practice.

2. In the preceding lesson, you contrasted your writing rate on a ten-minute timed writing with that of a five-minute writing. In this lesson, your goal is to bring your ten-minute rate to the same level of stroking as your five-minute rate.

3. Identify your half-minute and minute goals; then type at your goal rate for one minute. When you have achieved your goal for one minute, type for a minute and a half; then work up to a ten-minute writing by adding a half minute to each preceding timing.

4. If time permits, type for ten minutes without interruption and see if you have achieved your ten-minute goal.

LESSON 80

RECONSTRUCTION PRACTICE

5 minutes

Directions. 1. Use a 70-space line; single spacing.
2. Type each sentence of Technique Practice 76 three times without error.
3. Double-space between groups of errorless writings.

TECHNIQUE PRACTICE 80

8 minutes

Directions. 1. Use a 70-space line; single spacing.

2. Type each sentence of Technique Practice 78 three times without error. Double-space between groups of errorless writings. Errorless typing is important, but even more important is the technique you develop through this practice. Use the "hinge" wrist motion when controlling the shift keys. Make certain that you maintain the same hand alignment with the keyboard. Forearm and elbow movement should be held to a minimum.

EXERCISE 102

30 minutes

Directions. 1. Use a 70-space line; double spacing. Set the machine for a 5-space paragraph indention.

2. Use Exercise 98, page 149, for this practice. You are to type the three paragraphs for control. Retype the paragraphs until you have not more than an average of one error for each five lines typed. If you complete Exercise 98 satisfactorily, use the same procedures for typing Exercise 100.

OPTIONAL PRACTICE

If you feel that you have developed good control and want to take a timed writing, use each of the paragraphs of Exercise 100 for a five-minute writing. A bonus of an extra honor mark will be given for an errorless five-minute writing.

The dictator's official title should be typed four spaces (two double spaces) below the firm name to allow space for the penwritten signature, which should be a part of the closing lines of each letter. No punctuation mark is required after the official title.

Reference Initials. In a business letter the initials or the name of the dictator and the initials of the stenographer should be typed flush with the left margin, two spaces below the official title. The dictator's initials should be typed first and should be separated from those of the stenographer by a colon or some other mark of separation.

STYLE LETTERS

The style or form of letter to be used will be determined by the length of the letter or the custom of the office in which you work. Various letter forms are presented in this book. You will be held responsible for knowing how to arrange letters in these different forms. Study each illustration as it is presented; know the details of the form illustrated.

In the indented form, the second and third lines of the inside address are indented five spaces from the beginning of the preceding line. The first line of each paragraph also must be indented five spaces from the left margin.

FORMS OF PUNCTUATION
2 minutes

Three forms of punctuation are used: the close, the open, and the mixed.

Close punctuation requires a punctuation mark at the end of the date line, each line of the address, the salutation, and the complimentary close.

Open punctuation does not require any punctuation at the ends of lines except a period after abbreviations.

Mixed punctuation is the same as open punctuation except that a colon is placed after the salutation and a comma after the complimentary close.

In each form of punctuation, an abbreviation must be followed by a period; and the name of the city and of the state must be separated by a comma when typed on the same line.

The use of the close or open form of punctuation is a matter of personal preference or office custom. The open or the mixed form is preferred by most correspondents. Do not attempt to link a definite form of punctuation with a particular style of letter. Either the close or the open form of punctuation may be used with any style of letter.

EXERCISE 42
7 minutes

Directions. Now that you have had the experience of typing a letter and have studied the explanations of the setup of the letter, retype Style Letter No. 1. The repetition practice will add to your skill in handling the operative parts of the typewriter and in adapting your straight-copy speed to the typing of letters.

LESSON 42

RECONSTRUCTION PRACTICE
5 minutes

Directions. 1. Use a 70-space line; single spacing.
2. Type each line twice; then double-space.

He lives at 3948 Brandon Road.   His telephone number is Cedar 1472-J.
Have they answered your letter of April 26?   Has bill #501 been paid?
Marks & Logan sent a check for $2,195.   The bill amounts to $2,915.
I must keep my eyes on the copy and my elbows quiet as I typewrite.

TECHNIQUE PRACTICE 42
5 minutes

Directions. Type Technique Practice 41 as directed. You must learn to type figures and symbols with ease, rapidity, and accuracy. This repetition practice will add to your skill in typing figures and symbols.

[89]

great intelligence, but to be able to use that skill does call for intelligence. It   1031

is at this point that many students fail because they seem to feel that the   1107

ability to write at a high rate of speed is all that business requires of a be-   1185

ginner. This is far from the truth. You will have to realize that there are   1263

many other things of great importance. For one thing, you should know how   1338

to use the telephone in the correct way. A cheerful but quiet voice carries its   1419

message without fail, and at no point can an individual so reveal himself as   1496

in the use of the telephone.   1526

You must learn to type, of course; but more than that, you must learn to   1594

use your typing skill so that you can eventually lift yourself above routine   1671

work. Good typing means more than the correct copying of so many letters.   1747

Any typist should be able to copy what someone else has prepared for him.   1822

More than that will be expected of you in your business life. You must know   1899

how to arrange your work in a neat, correct form. Employers are willing   1972

to pay those who can do their work in a satisfactory manner without having   2047

to be taught the things that should have been learned in school. Show   2118

enthusiasm and zeal in learning your duties; be quick to find your own errors;   2197

and do your work in just the way you feel it should be done.   2257

LESSON 79

RECONSTRUCTION PRACTICE
5 minutes

Directions. Use a 70-space line; single spacing. Teach your fingers to spell the words by typing each word as many times as you feel you need to type it in order to have good control of it.

getting	ability	correct	intelligence
amount	one's	cheerful	individual
people	highest	quiet	enthusiasm
varied	business	carries	employers
trouble	great	message	expression
realize	speed	learning	required

EXERCISE 43 *18 minutes*

Directions. 1. Refer to the placement table for the length of line to be used.

2. Use single spacing and mixed punctuation.

3. The form of letter to be used is the same as that of Style Letter No. 1 on page 87. Use the current date and your reference initials in all letters. Type the letter twice.

The first figures at the end of each letter indicate the total strokes in the entire letter, counting an average of 15 strokes for the date line; the second figures indicate the number of actual words *in the body of the letter.* The exact number of strokes will be needed when the letter is used for a timed writing; the words in the body of the letter are used to determine, through reference to the letter placement chart, the exact length of writing line.

Mrs. John L. Ziegler 104 Lakewood Avenue Omaha, Nebraska Dear Madam: (P)* If we are somewhat persistent in calling to your attention the fact that your account has been inactive for some time, it is because of the value we place on your patronage. We want to do everything we can to retain your business. (P) Please let this informal letter persuade you to shop here again. We want to know that you are pleased with the quality of our goods and with the excellence of our service.

Yours very truly, LIPPINCOTT COMPANY (Dictated by W. T. Powell)** Credit Manager *(Strokes, 551; words, 75.)*

EXERCISE 44 *14 minutes*

Directions. 1. Use the same machine adjustments called for in the preceding exercise.

2. Type the letter once; then check it for placement as well as for accuracy of typing.

3. If time permits, retype the letter so as to improve the quality of the work and decrease the time required to type the letter.

Mr. William F. Dixon 610 Drake Street Lincoln, Nebraska Dear Mr. Dixon: (P) Most of our customers pay us promptly, but when they do not, we know that it is just because they have overlooked or forgotten the statement sent out for the previous month's purchases. (P) We are certain that this friendly request for the payment of your account is all that will be necessary. The size of your account is not large, but we must keep our collections up to date. (P) We shall expect a check from you by return mail. Yours very truly, LIPPINCOTT COMPANY (Dictated by W. T. Powell) Credit Manager *(Strokes, 575; words, 79.)*

* When this sign is used, begin a new paragraph.

** Do not type this information in parentheses. It is given in order that you may have the correct reference initials of the dictator.

LESSON 43

RECONSTRUCTION PRACTICE *5 minutes*

Directions. 1. Use a 70-space line; single spacing.

2. Type each line twice; then double-space.

3. Unless otherwise directed, follow the same instructions for succeeding reconstruction practices.

Italicized words are to be underscored when typed.

d3d j7j s2s k8k f5f 191 f4f j6j s2s ;0; f5f ;-; f5f ;-; d3d j6j s2s ;0;

Joe will be on leave until January 20, 1942.   He left here on the 10th.

What is the sum of 38 and 21 and 47 and 59?   The check is for $139.50.

He said, "Have you read this book, *War Clouds*?" Who wrote *War Clouds*?

TECHNIQUE PRACTICE 78

Directions. 1. Use a 70-space line; double spacing.

2. Type each sentence once; then select the sentences for repetition that provide the particular practice that you feel you need.

	STROKES
Nancy and Maxine could not go to Mexico in May as they went to Panama.	70
Robert Slaughter visited us in Algiers before sailing on the Algonquin.	71
Jack and Mattie will go to Maine in March. Is Janet in Maryland now?	69
The letter says Sue and Will went to Spain in April. Don is in Russia.	71
James lived in Dallas, Texas, for a year after he left Eugene, Oregon.	70

Remove the paper, reinsert it, and type over the last line. If you are not certain of the correct machine parts to use in aligning the sentence, read the instructions on page 57 for gauging the line and typing over it.

EXERCISE 100

25 minutes

Directions. 1. Use a 70-space line; double spacing. Set the machine for a 5-space paragraph indention.

2. Type the exercise for a five-minute writing. Check your gross writing rate.

3. Type the exercise for ten minutes. Check your writing rate and compare it with the gross writing rate on your five-minute writing. You will need this information in the next lesson.

Each paragraph has a syllable intensity of 1.30 and includes all letters of the alphabet.

	STROKES
There are many adjustments that the worker must make when he first goes	72
on a job, one of which is getting along with other members of the office force.	153
A good bit of common sense and no small amount of tact can take care of this	230
problem. One must admit that is a problem; for where there are so many	302
kinds of people from such varied kinds of homes, there will be an opening for	380
friction. If you have trouble with people you meet now, it is quite likely you	460
will have difficulty in your working life. If you like people; if you can see the	543
point of view of others; if you realize you have your part in keeping matters	621
running smoothly, you can excel without difficulty and make your own niche	696
in an office.	711
The ability to type is not an end; it is just a means to an end. Typing is	787
a tool of expression, and as such it is worth all the time and the effort that	866
are required to attain one's highest skill. To learn to type does not call for	946

[151]

TECHNIQUE PRACTICE 43

Directions. Use a 70-space line; single spacing. Type each sentence twice. Double-space after the second typing of each sentence.

Drill

STROKES

(a) An accountant has appealed for compensation on the basis of his accident. 73

(b) Bargains in bright book bindings can be bought by about doubling the bid. 73

(c) Can success be achieved except by checking unsocial characteristics? 68

(d) Deeds well done and knowledge well learned delivered Dick from boredom. 71

(e) European problems were followed by the men selected for the emergency. 70

EXERCISE 45 *17 minutes*

Directions. 1. Refer to the placement table for the length of line to be used.

2. Use single spacing and mixed punctuation.

3. The form of letter to be used is the same as that of Style Letter No. 1, page 87. Use the current date and your reference initials in all letters. Type the letter twice.

Mrs. Robert Maxton Smith 3875 Aliquippa Street Lincoln, Nebraska Dear Madam: (P) Announcements of our special sales to charge customers only will be sent to you from time to time. We hope this service will make it possible for you to buy to better advantage. (P) We again express our appreciation of the charge account that you opened with us during the early part of this month. Use this account just as often as you have shopping to do. (P) We have three deliveries in Lincoln each week. This delivery service is without extra charge. Yours very truly, LIPPINCOTT COMPANY (Dictated by W. T. Powell) Credit Manager *(Strokes, 606; words, 81.)*

EXERCISE 46 *15 minutes*

Directions. 1. Use the same machine adjustments called for in the preceding exercise.

2. Type the letter once; then check it for placement and for accuracy of typing.

3. If time permits, retype the letter.

Mr. G. J. Pritchard Sheffield Apartments Omaha, Nebraska Dear Sir: (P) Our records show an account in your name, but not at the address given above. It was this difference between the address in our records and that on your last purchase ticket which caused the delay in the delivery of the goods you bought. (P) You will recognize the necessity for our making a careful check on the use of all charge accounts. This care is exercised for the protection of our customers no less than for our own. Now that our records show your new address, you will have no further difficulty in using your charge account. Yours very truly, LIPPINCOTT COMPANY (Dictated by W. T. Powell) Credit Manager *(Strokes, 680; words, 97.)*

LESSON 44

RECONSTRUCTION PRACTICE: Type Technique Practice 41.

TECHNIQUE PRACTICE 44

Directions. Use a 70-space line; single spacing. Type each sentence twice. Double-space after the second typing of each sentence.

Drill

STROKES

(f) Fearful effort is futile effort, for fear frequently forces defeat. 67

(g) Good wages are going to bring greater opportunity for graceful living. 70

(h) Hear and think that which is right; then that which is right you can do. 72

(i) Identification of his kind of individuality is imperative if he wins. 69

(j) The majority judgment is that adjournment is justifiable in June or July. 73

SPEED EMPHASIS

5 minutes

Use the first paragraph of Exercise 98 for this practice. Select as your goal the same rate you made in typing the sentences of Technique Practice 76. Try to type this somewhat more difficult paragraph material at this fast stroking rate; to do this, first type for twelve seconds and then for twenty-four seconds, and so on until you can type the minute test at the rate of 70 words a minute. Use the stencil drill in this practice if you wish to do so.

LESSON 77

RECONSTRUCTION PRACTICE

5 minutes

Directions. Use a 70-space line; single spacing. Teach your fingers to spell the words by typing each word as many times as you feel you need to type it in order to have good control of it.

typewriter	kept	justification	preparations
expensive	should	carefully	carriage
properly	gummed	backward	difficulty
trouble	injury	benzene	adjustment
matter	realize	cautiously	expected
fluid	required	excess	absorbed

TECHNIQUE PRACTICE 77

8 minutes

Directions. 1. Use a 70-space line; single spacing.
2. Type Technique Practice 76 as directed. If you find you can type each sentence faster than called for, hold yourself to a slightly slower writing rate and emphasize exact control. First, though, you want to demonstrate your power to write a sentence each twelve seconds.

EXERCISE 99

30 minutes

Directions. 1. Use a 70-space line; double spacing. Set the machine for a 5-space paragraph indention. Use Exercise 98 for this practice.
2. In the preceding lesson, you contrasted your writing rate on a ten-minute timed writing with that of a five-minute writing. In this lesson, your goal is to bring your ten-minute rate to the same level of stroking as your five-minute rate.
3. Identify your half-minute and minute goals; then type at your goal rate for one minute. When you have achieved your goal for one minute, type for a minute and a half; then work up to a ten-minute writing by adding a half minute to each preceding timing.
4. If time permits, type for ten minutes without interruption and see if you have achieved your ten-minute goal.

LESSON 78

RECONSTRUCTION PRACTICE

5 minutes

Directions. Use a 70-space line; single spacing. Teach your fingers to spell the words by typing each word as many times as you feel you need to type it in order to have good control of it.

worker	difficulty	importance
members	smoothly	telephone
common	expression	individual
problem	required	eventually
adjustments	intelligence	employers

EXERCISE 47 *18 minutes*

Directions. Type Style Letter No. 2 as it is given in the illustration except for the date and the reference initials. Use the current date and your initials. Type the letter twice.

When the typed signature is used, the dictator's initials may be omitted from the reference notation.

When one enclosure is to be placed in a letter, type the word *Enclosure* at the left margin, two spaces below the reference initials. If there is more than one enclosure, type the word *Enclosures* and after it the figure representing the number of enclosures.

EXERCISE 48 *15 minutes*

Directions. Type the letter with the same form as Style Letter No. 2. If time permits, type the letter twice. Use open punctuation.

Mr. Baxter J. Luzerne 1210-1218 Clark Building Detroit, Michigan Dear Mr. Luzerne (P) In order that we may determine the best medium of advertising for our company, we want to know which newspapers are read regularly by our customers. We enclose an addressed postal card on which we have a list of the local newspapers. It will require but a little time to mark on this card the papers you read and to indicate by numbers (1, 2, 3, 4) the order of your preference for general and financial news. (P) As a customer of ours, will you help us to get this information? Yours truly SHIELDS & COMPANY John E. Lane Manager Enclosure (*Strokes, 640; words, 90.*)

LESSON 45

RECONSTRUCTION PRACTICE *5 minutes*

The letter is dated March 29. The note is for $3,500 at 6% interest.
Mr. Marshall owes 85 cents. Order #471-J must be shipped by July 15.
The judge said, "Who will win the prize?" Did Joe answer, "I will"?

TECHNIQUE PRACTICE 45 *5 minutes*

Directions. Use a 70-space line; single spacing. Type each sentence twice. Double-space after the second typing of each sentence.

Drill STROKES

(k) Karl knew his kinsmen went from Kentucky to Kansas and then to Keokuk. 70

(l) Let us all realize fully the practical side of the national call for help. 74

(m) Make most emphatic the import of the message you must give them tomorrow. 73

(n) Nations need to learn to understand each other just as individuals do. 70

(o) Orderly conduct often calls forth most favorable official commendation. 71

EXERCISE 49 *19 minutes*

Directions. Type the letter twice in the same form as Style Letter No. 2. Use open punctuation.

The title in the address should be placed on the second line and should be separated from the company name by a comma. If this placement of a title would make the second line disproportionately long, the title may be placed on the first line and separated from the individual's name by a comma.

Mr. Stanley C. Longstaff Manager, Morse & Company Ann Arbor, Michigan Dear Sir (P) Because of the recent scarcity of short-term securities, it has been difficult for many investors to diversify their holdings properly. (P) We have an attractive issue of Jertz Utilities that would afford you the opportunity of adding a high-grade short-term investment to your account on an excellent yield basis, and also of further diversifying your account as to type of industry. (P) We have studied your bondholdings, and we now recommend these 6½% sinking-fund gold notes to you as offering a splendid yield and quite exceptional investment safety. Yours truly SHIELDS & COMPANY John E. Lane Manager (*Strokes, 700; words, 93.*)

EXERCISE 50 *14 minutes*

Directions. Type Style Letters Nos. 1 and 2, pages 87 and 93. Use the directions for Exercise 41, page 86, when typing Style Letter No. 1; use the directions for Exercise 47 when typing Style Letter No. 2.

The typewriter is an expensive machine. When it is properly cared for,   72

it will aid you in your growth in typewriting skill. When dust and dirt are   149

allowed to get on the parts of the typewriter, they will cause trouble.   222

The carriage rods should be kept free from gummed matter. You may rub   293

the rods with an oiled cloth, but too much oil may cause as much injury as   368

too little oil and you may not realize how little oil will be required. Use an   448

oiled cloth to clean the dust from the surface and from the parts of the   521

typewriter. Dust your machine every day.   564

There can be no justification for failure to keep the typewriter clean. To   640

clean the type, brush it carefully with a stiff brush. Use a forward and back-   718

ward motion, from left to right. If certain letters are clogged, use a sharp   796

splinter to remove the caked dirt. Benzene should be used cautiously, if at   873

all. If it is used, place a blotter under all the type bars so that the excess   953

fluid will be absorbed. There are special preparations for cleaning the type.   1033

These give quite good service. Do not wait to be told to clean the type of   1109

your machine. Brush the type each day with a stiff, dry brush and use the   1184

cleaning fluid when the type gets clogged.   1228

If the carriage sticks or slows up at the right margin, the rods may be dry   1304

or gummed with dust. In this case a drop or two of oil will take care of the   1382

difficulty. If the carriage sticks at the left margin, the throw may be too hard   1464

or you may not be giving equal power to the throws. You may not realize   1537

just how much power you use in the throw. When something is wrong with   1609

your typewriter, try to make the adjustment. You are not expected to know   1684

how to make all repairs, but you can take care of minor troubles without help.   1764

The right care of the typewriter will reduce machine problems a great deal.   1841

Keep your typewriter covered when it is not in use.   1892

SHIELDS & COMPANY

INCORPORATED

INVESTMENT SECURITIES

DETROIT, MICHIGAN

April 2, 194-

STROKES

14

Mr. Charles J. Webster   37
2831 Beechwood Avenue   59
Detroit, Michigan   77

Dear Sir   86

    We know you are interested in having   123
all surplus funds work for you. We, how-   163
ever, realize that you want to be assured   205
of the safety and of the soundness of an   246
investment.   259

    The enclosed folder will interest   293
you, we are sure, as it will help to solve   336
this problem of finding a safe investment   378
for your money. If there is any feature   419
concerning this investment that you wish   460
to have explained, inquire by letter or   500
telephone and the information will be sent   543
to you without delay.   566

      Yours truly   578

    SHIELDS & COMPANY   596

John E. Lane
      John E. Lane   609
      Manager   617

mos   621

Enclosure   630

*When the typed signature is used, the dictator's
initials may be omitted from the reference notation.*

(*Strokes, 630; words, 86.*)

**Style Letter No. 2 — Single-Spaced Indented Form with Open Punctuation and the
Dictator's Name Typed with the Official Title**

UNIT VII — *THE IMPROVEMENT OF STROKING SKILL*

BUDGET VIII

The purpose of the work of this budget is to increase your typing power through speeding up your stroking rate and then improving your control. If you will work with right technique and right work habits, the improvement will necessarily follow. Practice alone is not enough; you must practice in the right way and with the right mind-set. How you feel about this work is one of the major determinants of the degree of success you achieve.

LESSON 76

RECONSTRUCTION PRACTICE   *5 minutes*

Directions. 1. Use a 70-space line; single spacing.

2. Type the sentence ten times. Give special attention to the continuity of stroking. Your writing rate will be high enough if you will keep the carriage moving continuously and rhythmically. Start typing the sentence immediately after the carriage is returned. One student found he was wasting five seconds after each carriage throw. The elimination of this waste of time increased his stroking rate considerably. HOLD YOUR EYES ON THE COPY.

STROKES

It is the way you do your work that makes you grow in power to do more.   71

TECHNIQUE PRACTICE 76   *8 minutes*

Directions. 1. Use a 70-space line; single spacing.

2. Type each sentence for a minute.

Note to Instructor: Call the throw each twelve seconds. This will give a stroking rate of approximately 70 words a minute. If a student cannot reach this stroking rate on the minute timings, check to see where his waste of time occurs.

STROKES

The boy did not get the old net and the new rod for our use for the day.   72

They said that they felt they must move that show club from your land.   70

Your girl will read that next long page from this fine book they have.   70

This is the kind of work I like to do and the work I think I do well.   69

No one is so futile as he who will not or cannot control his thoughts.   70

EXERCISE 98   *25 minutes*

Directions. 1. Use a 70-space line; double spacing. Set the machine for a 5-space paragraph indention.

2. Type the exercise for a five-minute writing. Check your gross writing rate.

3. Type the exercise for ten minutes. Check your writing rate and compare it with the gross writing rate on your five-minute writing. You will need this information in the next lesson.

BUDGET II
LESSON 46
RECONSTRUCTION PRACTICE

The * is used in footnotes. Use the hyphen (-) in compounds.

The ¢ and @ symbols are used most often in market quotations.

My brother was born May 16, 1911, at 16 East Rochelle Street.

FOR RENT: A 4-room apartment, 100 Farlan Street, $45 a month.

TECHNIQUE PRACTICE 46
5 minutes

Directions. Use a 70-space line; single spacing. Type each sentence twice. Double-space after the second typing of each sentence.

Each sentence illustrates a definite principle for expressing numbers. Study the following explanations in order that you will know how to express numbers when it is necessary for you to do so.

Sentence 1. After the name of a month, use figures to express the day. Note, too, the use of the comma in a series.

Sentence 2. Use *d, st,* or *th* when the day of the month stands alone or when it precedes the month. In expressing even sums of money, type without a decimal and ciphers.

Sentence 3. Express dimensions in figures and spell *by* in full. (Use the symbol *x* for *by* when typing specifications, but do not use it in business letters or ordinary reports.)

Sentence 4. When one number in a sentence immediately follows another, it is better to express the larger number in figures and to spell the smaller in full.

Sentence 5. At the beginning of a sentence, spell numbers in full, even when figures are used later in the sentence.

	STROKES
Your letters of April 7, 9, and 13 were answered in full on April 28.	69
In his letter of the 26th of May, he enclosed this check for $1,450.	68
A six-page pamphlet, 5½ by 8 inches, was sent to Portsmouth University.	71
We shall need 48 three-cent stamps and 36 two-cent stamped envelopes.	69
One hundred sixty-seven men reported their yearly earnings at $750.	67

FIVE-MINUTE TIMED WRITING
5 minutes for typing
3 minutes for checking

Directions. Use a 70-space line; double spacing. Set a tabulator stop for a five-space indention.

All letters of the alphabet are used in each paragraph. The syllable intensity for each paragraph is 1.25.

	STROKES
Each letter that you mail goes out to take your place as a message bearer. If	79
you were to send a man to take your place in a conference with others, would	156
you send one who was not well groomed? Of course not, for you realize that	232
good manners in dress and in speech are assets in a conference. You should	308
be just as eager, too, to have only the best work in typing go out to represent	388
the quality of the work you do. If you write a personal letter, you must think	468
of the style of expression as well as of the right form for the letter. If you	548

[94]

Stubbs gauge ⅜-inch copper tubing, ½-inch gas connection, and 1-inch water connection. (P) The cost of the heater is $21, f.o.b. Buffalo. *(Strokes, 781; words, 127.)*

EXERCISE 96 *16 minutes*

Directions. 1. You are to use the letter in Exercise 95 as the basis for this exercise. Address the letter and envelope to Mrs. John M. Jacobsen who lives at 417 E. 22d Street in Rochester, New York.

2. Type the letter with a carbon and make the following changes as you type:

a. Instead of typing the name of the heater in capitals, type it in capitals and small letters and underscore it.

b. Change the page number in the first paragraph from 25 to 19.

3. The cost of the heater given in the last paragraph is to be changed to $35.

LESSON 75

RECONSTRUCTION PRACTICE *5 minutes*

Directions. 1. Use a 70-space line; double spacing.

2. Type each word as many times as you feel you can profit from the immediate repetition. Note the correct spelling as you type. You can teach your fingers to spell as you teach them to type more rapidly and accurately.

mutually	month's	cycles	meters
profitable	radios	alternating	kilocycles
relationship	unusual	current	background
remittance	veneers	illuminated	electric

TECHNIQUE PRACTICE 75 *8 minutes*

Directions. 1. Use a 70-space line; double spacing.

2. Type each sentence for one minute. Try to bring the rate of stroking on the alphabetic sentences to the same level as the rate on sentences 2 and 4.

	STROKES
The boy quickly recognized that jumping was very good exercise for him.	71
You are always to do the finest work that it is possible for you to do.	71
Vim, pluck, zeal, and a wish to excel quickly brought joy to Frederick.	71
There is no better time than right now for you to show what you can do.	71
A dozen grave lawyers objected to the question of the remarkable expert.	72

EXERCISE 97 *24 minutes*

Directions. 1. It is important that you learn to type letters rapidly and accurately and to address envelopes without waste of time.

2. Type Style Letters No. 6, page 125, and No. 7, page 130, with carbon copy and address an envelope for each letter. You should be able to complete each letter and its envelope in ten minutes.

Machine adjustments, 2 mins. for each letter	4
Typing each letter and envelope, 10 mins. each	20

SPEED EMPHASIS *6 minutes*

Use the paragraph given for Technique Practice 73, page 144. Type the first one-minute writing at the rate of 50 words; type the second one-minute writing at the rate of 60 words; and type the third writing at the rate of 65 to 70 words.

				STROKES
110	115	120	125	

are the typist for another, the dictator will say what is to be in the letter, but   631

you must look after the details of expression and the form of the letter.   706

In writing your own letters or those of others, be sure that words are spelled   783

and capitalized correctly and that each sentence has the right punctuation.   860

All of this work must be done quickly, too. You will want to type letters at   938

exactly the rate you type paragraphs. You do not have any more time to   1010

type at a slow rate than a businessman has to wait for a slow worker. Fast   1086

typing is not just the rapid stroking of the keys; it is the even and constant   1165

stroking of the keys. You can do more work in the same time if you get rid   1241

of waste motions and learn to keep the carriage moving. Learn this when   1314

you are typing a timed test, a business letter, or a personal note. It is a good   1396

technique to set up, for it can be made a habit that will lead to typing   1469

power.   1475

EXERCISE 51   *14 minutes*

Directions. Type Style Letter No. 3, page 96, twice. Use the current date, and your initials in the reference notation. The dictator's initials are not used in the reference notation.

You will observe that the block form of letter (which must be typed with single spacing) and open punctuation are used. Type the dictator's name in the position for the official title, four spaces below the complimentary close.

SPEED EMPHASIS   *12 minutes*

Directions. 1. Type the paragraphs of the five-minute timed writing for three minutes. Determine your rate.

2. Type Style Letter No. 3 for three minutes. Determine your rate and contrast your letter-typing rate with your straight-copy rate.

3. Retype the letter for three minutes to see if you can bring this rate nearer to the straight-copy rate.

CHECK, AND DOUBLE CHECK, PLEASE!

Most workers can easily identify the big errors that are made in typed work, but it takes the seeing eye and the knowing mind to detect the small errors that creep in when work must be rushed through. Little errors often make work unmailable—and the office standard for business letters is mailability.

The following examples of typed work are taken from the letters of beginning office typ-

ists. Can you tell what is wrong with the examples? If time permits, type the material in correct form; if this is not possible, study the examples and know the correct forms so that you can avoid similar errors in your own work.

1. March 16th, 1941
2. Mr. Frances Sones
3. Mrs. Mark C. Black
   Colorado Springs,
   Colorado
   Dear Mrs. Blake
4. Miss Jesse Morrow,
   #409 Market St.
   Toledo, Ohio.
5. My Dear Miss Morrowe:
6. Your account for $50.00 is over-due.
7. Let this informel letter persuaded you
8. Your car is equiped for service now.
9. Yours Very truly
10. Leonard S McCausland,
    Manager

[95]

Manufacturers Distributing Company
567 Main Street
SYRACUSE, - - - - - - NEW YORK

February 1, 194-

Mr. Paul F. Ziegler   *126th*   *sp. in full*
5439 W. ~~One Hundred and Twenty-sixth~~ St.
Buffalo, N. Y   *sp. in full*

Dear Sir:

ed   *of last month*

In response to your request of the 30th, we
~~are~~ mailing you today our latest catalogue of mod~~ern~~
~~ern~~ plumbing and heating fixtures. As you look
through our catalogue, please keep in mind the fact
that we can furnish in colors any of the enamelware
shown. Any of the sinks ~~which we~~ illustrated can be   *in our catalogue*
furnished with stainless enamel, also. We wish to
call your special attention to illustration No. 26   *cap*
on page 9 showing one of the newest models of sinks
for a butler's pantry. This particular sink has ma~~ny~~   *ny*
~~ny~~ conveniences not to be found in any other sink   *at a similar price*
on the market. ~~The price is remarkably low, and~~
~~the cost of installing it is quite reasonable, too.~~

at your convenience

One of our salesmen will be glad to call on   *Mr. M. R. Zeitman,*
you and to make an estimate of the cost of your plumbing
and heating fixture needs. Our follow-up service
after the installation of a heating plant will help   *described on page 27 of our catalogue,*
in the ~~all~~ very important problem of what fuel to buy
and how to burn the fuel in order to get the maximum
heat at a minimum cost.

Yours Very Truly,   *l.c.*

l.c.   *all caps* → Manufacturers Distributing Co. *sp. out*

sp. out   Chas. A. Bruce, SALES MANAGER   *l.c.   l.c.*

dep

(Strokes, 1178, words, 188.)

JOHN BAXTER MORGAN

STROKES

November 15, 194-

18

Zueger Transfer Company 42
4801 Market Street 61
Cambridge, Ohio 77

Gentlemen 87

I should like to equip one of your trucks 129
with a 35 by 5 inch 8-ply cord tire for 169
a year's tryout. I want you to prove to 210
your own satisfaction that this tire will 252
give the extraordinary service claimed 291
for it. 300

If you will send one of your trucks to the 343
Longstaff Street entrance to the garage, 384
I shall have the tire mounted without cost 427
to you. 436

All tires sold by this garage are fully 476
guaranteed to give superior service. 514

Yours truly 526

John Baxter Morgan

John Baxter Morgan 545

mos 548

(Strokes, 548; words, 83.)

Style Letter No. 3 — Block Form of Letter with Open Punctuation and the
Dictator's Name Typed Four Spaces below the Complimentary Close

EXERCISE 94 *22 minutes*

Directions. Type the letter on page 146, making all the changes indicated. Use open punctuation. Make a carbon copy and address an envelope.

If the name of a street is a number above one hundred, use figures. Authorities agree that figures should be used when the name of a street is a number above one hundred, but they do not agree about names that are numbers below one hundred. Some place *ten* as the limit for writing the name in full; others, *twelve*; still others, *one hundred*.

SPEED EMPHASIS *8 minutes*

Use the paragraph given for the Technique Practice 73. Select a fifteen-second goal that is at least five words faster than you have been typing on minute writings; then when you have been able to write at this new rate, type at the same rate for thirty seconds; then type at the same rate for a minute. After you have pushed yourself to the new minute writing rate, type for a minute at a rate that is approximately five words slower so that you can pay attention to the letter sequences and type without error.

LESSON 74

RECONSTRUCTION PRACTICE *4 minutes*

Directions. Type each line of Technique Practice 72 once.

TECHNIQUE PRACTICE 74 *8 minutes*

Directions. 1. Use a 70-space line; double spacing.
2. Type each sentence once; then check the five sentences and retype those in which errors have been made.

Sentence 1.   Use the apostrophe to indicate contractions.
Sentence 2.   Note the difference between the possessive pronoun and the contraction.
Sentence 3.   The possessive form of *it* is *its*; the contraction of *it is* is *it's*.
Sentence 4.   *Principal* means chief; *principle*, rule or law.
Sentence 5.   *Stationery* means writing material; *stationary* means fixed, not movable.

	STROKES
Here's our paper to be read and O. K.'d when you're through with yours.	71
Theirs is a great work, and there's no chance that they will lose by it.	72
This doesn't give its complete meaning, but it's the best I can do now.	71
The title of the principal speaker's address is, "Principles of Law."	69
Business letters should be written on the best stationery obtainable.	69

EXERCISE 95 *9 minutes*

Directions. 1. Type this problem letter in the block form, with one carbon.
2. Use open punctuation.
3. Address an envelope. If your letter is mailable, sign the dictator's name with pen and ink and add your initials below the signature to show that you have signed for the dictator; then fold the letter and insert it into the envelope.

Add appropriate personal title, salutation, and closing lines. Mr. Charles A. Bruce dictated the letter and you will use the same closing form as you have used in the other letters of this budget.

If your typewriter does not have all the fractions used in a letter, employ the diagonal in writing all of them in order that uniformity may be maintained.

David 1 warner 593 lapsley drive niagara

falls newyork After studying the size and arrangement of your house, we recommend the TRIPLE - COPPER - COIL TANK WATER HEATER shown on page 25 of our catalogue, a copy of which was sent to you last week. (P) Our TRIPLE-COP-PER-COIL TANK WATER HEATER is made of a cast-iron jacket in two parts. The door half of the jacket is supported on hinges and fastens with a latch. This gives easy access to the inside of the heater. This heater, which may be made with a regulator, has $36\frac{2}{3}$ feet of No. 20

LESSON 47

RECONSTRUCTION PRACTICE

5 minutes

Directions. Use the sentences of Technique Practice 46.

TECHNIQUE PRACTICE 47

6 minutes

Directions. Use a 70-space line; single spacing. Type each sentence twice.

The sentences in this technique practice emphasize the control of figures and of special characters. Some basic principles for the expression of numbers are taught. Study these principles carefully.

Express in figures, not in words:

1. Distance, except a fraction of a mile. (Sentence 1.)
2. Measures. (Sentence 2.)
3. Dimensions and weights. (Sentence 3.)
   Do not separate by a comma the related parts of dimensions, weights, or measures; as, "8 feet 4 inches."

4. Diagonal. (Sentence 4.)
   If you use the diagonal for one fraction in a letter, use it for every other fraction in that letter.
5. Market quotations. (Sentence 5.)
   The plural of letters and figures is usually expressed by adding *'s*. In market quotations, however, it is permissible to form the plural of figures by adding merely *s*.
   Fractions for which there are no special keys should be typed with the diagonal as the mark of division. One space should be left between the whole number and the fraction.

	STROKES
It is approximately 20 to 25 miles from here to the Aliquippa plant.	68
The 9 gallons and 3 quarts of oil are to be used in the paint mixture.	70
This large box is 8 feet 4 inches wide and weighs 110 to 115 pounds.	68
Always use the diagonal (/) when typing fractions not on the keyboard.	70
I bought North Atlantic 4s at 65⅞ and sold them today for 77⅛.	68

EXERCISE 52 *15 minutes*

Directions. Type the following letter in the block form used in Style Letter No. 3 on page 96. Use open punctuation. Type the official title of Mr. Warner on the second line of the inside address, and separate the title from the company name by a comma. Type the dictator's name in the position for the official title.

In underscoring the name "Quick-Wax," underscore the hyphen as it is part of the name.

Mr. Robert M. Warner Manager, Warner Garage Massillon, Ohio Dear Sir (P) You can use *Quick-Wax* polish to bring back the lost luster and beauty of the original factory finish on your car. This polish removes all dullness and film, and it is equally effective on enamel and lacquer. (P) I can let you have *Quick-Wax* polish in 13-ounce cans at 65 cents a can if you order a dozen or more cans. This is a very low price on this high-grade polish. (P) This letter is written in answer to your card of the 16th. Yours truly John Baxter Morgan *(Strokes, 550; words, 87.)*

EXERCISE 53 *14 minutes*

Directions. Type the following letter twice in the block form used in Style Letter No. 3 on page 96. Use open punctuation. Type the dictator's name in the position for the official title.

DeLuxe Supply Company 410 Euclid Avenue Cleveland, Ohio Gentlemen (P) I have been handling automobile supplies for a great many years; but because of your merchandising policy, I have never been able to put in a supply of your goods. You do not have a local store in Cambridge, yet I believe that the quality of your goods and the price at which you sell even your best products would attract many buyers in this territory. (P) Would you be interested in letting me carry a trial stock of your goods? My credit rating can be obtained from Dun and Bradstreet. If you wish me to submit a report of the condition of my business, I shall be glad to do so. Yours truly John Baxter Morgan *(Strokes, 705; words, 111.)*

EXERCISE 92

Adjustments 3 min.
Letter 11 min.
Envelope 3 min.

Directions. 1. Type the letter, with carbon, in the block form; open punctuation.

2. Address an envelope. If your letter is mailable, sign the dictator's name with pen and ink and add your initials below the signature to show that you have signed for the dictator; then fold the letter and insert it into the envelope.

In a street address any number except *one* is written in figures.

Mrs. H. E. Obermayer One Marsden Road Tonawanda, New York Dear Madam In your letter of the 9th, you ask us to give you information with regard to the different styles of radiators suitable for heating your house, which is now being remodeled. (P) In the tube type of window radiator, the manufacturers have produced a radiator that gives a maximum amount of surface perfection without sacrificing the slender tube effect. The 14-inch model is especially adaptable to conditions under which window sills require unusually low radiators. (P) Ample air passages are maintained in all tube patterns, from the three-tube to the six- and seven-tube patterns. (P) Mr. J. K. Bridgeport, our radiator specialist, will be glad to call on you at your convenience to check with you the different styles and sizes of radiators. After inspecting your house, Mr. Bridgeport will make up a drawing based on his analysis. Yours very truly MANUFACTURERS DISTRIBUTING CO. Charles A. Bruce, Sales Manager *(Strokes, 1002; words, 138.)*

EXERCISE 93

14 minutes

Directions. 1. Type Exercise 92 in the form directed but do not make a carbon of the letter. Increase your typing rate.

2. Address an envelope and place the letter under the flap, but do not sign or fold the letter.

LESSON 73

RECONSTRUCTION PRACTICE

8 minutes

Directions. 1. Use a 70-space line; double spacing.
2. Type each sentence once. Retype those sentences in which errors have been made.

Sentence 2. Express page numbers in figures. Use Roman numerals to express major divisions.
Sentence 3. Use the abbreviation *No.* or the symbol # with a figure, never the word *number*.

	STROKES
Your book has 39 illustrations of numbers—21 of Arabic and 18 Roman.	69
The reference will be found on page 295 of Vol. VI, Section 47, I know.	71
The number of his references is not known. This report must be No. 27.	71

TECHNIQUE PRACTICE 73

5 minutes

Directions. 1. Use a 70-space line; double spacing.
2. Type the first one-minute writing at the rate of 40 words; type the second one-minute writing at the rate of 50 words; and type the third writing at the rate of 55 to 60 words.

	STROKES
If you can find your own errors you can be of real worth in almost any	71
business office. Be alert to the need for knowing when your work is right or	149
wrong. It does not require much intelligence or skill to copy a piece of work	228
that is correctly spaced, spelled, and punctuated. The real test of your ability	310
to do good office work will be found in your production ability when typing	386
problem material.	403

LESSON 48

RECONSTRUCTION PRACTICE
4 minutes

Directions. 1. Type Technique Practice 47 once.
2. Select for repetition the lines that seem to offer the practice you most need.

TECHNIQUE PRACTICE 48
5 minutes

Directions. Use a 70-space line; double spacing. Type each sentence once; then select for repetition the lines that seem to offer the practice you most need.

	STROKES
He studied abroad 3 years 8 months and 15 days at a cost of $6,000.	67
The package is 2 feet by 4 feet and will weigh from 250 to 300 pounds.	70
The $125 premium on Policy No. 168594 has been recorded on page 1370.	69
The law passed on June 3, 1897, is given in Vol. V, Sec. 2, page 12.	68
Robert works at 807 Eighth Street and rooms at 539 S. 146th Avenue.	67

EXERCISE 54 *17 minutes*

Directions. Type Style Letter No. 4 as it is given on page 99, except for the date and the reference initials. Use the current date and your initials. Use close punctuation.

In this modification of the block style, all lines of the inside address, the salutation, the body of the letter, and the reference initials are begun at the left margin. The closing lines are indented to the position for the complimentary close and blocked. Note that when the dictator's name is typed, it is unnecessary to include his initials in the reference notation.

EXERCISE 55 *14 minutes*

Directions. Type the following letter in the modified block form used in Style Letter No. 4 on page 99. Use close punctuation.

Mr. Ralph J. Brockton, R. D. 5, Canton, Ohio. Dear Mr. Brockton: (P) You have given me your tire business during the past three years, and I want you to know I fully appreciate your continued patronage. (P) During the cold weather, when the ground is covered with snow and ice, you will need tires that grip the road. You cannot afford to gamble on smooth tires when you need all the road-gripping and nonskid qualities that a good new tire will give you. (P) Let me inspect your tires and give you an estimate on their possible further service. If you do not need new tires, you will incur no expense in letting me check your present ones for you. Just be sure that your car is equipped for safe winter driving. Yours very truly, John Baxter Morgan *(Strokes, 764; words, 118.)*

LESSON 49

RECONSTRUCTION PRACTICE
4 minutes

Directions. Type each sentence once; then select for repetition the sentences that seem to offer the practice you most need.

"C. O. D." may be written with capitals; "f.o.b.," with small letters.

She rooms and boards at the Y. W. C. A. (This may be written "YWCA.")

Albert sailed to Spain at eleven o'clock on Friday, February 26.

Harry, Mack, and James visited Mr. Marshall in New York last January.

We take all our modern machines as a matter of course. A businessman 1861

dictates a letter and does not expect to think of it again until he signs it. His 1944

stenographer quietly and deftly types it and gets it ready for mailing. It 2020

whizzes down the mail chute, is handled expertly by the Post Office Depart- 2094

ment, is sent by train or airplane, and is delivered at the other end of the 2171

line just as expertly. Yes, we have come a long way from the runner who 2244

took a message by word of mouth; and too often we fail to wonder at the 2316

inventions that make our offices beehives of business. We take things as a 2392

matter of course, and most of us do not know the beginnings of the machines 2468

that make our work easy. Many men have given much thought and long hours 2542

of hard work to perfecting what we use so casually. 2593

EXERCISE 91   *10 minutes*

Directions. 1. Type the letter in the block form, similar to Style Letter No. 3, page 96.

2. Use open punctuation.

3. Make a carbon copy and address an envelope for the letter. Place the letter and the carbon copy under the flap of the envelope. Proofread the letter carefully. If it is mailable, sign the dictator's name with pen and ink and add your initials just below the signature to show that you have signed for the dictator; then fold the letter and insert it into the envelope.

Mr. George W. Schullman 573 Dixon Street Buffalo, New York Dear Sir We have checked your requirements carefully, and we think our 20 by 24 inch porcelain-enameled iron, square-apron lavatory will meet your needs. Please look at the illustration on page 19 of our catalogue, a copy of which we are sending to you in a separate package. (P) The lavatory illustrated on page 19 is furnished complete with our No. 928 solid-china cross-handle unit with china waste knob and nickel-plated raised nozzle. The lavatory with all fittings can be furnished for $56.75. This is a price that we think you cannot duplicate elsewhere in Buffalo. (P) If you place your order with us, we can make delivery very soon. Dial 47-593 if you are in a special hurry for delivery, and we shall rush your order. Yours very truly MANUFACTURERS DISTRIBUTING CO. Charles A. Bruce, Sales Manager *(Strokes, 884; words, 139.)*

LESSON 72   *4 minutes*

RECONSTRUCTION PRACTICE: Type each line of Technique Practice 71 twice.

TECHNIQUE PRACTICE 72   *8 minutes*

Directions. 1. Use a 70-space line; double spacing; type each sentence for one minute.

2. Goal: Errorless writings, with a minimum gross stroking rate of 50 words a minute.

	STROKES
From Life's assortment of habits, you must select only the good ones.	69
"Each good thought or action moves the dark world nearer to the sun."	69
So live that your afterself—the man you want to be—may be realized.	69
Ancient Babylon and the proud Roman Empire fell from love of luxury.	68
Thought is the property of those only who can entertain it.—Emerson.	69

JOHN BAXTER MORGAN

AUTOMOBILE SUPPLIES
CAMBRIDGE • OHIO

November 20, 194-.   20

Howell & Lang Paint Company,   49
361 Hobart Avenue,   68
Cincinnati, Ohio.   87

Gentlemen: 99

Please quote me your lowest price on your   141
painting and refinishing outfit No. 4703,   183
illustrated and described on page 572 of   224
your catalogue.   241

The outfit I need must have black paint,   282
top dressing, and at least a half pint of   324
running gear paint. I shall also require   366
steel wool and a brush for use in applying   409
the paint. I assume that your complete   449
outfit includes all supplies necessary   488
for a complete refinishing job.   521

Please quote in dozen lots and also on a   562
single outfit.   578

              Yours very truly,   596

              John Baxter Morgan
              John Baxter Morgan
                                                                     615
mos
                                                                     618

(Strokes, 618; words, 89.)

Style Letter No. 4 — Modification of the Block Form with the Closing Lines
Blocked at the Complimentary Close Position

[99]

TIMED WRITING

Directions. 1. Use a 70-space line; double spacing.

2. Set the typewriter for a 5-space paragraph indention.

3. Use the paragraphs for two 5-minute writings or for one 10-minute writing. Check the writing and figure gross and net words per minute.

	STROKES
Before writing was in use, messages were sent from place to place by	69
runners. Just how accurate these runners were, we do not know. The civili-	144
zations of long ago were quick to make use of writing when it evolved. No	219
doubt men found it a more exact means of communication than by the word	291
of mouth of a runner. For four thousand years the world's early letters were	369
"filed but not found." That must be some kind of record that can be equaled	446
by not more than a few of the file clerks employed in business now. At last,	523
in the land of Egypt and of Babylonia, bricks were uncovered on which	593
letters had been written. Some of these bricks have now been deciphered,	668
and the date of the beginning of the art of writing letters has been pushed	744
back to 2000 B. C.	764
It is queer that the art of letter writing has not changed much since the	838
time when letters were written on bricks. In the early times there were let-	914
ters that begged to acknowledge receipt and letters that thanked in advance,	991
just as there are today; for some men continue to use the old meaningless	1065
phrases in spite of all that can be said against such trite ways of expressing	1144
themselves. Despite all the changes that have come during the progress of	1219
mankind, it is said human nature has changed but little. Men are apt to	1293
follow in the ways of those who have gone before, and few dare to move out	1367
of the zone of action that has bounded the others. Still, there has been one	1445
great change in the writing of letters. The typewriter has speeded up letter	1523
production and added to the ease with which letters may be written, read,	1597
and filed. Think what would happen in business now if for one week not a	1671
typewriter could be used. Not many letters would be ready for the five	1743
o'clock mail, and business would be paralyzed.	1789

Directions. Type Technique Practice 48, page 98.

CARBON COPIES *2 minutes*

Records must be kept of communications in business. Carbon copies of all outgoing letters are therefore made. Carbon paper is used to make these copies.

Place the carbon paper, with the glossy side down, on a sheet of plain paper. (Second sheets of thin yellow paper are frequently used for carbon copies.) The letterhead paper is then laid on the carbon paper, and all the sheets are inserted into the typewriter so that the face of the letterhead is toward the typist. If you are using plain paper instead of a letterhead, check the insertion to see that the carbon paper is placed correctly. The dull surface of the carbon sheet will be toward you when the sheets are in the proper position for typing.

Handle the carbon sheets with care. Unsightly streaks .or smeared places on carbon copies indicate carelessness on the part of a typist. You cannot afford to permit yourself to neglect the quality of your work. Carbon copies of letters are kept in office files, and they thus become a permanent record of the quality of a stenographer's work.

You will not be asked to make carbon copies of all the letters to be typed in this budget, but you must learn how to use carbon paper effectively.

EXERCISE 56 *15 minutes*

Directions. Type the following letter twice in the modified block form used in Style Letter No. 4 on page 99. Use close punctuation. Make a carbon copy.

Mr. Roy T. Jackson, Box 415, Cadiz, Ohio. Dear Sir: (P) I do not now carry in stock the DeLuxe valve about which you inquire in your letter of the 12th. I hope to have the sales rights for this kind of automobile supplies, but final arrangements have not yet been made. (P) Have you tried a

UNION superpowered battery? I can guarantee this battery for three years' service. I have found that the installation of a UNION gives freedom from trouble and unusual expense. If you will tell me the make of car you are driving, I can quote you a low price for the battery of "longer life and more power." I am sure you will be pleased with the service you get from the UNION. Yours very truly, John Baxter Morgan (*Strokes, 725; words, 116.*)

EXERCISE 57 *10 minutes*

Directions. Type the following letter in the modified block form used in Style Letter No. 4 on page 99. Use open punctuation. Make a carbon copy.

Texark Oil Company 1372-1380 Ridgeway Street Cleveland, Ohio Gentlemen (P) I have been selling Texark motor oil for several months now, and I have had some complaints that the oil does not flow freely in cold weather. You have advertised that extra filtrations make your oil free from the gummy tar that causes faulty valve action, sticky piston rings, and excessive carbon. (P) It may be that the exact grade of oil for best performance in the particular cars that have been using your oil has not been determined. Perhaps you have a chart that shows just what grade of oil should be used in each make of car. If you have, please send me a copy of the chart at once. (P) Could you send a man to Cambridge to inspect some of the cars in which Texark oil has been used? I want to be certain that the trouble is not in the oil I have been getting. Yours very truly John Baxter Morgan (*Strokes, 895; words, 148.*)

with *Wear-Long* paint in our twenty years' business experience. (P) You know that linseed oil is the life of paint. The oil holds the pigment together and binds it to the surface. The formular for *Wear-Long* paint calls for 50 per cent pure lead ground in the linseed oil, combined with 50 per cent zinc. This combination gives a high-grade paint that has always been thoroughly satisfactory for painting jobs. (P) I wish you would make a personal investigation of this complaint. Try to get some of the leftover paint so that an analyses can be made of it. If you received a shipment of inferior paint, an adjustment will be made without delay. It is the policy of this company to make a refund or a substitute shipment whenever any of our paints, varnishes, enamels, or lacquers have proved unsatisfactory. very truly yours, harry m hill sales manager *(Strokes, 1214; words, 188.)*

EXERCISE 90 *14 minutes*

Directions. Retype Exercise 89 after you have checked your corrections and are certain that you have used the correct form of punctuation for the inside address (mixed punctuation), have made the correction in spelling the name *Burns,* and have correctly spelled *formula* and *analysis.* Type from the problem form in the textbook and not from your typed work. Pay attention to what you are typing so that you will establish the habit of typing meaning and not merely words.

BUDGET VII

LESSON 71

RECONSTRUCTION PRACTICE *5 minutes*

Directions. 1. Use a 70-space line; double spacing.
2. Type each word as many times as you feel you can profit from the immediate repetition. Note the correct spelling of the words as you type. This is a good way to speed up your fingering and at the same time teach your fingers to spell.

illustration	nozzle	civilizations	paralyzed
radiator	Buffalo	accurate	begged
sacrificing	quantities	communication	airplane
recommend	population	equaled	casually
arrangement	favorite	acknowledge	receipt

TECHNIQUE PRACTICE 71 *7 minutes*

Directions. 1. Use a 70-space line; double spacing.
2. Type each sentence once; then check for accuracy and for understanding of the principles illustrated. Retype the sentences in which errors are made. Goal: Each line without error and an extra line typed accurately for each error made.

	STROKES
I said, "He will borrow $5,000 from my wife's brother for the store."	69
Mr. Lane sold quantities of "Klean-Quick" to New Zealand's population.	70
On Wednesday, September 16, 1936, Robert reported for the fall term.	68
Ronald's father edited the *New England Gazette,* the farmers' favorite.	70
The Secretary of the Interior spoke to the Isleta Indians in Spanish.	69

DETERMINING YOUR NET WORDS PER MINUTE

In timed writings you may determine your net words per minute as follows: Count the total strokes written; divide by 5 to get gross words; deduct 10 words for each error (or whatever penalty your teacher establishes for your timed writings) to get the net words; divide net words by time to determine net words per minute.

Example: gross strokes 1367 divided by 5 equals 273, minus 30 (3 errors times 10) equals 243; divided by 10, equals 24 net words per minute.

LESSON 50

RECONSTRUCTION PRACTICE

4 minutes

Directions. Type each line once; then select for repetition the lines that offer practice on reaches that seem awkward for you.

fix mix six box fox wax cap car cad cup cut ace fob rob tub fib rib fig

zeal zone quiz next quit hazy lazy maze hump jump card pump dear mill

stump bride steel broke stone brick steam brook swell swear swore swamp

expect mainly exceed mighty expert ninety expose highly export richly

TECHNIQUE PRACTICE 50

5 minutes

Directions. 1. Use a 70-space line; single spacing.
2. Type each line for one minute.

	STROKES
The sum of 27 and 31 and 40 and 39 and 58 and 61 and 20 and 56 is what?	70
The stenographer needs 250 two-cent and 136 three-cent stamps at once.	69
Have you been able to find Edward Ryan's article, "Flying the Andes"?	68
The bond is for $1,000; it is a Marks & Hall 1956 (Series 2-B), isn't it?	73
Joe said that he had packed my sledge with five boxes of frozen quail.	70

EXERCISE 58

33 minutes

Directions. 1. You are to type with carbon copies each of the four style letters practiced in the preceding lessons.
2. You are to have exactly thirty minutes for typing this assignment. As soon as you have made the machine adjustments, wait for the signal to start before beginning to type. If you complete the four letters before time is called, retype as much of Style Letter No. 4 as possible, using the back of the letterhead. Under no circumstances are you to start over after beginning a letter. Type as accurately as you can, but work rapidly and without a sense of hurry.

Style Letter No. 1, page 87. Style Letter No. 3, page 96.
Style Letter No. 2, page 93. Style Letter No. 4, page 99.

BUDGET III

You have had sufficient practice in typing four letter forms to be able to set up letters from problem situations. In typing the exercises of this budget, you are expected to check the four style letters already typed whenever you need to verify your understanding of points in the setup of the letters; but you should be able to determine the exact placement of the parts of the letter if you have studied letter styles as you have typed the letter exercises.

LESSON 70

RECONSTRUCTION PRACTICE

5 minutes

Directions. Use a 70-space line; double spacing; 5-space indention.

STROKES

If you are making errors in typewriting form, you probably will find that	74
you have not been thorough in the study of the basic principles or that you	150
have been too limited in the application of the principles to typing problems.	230
Do you know how to address an envelope and can you address the envelope	302
in a minimum of time? The office production rate is an average of 120 to 150	380
envelopes an hour. Just how many can you address in an hour? Organize	452
your effort for better production; excel in exacting of yourself expert per-	527
formance in all you do. Know what you are to do—then do it with quiet but	603
quick efficiency.	620

TECHNIQUE PRACTICE 70

7 minutes

Directions. 1. Use a 70-space line; double spacing.

2. Type each sentence once; then check for accuracy. Retype the sentences in which errors are made. Goal: Each line without error and an extra line typed accurately for each error made.

Sentence 1.   Begin a sentence with words—never with figures. If the number cannot be expressed in one or two words, rearrange the sentence to express the number in figures in the body of the sentence.

Sentences 2 and 3.   When two numbers come together, separate the numbers by a comma or, better still, rearrange the sentence.

Sentences 4 and 5.   Write round numbers in words. In spelling out round numbers more than a thousand, use the shorter form "fifteen hundred" and not "one thousand five hundred."

STROKES

Seventy-five words a minute is now considered a good typewriting speed.	71
We have spent $957, $350 of which was used for food for needy refugees.	71
We have spent $957, of which $350 was used for food for needy refugees.	71
More than two thousand students have been graduated from this college.	70
Fifteen hundred, NOT "One thousand five hundred," is the correct form.	70

EXERCISE 89

14 minutes

Directions. 1. Type this problem letter in the modification of the block form shown in Style Letter No. 6, page 125; but block the closing lines as shown in Illustration No. 56.

2. Use mixed punctuation.

3. Type the date to end at the right margin and place the subject of the letter in the position shown in Illustration No. 54.

4. In this problem letter you must correct the errors in punctuating the inside address, in spelling the proper name in the body of the letter, and in the spelling of words in the body of the letter.

Place the title in the inside address on the first line and separate it from the person's name by a comma. This placement of the title is permitted when the second line would be extended too far to the right by writing the title on the second line.

In the body of the letter, note the use of *s'* to indicate the plural possessive form in *years'*.

As this letter is written in the first person ("I"), it is correct to omit the company signature from the closing lines.

```
                    Very truly yours,


                    Harry M. Hill
                    Sales Manager

rfs
```

Illustration No. 56 — Closing Lines Containing the Dictator's Name Typed Four Spaces Below the Complimentary Close and One Space Above the Official Title

Subject: Complaint on *Wear-Long* (P)
Mr. A. O. Burns, President, Painters Supply Company, Bowling Green, Kentucky
Dear Sir: In your letter of the 16th you say that one of your customers has made a complaint about the failure to get a smooth, glossy finish with our paint. I am quite amazed at this complaint, Mr. Burn's, for we have not had this difficulty

LESSON 51

RECONSTRUCTION PRACTICE

5 minutes

Directions. Type each line once; then select for repetition the lines that need further practice in order for you to type them with ease and control.

were only card jump dear mill case pull fast hymn best milk ever hill
swear brave fears imply bread raved lumpy dazed great holly weave fever
He will be here at 8:35 p.m. We sail for the cruise on January 29.
Have you read *Social-Economic Problems*? The article is "Interest at 3%."

TECHNIQUE PRACTICE 51

6 minutes

Directions. Use a 70-space line; double spacing. Type each line once; then select for repetition the sentences that need further practice for you to type them with ease and control.

Drill		STROKES
(p)	Perhaps Phillip will postpone his appearance until April if you persist.	72
(q)	Qualified questioners required the quiz questions to be read quickly.	69
(r)	Reporters frequently remark about the task of rewriting or revising work.	73
(s)	Sensible persons seldom switch their sense of direction without a reason.	73
(t)	Thwarted ambitions and twisted attitudes often stunt one's achievement.	71

EXERCISE 59

9 minutes

Directions. 1. The form in which the letter is to be typed is the same as that of Style Letter No. 2, page 93.

2. Use single spacing and open punctuation.

3. Make a carbon of the letter.

4. Type the letter once.

mr james a warring treasurer, ward company lansing, michigan dear mr warring (P) In this morning's mail, we received from you coupons Nos. 9 and 10 for $27.50 each, due November 1 and May 1, which you have detached from your West Service Company Series B 5½% bonds due November 1, 1956. (P) We are forwarding these coupons for deposit. When the certificate of deposit for the coupons is received by us, it will be held until you call for it. yours truly jackson & company jack e long manager *(Strokes, 512; words, 75.)*

EXERCISE 60

10 minutes

Directions. 1. Type the letter in the single-spaced indented form, similar to Style Letter No. 1, page 87. Use mixed punctuation.

2. Make a carbon of the letter.

3. Type the letter once.

Words that appear in italics are to be underscored when typed.

mr thomas g mcmahon 1356 pointview place detroit, michigan dear sir (P) Coupon bonds of the Arizona Utility 6% issue are ready to be exchanged in New York for the temporary certificates. This exchange will be quickly made for you if you will forward your certificates by *registered mail* directly to our New York office, 34 Wall Street, New York, New York. Use the enclosed forms in sending in these bonds. (P) In order that we may insure your shipment, Form 57-A should be mailed one day in advance of the mailing of the temporary certificates. yours truly michaelson company (Dictated by O. S. Michaelson) credit manager enclosures 2 *(Strokes, 625; words, 87.)*

EXERCISE 61

11 minutes

Directions. If you feel that you can do better work in typing the preceding exercises, retype either or both of the letters without carbons. Submit the better of the two writings for each exercise to your teacher.

If time permits, practice control drills from pages 118 to 120. You must show measurable improvement in the ease and control with which you type your daily lessons.

LESSON 69

RECONSTRUCTION PRACTICE

5 minutes

Directions. Use the reconstruction practice for Lesson 68.

TECHNIQUE PRACTICE 69

7 minutes

Directions. 1. Use a 70-space line; double spacing.

2. Type each sentence five times; or, if your teacher so directs, type each sentence for one minute. Type for control.

	STROKES
No matter how many years you may live, there isn't time for worry.	66
Ever to keep your promise, cost what it may, is to be "true as steel."	70
Thrift has four aspects—earning, saving, investing, and spending.	66
"Eighty per cent of the successful men of this country began poor."	67
Always dream lofty dreams, and as you dream, so shall you become.	65

EXERCISE 88   *15 minutes*

Directions. 1. Type this problem letter in the modification of the block form shown in Style Letter No. 6, page 125; but block the closing lines as shown in Illustration No. 55.

2. Use mixed punctuation.

3. It is the responsibility of a typist to check names, dates, and figures. In this problem letter, there is an inaccuracy in the use of the name, an inconsistency in the expression of numbers, and an inaccuracy in figuring the amount for which the check should be written. Make these corrections as you type the letter.

Mr. Tom M. Hunter R. D. 6 Danville, Indiana Dear Mr. Hunter: We thank you for your order for 2 gallons of dark lead porch floor paint. This paint is being shipped to you today by parcel post. (P) Be sure to mix the paint thoroughly, Mr. Thomas. Pour off the linseed oil and then empty your paint into another container. Use a large wooden paddle and add the linseed oil as you stir. For the first coat you should add an extra quart of linseed oil to a gallon of paint. For the second coat use the paint as it comes from the can. This paint will wear like iron if you take the proper precautions in preparing your floor for painting and if you mix your paint properly. These two items are absolutely necessary in order to get the proper results. If one follows instructions, it is a simple matter to get good results in painting. (P) We appreciate your order, and we hope that you will let us supply the paint, varnish, and enamel you may need. Our terms are 2% 10 days; ~~thirty~~ 30 days net. If you care to take advantage of the discount, send us your check within ten days for $17.41, the cost of 2 gallons of the porch floor paint, which sells at $3.78 a gallon, less 2%. Very truly yours, McCausland-Hill Paint Company (Leslie G. McCausland, Jr.) Vice-President and Treasurer *(Strokes, 1279; words, 219.)*

OPTIONAL PRACTICE   *11 minutes*

Directions. 1. If you have not typed a mailable letter for Exercise 88, retype the letter as directed. Be sure of the *meaning* of what you type and check for the inconsistencies that you are told are in the letter. Copying words without thought of what the words mean will increase your speed of typing but it will not increase your office efficiency.

2. If you do not need to retype Exercise 88, practice the material listed below:

a. Type each sentence of Technique Practice 69 three times *without error*. Keep the carriage moving continuously, but type with a sense of easy control.

b. Turn to Lesson 70, and type the reconstruction paragraph without error.

LESSON 52

RECONSTRUCTION PRACTICE

4 minutes

Directions. Type each line of Technique Practice 51 once; then select for repetition the lines that need further practice in order for you to type them with ease and control.

TECHNIQUE PRACTICE 52

5 minutes

Directions. Use a 70-space line; double spacing. Type each line once; then select for repetition the sentences that need further practice for you to type them with ease and control.

Drill · STROKES

(u) Uncles and aunts must understand hundreds of humorous questions of youth. · 73

(v) Valid voters very vigorously vindicated their views on various vocations. · 73

(w) Words without wisdom seldom win such worth-while rewards as wise work. · 70

(x) Max fixed the six wax dolls but did not expect to be called an expert. · 70

(z) He was puzzled that his zeal and zest did not help him to seize power. · 70

EXERCISE 62

10 minutes

Directions. 1. Type the letter in the block form similar to Style Letter No. 3, page 96. Use open punctuation. Type the dictator's name four spaces below the complimentary close.

2. Make a carbon of the letter.

3. Type the letter once.

If the dictator fails to give the salutation, the complimentary close, or the enclosure notation, the typist must supply this information when typing the letter.

20-64

mr william e heilman national bank building monroe, michigan dear sir (P) "Two New Fields for Bond Investors," an advertisement that quite recently appeared in Detroit papers, is enclosed. These two new fields are made up of the magazine industry and the motion-picture industry. (P) I know that you are interested in bonds that give a representative yield with maximum safety. For this reason I am sending to you the announcement of the bonds, which, in my judgment, offer you an excellent opportunity for a sound investment. (P) If you wish further information concerning the bonds, do not hesitate to call on me. yours very truly thomas crawford marks *(Strokes, 668; words, 89.)*

EXERCISE 63

10 minutes

Directions. Type one copy of the letter with carbon copy in the modified block form, similar to Style Letter No. 4, page 99. Use close punctuation.

17-67

miss emma louise chadwick marchand-ritz towers flint, michigan dear madam (P) In your letter of the 15th, you ask the price of the Jackson Electric and Gas Company First Mortgage $4\frac{1}{2}$s due in 1960, which we have offered for sale. We are today quoting these bonds at $101\frac{1}{2}$ and interest. (P) In view of the company's conservative funded-debt structure and ample coverage of fixed charges, these bonds should prove a satisfactory addition to your list of investments. The price quoted is subject to changes in the market. (P) We shall be glad to place your order for these bonds. They are issued in either $500 or $1,000 denominations. yours very truly michaelson company thomas crawford marks *(Strokes, 708; words, 106.)*

EXERCISE 64

12 minutes

Directions. If time permits and you feel that you can do better work in typing the preceding exercises, retype either or both of the letters without carbons. Submit the better of the two writings of each exercise to your teacher.

```
Subject: Guaranty                    March 19, 194-



J. H. Turner & Company
Hiseville
Kentucky

       Attention Mr. J. H. Turner

Gentlemen:
```

Illustration No. 54 — Placement of the Subject Line on a Letterhead Having a Printed Subject Heading

```
Very truly yours,

McCausland-Hill Paint Company


Vice-President and Treasurer

LGMcC,Jr/rfs
```

Illustration No. 55 — Closing Lines Blocked at the Left Margin

In the body of the letter, the trade name *Wear-Long* is printed in italics. Words that are italicized in type should be underscored when they are typewritten.. In underscoring a word containing a hyphen, underscore the hyphen as it is considered a mark of spelling and not of punctuation.

Subject: Guaranty (P) J. H. Turner & Company Hiseville Kentucky Attention Mr. J. H. Turner Gentlemen: Our salesman, W. E. Conklin, reports that you have most of the paint business in your community and that you are interested in putting in a supply of our *Wear-Long* products. (P) We guarantee our paints, varnishes, lacquers, and enamels to be equal in quality to any others sold at a price of 75 cents to $1.20 a gallon higher than the prices we charge. We guarantee that our products, when properly applied according to the simple directions on each can, cover as much surface, can be applied as easily, look as well, and last as long as any other brand of paint now on the market. A customer who follows our directions but reports to you a dissatisfaction with *Wear-Long* products will have his money refunded upon the return to this office of a signed application stating the nature of the dissatisfaction. (P) We shall be glad to have your business. Your orders will be taken care of promptly. With every shipment a signed guaranty will be sent to you so that you will be protected fully on each item of our merchandise that you sell. Very truly yours, McCausland-Hill Paint Company (Leslie G. McCausland, Jr.) Vice-President and Treasurer *(Strokes, 1234; words, 190.)*

EXERCISE 87   *12 minutes*

Directions. 1. Type this problem letter in the modification of the block form shown in Style Letter No. 6, page 125; but block the closing lines at the left margin as shown in Illustration No. 55.

2. Use mixed punctuation.

3. Type the inside address in correct order and with an appropriate title; add an appropriate salutation and complimentary close; type the closing lines in the same style as the preceding letter.

c m wadsworth franklin kentucky box 105 Your letter of the 12th to the Painters Supply Company, of Bowling Green, has been sent to us with the request that we give the information you desire. (P) We think our *Wear-Long Albaglaze* paint will be durable and satisfactory for the job. *Albaglaze* is an excellent exterior house paint. The unusual whiteness and clarity of the paint will assure satisfaction after you have completed the painting of your house. (P) *Wear-Long Albaglaze* is not furnished in tints. We can supply the white *Albaglaze* in 1-gallon cans at $4.25 a can. One-half gallon cans of this paint are sold at $2.30 a can. (P) Our paints can be ordered through the Painters Supply Company, of Bowling Green, or directly from us. Your local hardware store in Franklin can take care of your order if you prefer to deal with a home-town merchant. Shipment will be made promptly upon receipt of your order. mccausland hill paint company (Leslie G. McCausland, Jr.) vice-president and treasurer *(Strokes, 1025; words, 159.)*

LESSON 53

RECONSTRUCTION PRACTICE   *4 minutes*

Directions. Type each line of Technique Practice 52 once; then retype the lines that you feel will help you to develop good control.

TECHNIQUE PRACTICE 53   *5 minutes*

Directions. Use a 70-space line; double spacing. Type each line once; then select for repetition the sentences that need further practice.

	STROKES
Joe said that he packed my sledge with five boxes of frozen quail.	66
I could not wait to see Liza quickly mix the very big jar of new soap.	70
Life is short, you know. You can't afford to waste a minute of time.	69
The man who learns to take orders and to follow them will make good.	68
Do you use all of your time just as well as you can use a single hour?	71

EXERCISE 65   *11 minutes*

The Personal Letter. In typing the personal letter, modification of the business letter forms may be made. The inside address may be omitted entirely if you are writing to an intimate friend; and the comma may be used after the salutation, as in penwritten personal letters.

Style Letter No. 5 shows one form for the personal letter with the inside address placed at the left margin six spaces below the complimentary close. As the letter is typed on plain paper, the complete return address is typed in the date-line position.

Directions. 1. Type Style Letter No. 5 as it is given on page 105. Use current date.

2. Set a tabulator stop so the return address can be blocked five spaces to the right of the center of the paper. The first line of the return address should be typed on the tenth line. (Insert the paper to the first line writing position; then space down nine line spaces.)

3. Use single spacing and open punctuation.

4. Type the complimentary close five spaces to the left of the center of the paper. Type the inside address in block form at the left margin, six line spaces below the complimentary form.

EXERCISE 66   *20 minutes*

Directions. 1. Set a tabulator stop for a five-space paragraph indention. Also set tabulator stops so that the return address, which consists of only one line, can be begun at the center of the sheet, and the date can be indented five spaces on the next line. Space down eleven spaces from the top of the sheet before typing the return address.

2. Use single spacing and mixed punctuation. In a personal letter a comma may be used as the mark of punctuation after the salutation, but in a business letter only the colon should be used.

3. Type the complimentary close five spaces to the left of the center of the sheet. You will observe that in this letter the inside address is omitted. The letter is written to Mr. Donald W. Taggert, Box 496, Zanesville, Ohio.

Silver Creek, Arizona (current date) Hello Don, (P) Maybe you think I have forgotten you, but I have not. Until now I have simply been too busy to do any writing. (P) First of all, I'll tell you a little about the trip out. On the first day I drove to Nashville, Tennessee, 510 miles; on the second day, to Little Rock, Arkansas, 434 miles; on the third day, to Mineral Wells, Texas, 427 miles; on the fourth day, to Las Cruces, New Mexico, 600 miles; and on the fifth day to Tucson, just 352 miles. I could have made the trip to Silver Creek; but as I needed to remain overnight at Tucson, I completed the 60 miles the next day. You see I did not waste much time between quitting work in Zanesville on one Friday and beginning work here on Friday of the next week. (P) The mines around here were originally prospected and worked for copper. On account of the low market, copper has become a by-product and molybdenum is what we are after. The mines are bringing in plenty of money, too. (P) I am busy and like it here. I shall send you some pictures soon if they turn out well. I realize how busy you are, but I'd like to hear from you when you can write. More later. As ever, (Strokes, 1205; words, 214.)

BUDGET VI

LESSON 68

RECONSTRUCTION PRACTICE

5 *minutes*

Directions. Use a 70-space line; double spacing. Set the machine for a 5-space indention.

STROKES

(Emphasizing letters *c, p, r, s*)

	STROKES
Accuracy is the keynote of success in the typing classroom as	62
it is in the office. Accuracy is cultivated most quickly by con-	126
scientious co-operation between pupil and teacher. The pupil	188
must realize that the teacher must make a constant check on the	252
accuracy of the work just as well as on the clean-cut, quick strok-	319
ing of the keys. This careful checking by the teacher does not	383
release the pupil from the necessity of proofreading each typed	447
page. In some way pupils must learn that this is a problem that	512
exacts from each one who would become proficient in typing,	572
constant and careful study of ways to hold thought to the work	635
at hand.	643

TECHNIQUE PRACTICE 68

7 *minutes*

Directions. 1. Use a 70-space line; double spacing.

2. Type each sentence once; then check for accuracy. Retype the sentences in which errors are made. Goal: Each line without error and an extra line typed accurately for each error made.

Sentence 1. An apostrophe may indicate the omission of a letter. The parentheses may be used for an expression given as an explanation. When *o'clock* is used, spell out expressions of time. *B&O* is used as a symbol of a name, not as an abbreviation; therefore, type it without periods. (It is equally correct to type *B & O.*)

Sentence 2. The period is ALWAYS written inside the quotation mark. In typed material the underscore is used to indicate the title of a book. When common possession is to be shown, use the apostrophe with the last noun only.

Sentence 3. Add *'s* to form the singular possessive when the noun does not end in *s*.

Sentence 4. When plural nouns do not end in *s*, add *'s* to form the possessive.

Sentence 5. It is better not to attribute possession to inanimate objects, but business sanctions the use of the possessive with *day, month, year,* and like words.

STROKES

	STROKES
They're to be at the B&O station (an emergency call) at four o'clock.	69
He said, "Have you read *Hi-Tide?* Joe and May's mother sent it to me."	70
The nation's response to the people's need aroused the world's wonder.	70
Children's shoes, women's dresses, and boys' shirts are on sale now.	68
In one day's time, ten years' work was wrecked by that terrible flood.	70

EXERCISE 86

17 *minutes*

Directions. 1. Type the letter in the modification of the block form shown in Style Letter No. 6, page 125; but block the closing lines at the left margin as shown in Illustration No. 55.

2. Use mixed punctuation.

3. Study Illustration No. 54 of the placement of the subject when the letterhead carries a printed subject heading.

4. Through the use of the variable line spacer, gauge the line of typing with the printed heading "Subject" and type the subject of the letter.

Type the date on a line with "Subject." Place the date so that it will end at the right margin of the letter. To do this, move the carriage to the approximate point at which the right margin should end; then backspace once for each stroke in the date line.

Because "Mc" and the hyphen are part of the company name, type the signature in capital and small letters. Note the placement of, and the correct way to type, the reference initials for the letters dictated by Mr. McCausland, Jr. The company name and the official title of the dictator are treated as headings and are therefore typed **without end** punctuation.

5728 Marizona Drive   20
Phoenix, Arizona   37
August 28, 194-   53

My dear Miss Alma   71

A letter is an insidious thing, for it has a way of   123
creeping into your attention at a time when, wishing   176
to hear and see no one, you may plug the telephone   227
and ignore the doorbell. The nicest part of this   277
letter is that it will not interrupt you for longer   329
than a few minutes and it requires no answer.   376

When you return here after your summer in Vermont,   427
I want to come to see you, if I may, to bring you   477
two little volumes you expressed a desire to read.   529

As an answer to your not-so-recent communication,   579
this letter is sadly out of time. As we jettisoned   631
the idea of time long ago, you are to imagine that   682
this letter immediately follows your own.   725

                    Your affectionate pupil   749

                    Jane Lang

Miss Alma Madison   767
1496 Prescott Street   788
Burlington, Vermont   807

(Strokes, 807; words, 127.)

Style Letter No. 5 — Personal Letter Typed in a Modified Block Form with the Inside Address
Placed at the Left Margin Six Spaces below the Complimentary Close

[105]

Directions. Make all the corrections indicated. Type the letter once. Study the following proofreader's marks:

lc   Lower case (or, put in small letters).   ⌐ Bring words to beginning of line.   ¶ Begin new paragraph.

THE RADIO SHOP

1249 CASA GRANDE AVENUE
PHOENIX, ARIZONA

May 15, 194-

42
27
15 - 69

Head, Commercial Department
Senior High School
Temple, Arizona

~~Attention~~ Miss Mary Frances Wynne

My Dear Miss Wynne:

The enclosed folder is the *only* printed material I
have that tells of the history of radio communication. This folder was published a few years ago by
a manufacturers of radios. Radio broadcasting is of
very recent origin. *modern* The first experiments that led
directly to radio communication was made by Hertz
in 1888. I understand that *even* as early as 1842 Joseph
Henry ~~found~~ something in radiation and that in 1875
Edison also made some discoveries, which, however,
were not followed up. *the nature of electromagnetic*

one of the
the development of
discovered
Thomas

From 1916 on, musical broadcasting took place; but *regular*
the first programs to be given on schedule were presented over station KDKA beginning on Nov. 2, 1920.
If there is any other way in which I can be of service
to you, call on me. *sp in full*

preannounced

further the broadcasting of the Harding-Cox election returns

Sincerely Yours,
lc

MOPayne/lmr
enclosure

(Strokes, 901; words, 175.)

In the salutation, capitalize the first word and the title of the person addressed. Since "dear" is not a title, it should not be capitalized when preceded by "My."

LESSON 54

RECONSTRUCTION PRACTICE

4 minutes

Directions. Type each line of Technique Practice 53 once; then retype the lines that you feel will help you to develop good control.

TECHNIQUE PRACTICE 54

5 minutes

STROKES

My office hours will be 9:30-11:30 a.m. and 2:00-4:30 p.m. in April.	68
Policy No. 472385 for $1,000, issued to Mr. Lange, is listed on page 6.	71
Mary's policy matures when she is 48 years 7 months and 26 days old.	68
Spell the number in full with "o'clock"; as, "It is eleven o'clock."	68
The dimensions of this box are 6 by 8 feet; and it weighs 265 pounds.	69

Can you state the principle governing the writing of figures in each of the above sentences? It will pay you to check the explanations for similar sentences in Technique Practice 41, page 85. The explanations are not in order, but you can easily identify the explanation that fits the sentence.

EXERCISE 67

15 minutes

Directions. Use a 60-space line. Specific directions will be given for each problem. You should be able to type each problem without difficulty; but you are to refer to preceding lessons for illustrations of form if you feel it is necessary to do so.

Problem 1. Directions. Type the current date 2 inches from the top of the paper. Use the open form of punctuation and begin the line approximately 5 spaces to the right of the center of the paper.

Problem 2. Directions. Type the following inside address correctly placed and in correct order, 6 spaces below the date line.

496 marshall avenue
mr c o blackwood
lexington kentucky

Problem 3. Directions. Type the closing lines in correct placement and correct order, 8 spaces below the inside address typed in Problem 2. Use the single-spaced indented style and open punctuation.

united coal and oil company
yours very truly
superintendent of mines

Problem 4. Directions. Type the reference and enclosure notations for a letter dictated by J. O. Depp. Two enclosures are mentioned in the letter.

Problem 5. Directions. Type in correct order and blocked 5 spaces to the right of the center of the paper, the return address for a personal letter. Use close punctuation.

october 28 194—
springfield illinois
3856 levergood street

Problem 6. Directions. Type the salutation with mixed punctuation.

my dear miss black

Problem 7. Directions. Type in correct order the inside address and salutation for a block form of letter with close punctuation.

gentlemen
littleford manufacturing company
st. anthony plaza
san antonio texas

EXERCISE 68 (Optional)

19 minutes

Directions. Use single spacing and mixed punctuation.

mr louis h rickard 105 e. bryant street fremont nebraska dear sir (P) On the 20th of last month, you returned an overcoat that you had previously bought in our Men's Department. After this credit of $55 has been deducted, the balance due on your account is $60.50. (P) It is probably just an oversight that payment of your account has not been made. Further delay, however, will impair your credit standing, and this you cannot therefore afford to permit. Now that you realize the importance of this matter, we know that you will arrange to take care of the account immediately. (P) We shall expect to receive a check from you by return mail. yours very truly longstaff company (Dictated by C. O. Phillips) credit manager *(Strokes, 699; words, 104.)*

LESSON 67

competition

RECONSTRUCTION PRACTICE

4 minutes

Directions. Use a 70-space line; double spacing. Type on the stroke level.

	STROKES
One of the prerequisites of success in typing is the development of speed	74
and accuracy, and that development depends upon purposeful practice. Please	151
notice that only the right type of practice makes perfect. Persistence in push-	230
ing the keys down pays dividends only in poor technique. Pupils who are lax	307
or lazy, who do not persevere, will be quite justly disappointed in their results.	389

TECHNIQUE PRACTICE 67

7 minutes

Directions. 1. Use a 70-space line; double spacing.

2. Type each sentence until you feel you have developed ease and control. Select certain sentences for repetition if you feel that it is helpful to retype the sentences.

Sentence 1.   Use a question mark after an interrogative thought.

Sentence 2.   A request in the form of a question is usually punctuated with a period. Some writers prefer the use of the question mark. Either form of punctuation is acceptable.

Sentence 3.   The question mark within parentheses after a word or a phrase indicates doubt as to its accuracy.

Sentence 4.   After an indirect question, use the period—not the question mark.

Sentence 5.   If the quoted matter is a question, type the question mark before the quotation mark. If the quoted matter is not a question, place the question mark after the quotation mark.

	STROKES
Larry asked Mr. Martin, "What suggestion can you make to them? When?"	70
Will you please send me a copy of the reference you quoted yesterday.	69
His ingenuity (?) was not proved by the performance he gave last night.	71
The principal asked when the students would master the principle.	69
He said, "Did you study hard?" Did he believe me when I said "Yes"?	68

EXERCISE 84   *11 minutes*

Directions. 1. Type the letter once. Do not address an envelope.

2. It is customary for the typist to supply the closing lines when the dictator fails to indicate the specific complimentary close preferred. In such case, the usual expression of the dictator would be typed. It is the responsibility of the typist to add the enclosure notation whether or not the dictator indicates this notation at the close of the dictation.

You would not address the envelope until you knew the size of the enclosure referred to in the first paragraph.

Type the title of Mr. Austin on the second line and place a comma after it. This placement of the title is used in all letters, unless it would make the second line of disproportionate length. In such a case, the title should be placed on the line with the personal name and should be separated from the name by a comma.

Mr. Lawrence B. Austin Principal, Austin Academy Chandler, Arizona Dear Sir:

The enclosed pamphlet, describing and illustrating the SIMPLEX radios, is sent to you in response to your request of the 24th. (P) Model No. 380, shown on page 5 of the pamphlet, is, I believe, most suitable for use in your school. The radio cabinet is of beautiful design. The linenfold pattern illustrated on the cabinet doors, so-called because of its resemblance to a folded napkin, was a favored form of decorating panels of furniture in the fifteenth and sixteenth centuries. (P) Radio Model 380, operating on alternating current, 110 volts, 60 cycles, and employing 7 AC tubes (including a rectifier), is quoted at $275 (less tubes). This quotation is subject to your usual school discount of 5%, in addition to which the regular discount of 2% 10 days may be taken. *(Strokes, 896; words, 140.)*

UNIT V — *SPEED EMPHASIS*

The aim of the work of this unit is to demonstrate measurable improvement in your stroking rate. To do this, you must use the right practice procedures; and your practice for improvement must be founded on right technique. Seven fundamental techniques for typewriting are listed below as guides for your self-appraisal of your typing form. Check the way you type to see that you have these techniques as established parts of the whole pattern of your typing form.

1. **Stroking.** You must have correct fingering. You must know the right finger for the right key and you must also have a quick stroke, with the finger pulled slightly toward the palm of the hand. Emphasize the release of the key. All strokes must be made with quiet hands and motionless arms.

2. **Relaxation.** Relaxation of shoulder and arm muscles is necessary. This does not mean that you can assume a slouched position. The fingers will not be relaxed while you are typing because they must be tense in order to have the power to deliver the stroke; but the forearm and shoulder muscles must be relaxed.

3. **Quiet Control.** Your hands and forearms should be held almost motionless; let the fingers do the work. Check to see that the elbows do not weave in and out.

4. **Carriage Return.** Throw the carriage with a swift wrist and finger movement; start typewriting immediately after the throw is made.

5. **Finger Weight.** Poise the fingers lightly on the keys.

6. **Shifting for Capitals.** Make the reach to the shift key with the "hinge" movement at the wrist. (All machine parts must be controlled as much as possible by touch rather than by sight.)

7. **Letter and Word Typing.** You must know when to type on the stroke or letter level and when to type on the word level. How the copy is read is of great importance. For accurate reading of the copy, your eyes must be held on the copy all the time you are typing.

LESSON 55

RECONSTRUCTION PRACTICE
5 minutes

Directions. 1. Use a full-sized sheet of paper.
2. Set the typewriter for a 70-space line and double spacing.
3. Operate the carriage lever an extra time to provide space between the different drills and the repeated timed writings.

sign wish work town form make such both down paid hand then when firm
while claim words ought bring those leave those while found learn doubt
fell miss tell pass well mass call took seem book good been poor keep
fact date mill card were jump fast care save dear pull fear gave mull

TECHNIQUE PRACTICE 55
8 minutes

Directions. 1. Use a 70-space line; single spacing.
2. Type each sentence for one minute.
3. Check each minute writing and select as your goal for the timed writing of Exercise 69, the rate of the most accurate minute writing.

	STROKES
One must always do good work no matter how little the pay may be.	65
You may lose money and get it again; lost time is never found again.	68
It is the way you stick to work that makes you a success or a failure.	70
Each man's future is his to make it what he will through his good work.	71
The goal for this work is to learn how to make the fingers move rapidly.	72

LESSON 66

RECONSTRUCTION PRACTICE

4 minutes

Directions. 1. Use a 70-space line; double spacing.
2. Type one line of each column of words. These words are taken from a list of commonly misspelled words. Teach your fingers to spell correctly!

accommodate	separate	attendant	interfered	aluminum
embarrassed	accidentally	recommend	auxiliary	sympathies
dissension	occurred	principal	privileged	transferred

TECHNIQUE PRACTICE 66

7 minutes

Directions. 1. Use a 70-space line; double spacing. Center the heading.
2. Type each sentence once; then check the five lines. Retype the sentences in which you find errors. Goal: Each line without error and an extra line typed accurately for each error made.

Sentence 1. Company and organization names usually omit the apostrophe.
Sentence 2. Form the possessive of a singular noun by adding the apostrophe and *s*; form the possessive of a plural noun ending in *s* by adding the apostrophe.
Sentence 3. When a preposition follows the noun, the apostrophe is not used.
Sentence 4. The possessive of an abbreviation is indicated by the apostrophe and *s* placed after the period.
Sentence 5. The possessive pronouns *ours*, *theirs*, *yours*, *its*, and *hers* do not take an apostrophe. *It's* is a contraction for *it is*.

	STROKES
The Farmers National Bank made the loan to the Trent Teachers College.	70
He pays quite well for either one day's work or for several days' work.	71
Joe has had ten years of experience as principal of their high school.	70
Mr. Jack Marshall, Jr.'s speech was given before the men's club of York.	72
Ours is a glorious challenge. It's certain to give us plenty of work.	70

EXERCISE 83

23 minutes

Directions. 1. Type the letter twice. The inside address and salutation are printed in problem form. You are to type them in correct order.
2. Address one envelope for the letters.

Letters that are a part of a serial number may be typed without spacing before them (as, 37A) or joined to the figures with a hyphen (as, 37-A). Letters used as symbols (as, AC tubes) are typed without a period or space between the letters.

Express per cent in figures. Use *per cent* instead of the symbol % except in tabulated work and in the quotation of terms (as, 2% 10 days).

attention mr j r brown, sales manager simplex radios, inc los angeles, california gentlemen Please send to me your latest price list for all the models of SIMPLEX radios listed in Pamphlet No. 59. The price list that I have quotes Model 37-A, chassis G, operating on alternating current of 110 volts, 60 cycles, and using AC tubes, at $385, less 2% in 10 days or 30 days net. Is this your latest quotation on this model of radio? (P) The superior quality of tone and of design of the SIMPLEX radios is recognized by most of my customers, but some of them object to the cost of the SIMPLEX and say that they can get radios of equal value for $50 to $60 less than the price I must quote to them. Are you now manufacturing any models of radios that will sell in competition with the medium-priced Supertone? Yours very truly, (M. O. Payne) *(Strokes, 856; words, 148.)*

TYPING FOR CONTROL

7 minutes

Turn to page 119 and type the control sentences that you feel will aid you in developing the power to type accurately. You are to determine the number of repetitions that are desirable. Check your typing form. See to it that this practice brings measurable improvement in your skill.

EXERCISE 69

Directions. 1. Use a 70-space line; double spacing.

2. For your goal, select the number of words you typed most accurately in one of the sentences of Technique Practice 55.

3. Type for one minute. When you are able to type for one minute at the rate you have set as your goal, type at the same rate for two minutes; then when you have achieved your two-minute goal, type at the same rate for three minutes; then type at the same rate for five minutes. You can select your half-minute goal and your minute goal and in this way be guided in the rate at which you type.

The total strokes shown at the end at each line of the exercises in this unit should be used in determining the writing rate. The figures above words indicate the 5-word groups. Use these figures in selecting the half-minute and minute goals for your timed writings. If your goal is to type 50 words a minute, place a small check mark at 25 for the half-minute goal and the figure 1 at 50 for the minute goal. Continue to indicate the half-minute and minute goals for the entire timed writing.

	STROKES
The other day I was in an office at a time when the manager was acting	71
like a stark lunatic. He barked orders right and left; he growled about	144
everything. He was all out of sorts. When the man had cooled down a bit, he	222
explained what was wrong. I had some understanding of what he was up	292
against. I realized quite well the cause of his temper. He had in his office	371
the great pest—the man who always borrowed something for "just a minute"	445
but never put it back where it belonged.	487
This problem is the same whether it is met in an office or in a school; the	563
difference is in the way in which the employer and the teacher act. Teachers	641
grin and bear it; or at times they give the students the fireworks, and the	717
students grin and enjoy the show. But the next day the same thing has to	791
be met once more. The truth is, no employer should have to put up with one	867
who has not learned to put things back where they belong. The required	939
training in right work habits must be a part of the school work. It may be	1015
that teachers will have to go on the warpath to get lazy pupils to learn this	1093
lesson; if so, they should forego the smile of "sweetness and light" and put	1170
on a show like an office manager behaving much as a raving lunatic.	1237

LESSON 65

RECONSTRUCTION PRACTICE

4 minutes

Directions. Use the reconstruction practice for Lesson 64.

TECHNIQUE PRACTICE 65

7 minutes

Directions. 1. Use a 70-space line; double spacing.

2. Center the heading, Technique Practice 65, in capitals. Triple-space after typing the centered heading.

3. Type each sentence once; then check the five lines. Retype sentences that have errors. Goal: Each line without error and an extra line typed accurately for each error made.

	STROKES
He was insured for $5,000 at the age of 17 years 8 months and 20 days.	70
The box is 6 by 9 feet and it weighs more than 250 pounds, I am sure.	69
They may call to see Dr. M. C. West on Wednesday from 9:45 to 11:30.	68
When "o'clock" is used, spell the hour; as, "Come at two o'clock."	66
His policy No. 284236 for $5,000 was made to his son, Joe Thompson.	67

EXERCISE 82   *25 minutes*

Directions. 1. Type the letter twice.

2. Address one envelope for the letters.

In the names of corporate organizations or companies, the apostrophe may be omitted from the plural possessive form. See the second line of the following inside address, in which "Farmers" is written without an apostrophe.

```
School of Business Administration
Farmers Bank Building
Phoenix, Arizona

Attention Dr. Charles E. Woodring

Gentlemen:
```

Illustration No. 53 — Placement of the Attention Line

Letters addressed to a company may be called to the attention of a particular individual through the use of an attention line. Type the attention line two spaces below the last line of the inside address proper and two spaces above the salutation. As the letter is addressed to the company and is merely called to the attention of a particular individual, use the salutation called for in addressing the company.

Spell in full expressions of time when *o'clock* is used and when only approximate time is given. Express time in figures when *p.m.* and *a.m.* (or *P.M.* and *A.M.*) are used.

Express dimensions in figures. See the second paragraph of the following letter.

School of Business Administration Farmers Bank Building Phoenix, Arizona Attention Dr. Charles E. Woodring Gentlemen: I shall be happy to have a DYNAMIC radio installed for your school assembly to be held at ten o'clock on Thursday morning of next week. I shall be at your office on Wednesday, sometime between 2:30 and 3:00 p.m., to check details of this installation. (P) Because of the size of your auditorium, I consider a large console radio with Symphonic speaker most suitable for your use. Model 469 is equipped with the Symphonic speaker, and it operates on 110 volts, alternating current. This radio is 49½ inches high, 34½ inches wide, and 17½ inches deep. For auditorium use it is unexcelled. (P) I am glad to have the opportunity of furnishing you with this radio service. Yours very truly, (M. O. Payne) *(Strokes, 830; words, 126.)*

TYPING FOR CONTROL   *7 minutes*

Turn to page 127, Exercise 79, and type the paragraphs at a controlled rate. You have no definite speed goal to attain; but your control goal is to type with an average of not more than one error for each four lines of typing.

SPEED EMPHASIS

10 minutes

Select a fifteen-second goal and let the goal be the highest typing rate you have attempted. For example, if you want to type at 60 words a minute, you will determine to type 15 words in the first fifteen-second writing. When you have made your fifteen-second goal, try to maintain the same rate for thirty seconds; then type at the same rate for a minute. *Type with good technique.*

	STROKES
You cannot build your speed on the wrong kind of typing habits. If you	72
have not checked the way you type more than the number of words you	140
type, you are missing your finest chance to improve your work. The key to	215
improved work is often found in some little thing that is not being done as	292
well as it can be done. Make sure that you are working up to your finest	366
skill and that you are working with your finest typing form. Nothing less	441
will pay.	450

LESSON 56

RECONSTRUCTION PRACTICE

2 minutes

Directions. 1. Use a full-sized sheet of paper for the drill and the technique practice. 2. Set the typewriter for a 70-space line and double spacing.

a;sldkfjgh a;sldkfjghfjdksla;sldkfjgh abcdefg hijklmnop qrstuvwxyz

for the and and for the pay man sir rug for and the rob rob fob fib

SYLLABICATION CHECKUP

5 minutes

Directions. Type the hyphen at the point where you might first divide the word after the ringing of the bell. If a word cannot be divided, type it solid.

Bell Rings on the Typing of the Fifth Letter of Each Word

1. department
2. consisting
3. commercial
4. organization
5. effective
6. division
7. knowledge
8. important
9. fundamentals
10. techniques

Bell Rings on the Typing of the Seventh Letter of Each Word

1. approximately
2. themselves
3. associations
4. satisfactory
5. production
6. registration
7. responsibility
8. performance
9. permitted
10. attractive

THREE COMMON FAULTS AND HOW TO OVERCOME THEM

Wasteful Arm Motion. Movement of the arms while the fingers are operating the keys will definitely limit your speed. Hold the arms quiet and let the fingers do the work.

Faulty Space Bar Operation. Failure to space between words often results because of the lingering thumb that is not removed from the space bar quickly after the stroke is made.

Wrists Too High. Low wrists tend to aid in the quick release of the keys. Many typists have been able to increase their speed a great deal by operating with relaxed and low shoulders and with the wrists held in a position that will give a natural drop from the back of the wrist to the tip of the elbow. This position lessens fatigue.

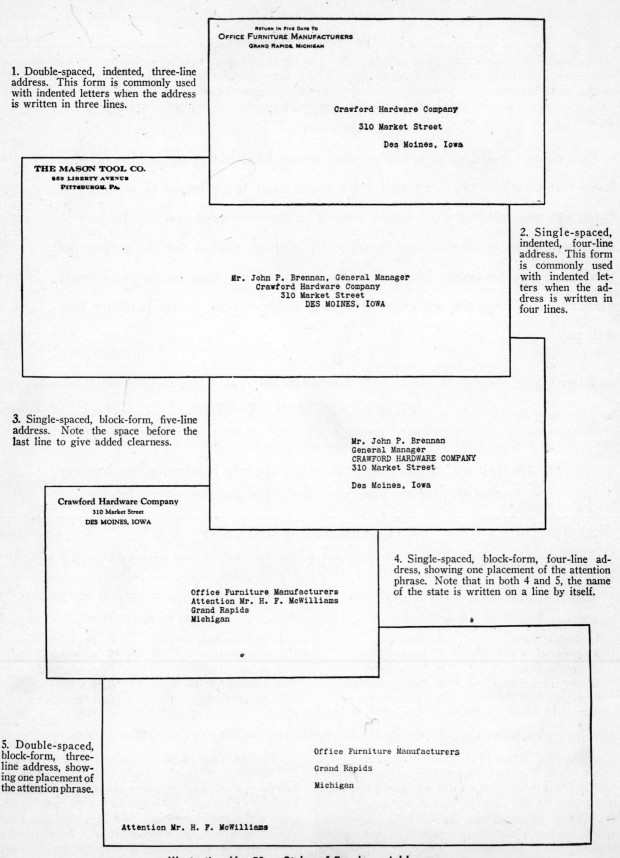

1. Double-spaced, indented, three-line address. This form is commonly used with indented letters when the address is written in three lines.

RETURN IN FIVE DAYS TO
OFFICE FURNITURE MANUFACTURERS
GRAND RAPIDS, MICHIGAN

Crawford Hardware Company
310 Market Street
Des Moines, Iowa

THE MASON TOOL CO.
659 LIBERTY AVENUE
PITTSBURGH, PA.

Mr. John P. Brennan, General Manager
Crawford Hardware Company
310 Market Street
DES MOINES, IOWA

2. Single-spaced, indented, four-line address. This form is commonly used with indented letters when the address is written in four lines.

3. Single-spaced, block-form, five-line address. Note the space before the last line to give added clearness.

Mr. John P. Brennan
General Manager
CRAWFORD HARDWARE COMPANY
310 Market Street

Des Moines, Iowa

Crawford Hardware Company
310 Market Street
DES MOINES, IOWA

Office Furniture Manufacturers
Attention Mr. H. F. McWilliams
Grand Rapids
Michigan

4. Single-spaced, block-form, four-line address, showing one placement of the attention phrase. Note that in both 4 and 5, the name of the state is written on a line by itself.

5. Double-spaced, block-form, three-line address, showing one placement of the attention phrase.

Office Furniture Manufacturers

Grand Rapids

Michigan

Attention Mr. H. F. McWilliams

Illustration No. 52 — Styles of Envelope Addresses

〖 132 〗

TECHNIQUE PRACTICE 56

8 minutes

Directions. Use a 70-space line; single spacing. Type each sentence for one minute.

	STROKES
Success is doing what you can do well and doing well whatever you do.	69
A man's fortune is in his own hands, and he may shape it as he wills.	69
Many a man has succeeded at the last hour because he would not let go.	70
Begin each day with the firm vow to do better work than ever before.	68
If you plan your work well and work your plan well, you will do well.	69

EXERCISE 70

20 minutes

Directions. 1. Use a 70-space line; double spacing.

2. Select as your goal the number of words you typed most accurately in one of the sentences of the preceding technique practice.

3. Type for one minute. When you can type for one minute at the rate you have set as your goal, type at the same rate for two minutes; then when you have achieved your two-minute goal, type at the same rate for three minutes; then type at the same rate for five minutes.

	STROKES
Details are worth while, to be sure, but they are not ends in them-	66
selves. They are worth while only when they are seen as a part of the whole	143
problem. You would not expect to know an engine from studying merely a	215
bolt or a spoke in the wheel. No matter how well you analyzed the bolt or	290
the spoke, you would not be able to acquire a knowledge of the engine until	366
you had studied it as a whole, until you had seen the part in relation to the	444
whole engine. This is why details must be right; they have relation to other	522
details, and when all are put together they make up the whole.	586
Have you analyzed your typing to see if there are some details that tend	659
to weaken your whole typing skill? A detail means little except when it fails	738
to fit into the pattern of your typing power. If it is not just in keeping with	819
the best of your skill, it will bring your rate and your control down. You	895
should quickly find the skill that is giving you trouble and practice to	968
bring this skill to your finest rate of performance. This is the way to make	1046
details fit into the whole pattern of typing skill.	1097

SPEED EMPHASIS

8 minutes

Select a fifteen-second goal and let the goal be the highest typing rate you have attempted. As a rule, it is wise to choose a speed improvement goal of approximately five words more than your usual writing rate. When you have made your fifteen-second goal, try to maintain the same rate for thirty seconds; then type at the same rate for a minute; then increase your time to two- and three-minute writings through the same method of practicing for a half minute longer each timed writing. Use the material of Exercise 71 for this speed emphasis practice.

ADDRESSING THE ENVELOPE

Spacing. Three-line addresses for envelopes should be typed with double spacing, even though the letter is single-spaced. When four or more lines are used for the envelope address, single-space the address. Always use at least three lines for an envelope address. If no street address is given, type the name of the city and that of the state on separate lines. The city and state names should be separated by a comma when they are typed on the same line. Never use *City* in the place of the city's correct name.

The Attention Line. The attention phrase may be typed on the line immediately following the company name, or it may be placed in the lower left corner of the envelope.

In Care of, or the special symbol *c/o*, should be typed in either of the positions indicated for the attention phrase. If space permits, it is better to spell out *In Care of* instead of using the symbol *c/o*. Never use the sign %.

Placement of the Address. When the ordinary business envelope, 3⅝ by 6½ inches, is used, the first line of the address should be typed approximately 2 inches (four triple spaces) from the top of the envelope and approximately 2½ inches (twenty-five thumb spaces) from the left edge of the envelope.

When using a large envelope, 4⅛ by 9½ inches, type the first line of the address 2½ inches (five triple spaces) from the top of the envelope and 4 inches (forty thumb spaces) from the left edge of the envelope.

These definite instructions for the placement of the address should be followed carefully until you have trained your eyes to judge the correct placement of the address. Once you have trained yourself to estimate the correct placement of the address, you can then simply twirl the envelope to the correct position without loss of time.

INSERTING THE ENVELOPE INTO THE TYPEWRITER

Insert the envelope into the typewriter so that the left edge of the envelope will be against the paper guide. If your typewriter does not have an envelope or card holder, move the right paper clamp over the right edge of the envelope. This will not be necessary, however, unless you are addressing a number of envelopes consecutively.

FOLDING AND INSERTING LETTERS INTO ENVELOPES

Fold the lower edge of the letterhead to within half an inch of the top edge of the sheet (Illustration No. 51, Step 2); fold from the right to the left, making the fold approximately one-third the width of the sheet (Step 3); fold from the left to the right, making the fold slightly less than a third of the width of the sheet and leaving a half-inch margin at the right in order that the letter may be opened easily (Step 4).

Insert the letter into the envelope in such a way that it will be in its normal reading position when it is removed from the envelope. Study the part of Illustration No. 51 showing the correct way to hold a folded letter when it is to be inserted into an envelope. Notice that the last fold of the letter is under the thumb and that the left-hand creased edge is inserted into the envelope first.

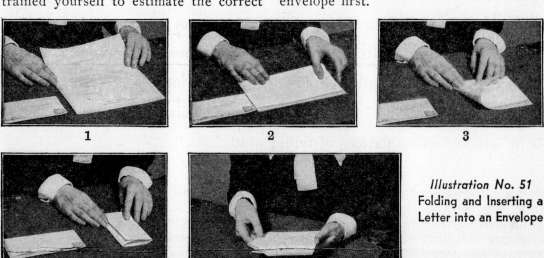

1   2   3

4   5

Illustration No. 51
Folding and Inserting a
Letter into an Envelope

LESSON 57

RECONSTRUCTION PRACTICE

4 minutes

Directions. 1. Use a full-sized sheet of paper for the drill and the technique practice.
2. Set the typewriter for a 70-space line and double spacing.
3. Follow the same directions for succeeding reconstruction practices unless otherwise directed.

	STROKES
It is the duty of a man to do me a turn and he is to do so if he can.	69
When I wish to do good work, I can do it; but I must want to do well.	69
act him bad you beg was car pin eat hum fee nun set pun war hum get are	72
card look case milk dear lump fact junk face link cars hulk case jump	70
of the of them of the of them of such of such to work of them to work	70

SYLLABICATION CHECKUP

4 minutes

Directions. Type the hyphen at the point where you might first divide the word after the ringing of the bell. If a word cannot be divided, type it solid.

Bell Rings on the Typing of the First Letter of Each Word

1. about
2. missing
3. properly
4. preparations
5. education

Bell Rings on the Typing of the Fourth Letter of Each Word

1. necessary
2. justification
3. intelligence
4. punctuation
5. condition
6. noticeable
7. classification
8. occurrence
9. according
10. distribution

TECHNIQUE PRACTICE 57

8 minutes

Directions. 1. Use a 70-space line; single spacing.
2. Type each sentence for one minute.
3. Your goal for the timed writings of Exercise 72 will be the rate of the most accurate minute writing.

	STROKES
Work and play do not go together well; you cannot do both at once.	66
I must learn to do well what I do, and I must know what I can do well.	70
We have more good than we use wisely, yet we reach out for still more.	70
If a task is once begun, do not leave it until it is completely done.	69
If you would get ahead in the world, be ahead of others in doing good.	70

EXERCISE 71

20 minutes

Directions. 1. Use a 70-space line; double spacing.
2. Your goal is the number of words you typed most accurately in one of the sentences of the preceding technique practice.
3. Type for one minute. When you can type for one minute at the rate you have set as your goal, type at the same rate for two minutes; then when you have achieved your two-minute goal, type at the same rate for three minutes; then type at the same rate for five minutes.

THE RADIO SHOP

1249 CASA GRANDE AVENUE

PHOENIX, ARIZONA

May 14, 194-

January 14, 1949
5⅛/43

Mr. H. B. Oliver
Marizona Lodge
Mesa, Arizona

My dear Mr. Oliver:

When you were in the store last Saturday, you looked
at different models of radios that we have in stock.
Today we received a new shipment of SIMPLEX radios
with several new cabinet designs of unusual beauty.

SIMPLEX No. 362, a six-tube complete electric radio
with a cabinet of beautifully shaded walnut veneer,
is new in design and low in cost. This radio is to
operate on 25 cycles of alternating current; and it
has the illuminated dial with calibrations, in both
meters and kilocycles, showing in white on a dark
brown background. The price of this SIMPLEX 362 is
$89 (less tubes).

Would you like to have the radio sent out for a two
weeks' trial? The trial use of the radio will not
obligate you to buy it.

Yours very truly,

M. O. Payne

MOPayne/lmr

30
45
59

80

133
187
238
291

343
395
447
499
551
601
653
672

724
775
800

818

829

*Type the reference initials six to eight spaces below the
complimentary close when no company signature, personal
title, or typed signature is used.*

(Strokes, 829; words, 138.)

Style Letter No. 7 — Modification of the Block Form of Letter with an Indented Complimentary Close

	STROKES
How do you study? Do you sit at your table quietly, but with your	67
thoughts wandering in dizzy heights, and find at the end of some hours that	143
you have not covered the lesson nor added to the sum total of your knowl-	215
edge? If, when you start to prepare your lessons, you can control your	287
thoughts in such a way that you give full heed to the exact work at hand,	361
you will find that you can cover the work in just half of the time. Make a	437
plan for those hours and stick to it. Do not let small things come in and rob	516
you of this channel of growth. We are such creatures of habit that we do not	594
change with ease. Once this habit becomes yours, it will be a simple thing	670
to keep.	680
Each of us must learn to concentrate if he would do his work well	746
and quickly. It is not easy to say just what we must do to learn how to	819
concentrate. We know that we must have the desire to pay attention if we	893
would block out of our immediate experience sounds, objects, and thoughts	967
that do not have a bearing on the work on which we are to concentrate.	1039
Interest can be forced if it does not come of its own accord because of the	1115
nature of the thing on which we are to concentrate. If we are reading a book	1193
that is compelling, we will forget our surroundings and be unaware of what is	1271
going on around us; then suddenly we will realize that we have been lost in	1347
thought or in the study of the written page. The best study comes from	1419
wanting to do the work, for interest will not need to be forced and maximum	1495
learning will take place in a minimum of time.	1541

SPEED EMPHASIS

7 minutes

Select a fifteen-second goal that will call for a five-word increase in your minute writing rate. When you have typed at the goal rate, type at the same rate for thirty seconds; then type at the same rate for a minute; then increase your time to two- and three-minute writings through the same method of practicing for a half minute longer each time. Use the material of Exercise 72 for this speed emphasis practice. Each time you add fifteen seconds to the length of time you type, begin at the first of the paragraph so that the repetition typing will add to the ease with which you handle the words.

BUDGET V

LESSON 64

RECONSTRUCTION PRACTICE

4 minutes

Directions. Use a 70-space line; double spacing. Type each sentence once without error.

STROKES

There are a great many rules for writing numbers that must be learned.　70

No matter how large it is, spell out a number that begins a sentence.　69

Two or three of the dozen or more men who were here were put to work.　69

We hope to increase the class to sixteen by the last of this week.　66

Their next article should have not more than eight thousand words.　66

TECHNIQUE PRACTICE 64

7 minutes

Directions. 1. Use a 70-space line; double spacing.

2. Center the heading, Technique Practice 64, in capitals. Triple-space after the heading.

3. Type each sentence once; then check the five lines. Retype sentences that have errors.

Goal: Each line without error and an extra line typed accurately for each error made.

Sentences 1 and 2.　Spell out round numbers unless such numbers come in connection with some that are not spelled out. In the latter case use figures. Use figures for numbers greater than one hundred, except in the case of isolated round numbers. Underscore italicized words.

Sentence 3.　Use figures for all numbers in a group if the largest has three or more digits and is not a round number.

Sentence 4.　Amounts of money, whether expressed in dollars or cents or in foreign denominations, should be written in figures (except in legal documents). Sums of money expressed in dollars should be written without the decimal and ciphers. Note the use of *'s* to form the singular possessive.

Sentence 5.　Express decimals and percentages in figures.

STROKES

Letters were sent to 125 grocers and to 40 wholesale produce dealers.　69

In May we sold 639 copies of the book, *His Quest;* in June, only 490.　68

I bought 6 azaleas, 18 spiraeas, 36 laurels, and 120 Radiance roses.　68

She paid a bill of $49 at Ziegler's and another of 75 cents at Ray's.　69

Syllable intensity of 1.30 is used for 98 per cent of the paragraphs.　69

LETTER EXERCISES

1 minute

The letters in this budget were dictated by Mr. M. O. Payne, the owner and manager of a radio store in Phoenix, Arizona. Mr. Payne uses mixed punctuation and a modification of the block form of letter. With the mixed form of punctuation, use a colon after the salutation and a comma after the complimentary close. Style Letter No. 7 illustrates one form of typing the reference notation at the bottom of a letter. Use this form in typing all the letters in this budget, but use your initials for those of the stenographer.

Directions for Typing Exercises 82, 83, and 84.

1. Refer to the placement table on page 86 for the margin adjustments.

2. Use single spacing; mixed punctuation; and the modification of the block style of letter that is used for Style Letter No. 7.

EXERCISE 81

3 minutes for studying Style Letter No. 7
5 minutes for studying envelope addressing
21 minutes for typing the letter twice and the envelope once

Directions. 1. Type the letter on page 130 twice. 2. Address only one envelope. Study the directions for addressing envelopes and folding letters given on pages 131-132.

LESSON 58

RECONSTRUCTION PRACTICE

4 minutes

Directions. Type on the stroke level.

	STROKES
Semiasphyxiation left Major Bucque very weak and exceedingly dizzy.	67
Dick was jubilant in exhibiting four queer zoology specimens in vases.	70
A king and a quaint wax lady from Zurich sat upon a carved jade table.	70
Jim Brown expected to analyze and to verify the graphs in his quiz book.	72
Poor lazy Jack very quickly relaxed after his big day at the new mill.	70

SYLLABICATION CHECKUP

4 minutes

Directions. Type the hyphen at the point where you might first divide the word after the ringing of the bell. If a word cannot be divided, type it solid.

Bell Rings on the Typing of the Sixth Letter of Each Word

1. constitution
2. experienced
3. interpretation
4. self-conceit
5. mentioned

Bell Rings on the Typing of the Third Letter of Each Word

1. graduate
2. clerical
3. division
4. wouldn't
5. referring

TECHNIQUE PRACTICE 58

8 minutes

Directions. 1. Use a 70-space line; single spacing.
2. Type each sentence three times. You should type at a controlled rate. Goal: an average of not more than one error for each three lines.

	STROKES
Jacob, who quickly won the prize, may visit the grand fair on the sixth.	72
Jack's mother was quite vexed and angry because he was just a lazy fop.	71
Joseph Forge made a very quick ride to the zone when the box was lost.	70
Please have him get me four dozen quarts of lemon juice by next week.	69
Jim and he can get but very few boxes of this size opened that quickly.	71

EXERCISE 72

27 minutes

Directions. 1. Use a 70-space line; single spacing.
2. Type each paragraph; then check for accuracy. If you have made errors, list them on the error-analysis chart similar to Illustration No. 50, page 79.*
3. Retype the paragraphs in which there are more errors than an average of one for each three lines of typing. This typing is not to be timed. Goal: Continuous typing with attention to letter sequences and a maximum of not more than one error for each three lines.

	STROKES
Have you ever visited Veracruz, a city of Mexico? This city is some 265	73
miles southeast of Mexico City, in Veracruz, a state of Mexico that has some	150
lofty mountains enclosing quite fertile valleys. The capital of the state is	228
Jalapa, and other cities are Orizaba, Cordoba, and Puerto Mexico.	293

* An error-analysis chart is provided in the workbook accompanying this textbook. If you do not have the workbook, prepare the form on blank paper.

2 minutes for study of proofreader's marks
3 minutes for study of letter
14 minutes for typing letter

Directions. Make all the corrections indicated. Study the following proofreader's marks:

# Insert space between words, characters, or lines.	**∧** Indicates inferior marks, letters, or figures.	*No ¶* No paragraph.
⌐ Omit.	**⊐** Indent.	*caps* or ≡ All capitals.
tr Transpose.	**∨** Indicates superior marks, letters, or figures.	

ELECTRIC
MANUFACTURERS, INC.

SERVING PRINCIPAL CITIES

BROUGHTON TERMINAL

NEWARK ∘ NEW JERSEY

February 17, 194—

Keenan Building

Mr. Harry M. Stoddard,
Attorney at Law,
Lancaster, Pa *sp. in full*

Dear Sir:

We attach for collection a statement of our account against B. O. Trimble, amounting to $531.42. Will you please acknowledge the receipt of this statement and then proceed to effect a prompt and, if possible, amicable settlement *of the account.* *in order to make collection from Mr. Trimble*

If a suit is necessary, please inform us of the debtors tangible assets so that we may determine whether or not the assets justify incurring the expense of the suit. *instituting legal proceedings.*

No ¶ Do not enter suit or incur any expense without our written authority.

If our claim is uncollectible, please return it to us promptly and give us detailed advice as to the credit standing of Mr. Trimble. *the papers* *information* *concerning the*

Yours very truly

all caps → Electric Manufacturers, Inc.

3 spaces Mr. Sleighter, Treasurer
M.R.

hbf
Enclosure

(Strokes, 895; words, 120.)

Because Bell, Edison, and Marconi believed more than they knew exactly,   72
the telephone has extended our voice, electricity has become our beast of bur-   149
den, and our messages are sent to the ends of the world without benefit of   224
wires. Had the zeal of these scientists to prove more than had been proved   300
been quenched, our daily life would be vastly different than it is.   367

If I had the freedom of an advertiser who talks about Krazy Kat Krackers   73
partaken of in the Kozy Korner Koffee Kup, my task of emphasizing a specific   150
letter would be exceedingly simple. I could write about keeping the eyes on   227
the kopy and the fingers kurved, or I might just write about korrekt teknique   305
for key stroking. This liberty is not mine, so I must be content with fewer k's   386
and hope this typing brings better technique.   431

> If time permits after you complete the paragraphs once with not more than one error
> for each three lines of typing, retype the paragraphs to attain the goal of errorless writings.
> Additional paragraphs for control will be found on page 120.

LESSON 59

RECONSTRUCTION PRACTICE   *4 minutes*

Directions. Type on the stroke level.

It is queer that people who would frequently quail at the idea of stealing   75
money will, without a qualm, quietly steal an hour's time from their employer   153
and be quite piqued when he is vexed. In your quest for success, quickly ac-   229
quire the habit of giving an equal return for everything you receive. Just   305
develop zest for your work, and you will not squander time. Learn to quit   380
quibbling over ten minutes of extra work; then you will have the first requi-   456
site for advancement.   477

TECHNIQUE PRACTICE 59   *6 minutes*

Directions. 1. Use a 70-space line; double spacing.
2. Type each sentence once; then check the five lines. Retype the sentences that have errors.
Goal: each line without error and for each error, an extra line typed accurately.

"Have you read the article 'Marching On'?" he asked. "It's great!"   66
Get that five-page 8½ by 11-inch folder on "How to Get a Position."   67
The girl's father is to address the men's club at 8:00 p.m. Wednesday.   70
The terms of invoice #510, dated May 12, are 2% 10 days, 30 days net.   69
He conquers who believes he can. "I will succeed; nothing can stop me."   72

EXERCISE 73   *33 minutes*

Directions. 1. Use a 70-space line; double spacing.
2. Your speed goal is to type 15 words a minute slower than your normal speed rate. Your control goal is to type without error.
3. Determine the rate at which you are to type; then check the half-minute goal and place a figure 1 at the minute goal. Type the half minute without error; then begin at the same paragraph and type the minute goal without error. Continue this for the two-minute, three-minute, and the five-minute goals. If you feel you can do better work by using a different starting point in the paragraph, select a starting point that is near the point of one of the five-word groups.

	STROKES
Can you find your errors in your completed typing work? If you can, you	73
have one skill that will be quite valuable in your personal correspondence	148
as well as in the office position that you may hold some day. "Eyes that	222
see" when they are looking at one's own work are rare exceptions, indeed.	297
Your mental picture of the word is much stronger than the visual picture.	372
You know you want to use a certain word, and the impulse is so strong that	447
you fail to realize you have struck the wrong key. Then you let your eyes	522
glance over the typed page and fail to see that incorrect letter. What is	597
this but just carelessness?	625
It may be that the classroom practice of penalizing you for each error tends	703
to cause you to close your eyes when you check your papers. You may take	777
the attitude that finding the errors is something of a game between you and	853
the teacher. If the teacher wins, he is denominated "old eagle eyes"; if you	931
win, you pat yourself on the back and express delight that you put that one	1001
over quite neatly. That is the child's way of acting, and you need to take	1083
yourself in hand and give the matter thought. Your teacher does not enjoy	1158
finding errors; he finds them and calls them to your attention only with the	1235
expectation that you will be more careful the next time you check your work.	1313
Businessmen say it is very hard to get workers who can find their own	1383
errors. They say the beginning worker can neither read nor check when	1454
someone else reads. Try the method of having someone read to you two or	1527
three columns of figures while you check the lists in which some corrections	1604
appear. You will find this to be good training. You may ask someone to read	1682
a paragraph of directions to you; and after the paragraph has been read, you	1759
may try to answer a half dozen questions on the directions. In this way you	1836
may find out just how well you listen and how exactly you report. Such	1908
methods will train you to work quickly and accurately if you will use them	1983
daily in your school work.	2009

Etiquette is much more than knowing how to drink tea with the right   68

flourish or how to use forks and spoons at a state dinner. There is more to   145

be said on how to behave than will be found in the list of things our "best   221

people" say and do. The acts of the major groups of people are no sanction   297

for bad manners, but such acts at times put the stamp of approval on   368

borderline actions. Today the one who uses a comb in public is justly criti-   441

cized. Some people consider the powdering of the nose in public as much a   517

breach of good manners as the cleaning of one's nails or the picking of one's   595

teeth in public. There are some things that simply are not done except by   670

those who are uncouth. Good taste has not yet gone over to the theory that   746

each may do as he pleases.   774

This whole subject of what is good taste may have to be answered in terms   848

of the place as well as the occasion. A dress that would be right for a garden   928

party would likely be quite out of place in a business office. In late years,   1007

business people have grown rather lax in the matter of appropriate clothes,   1083

matched by still more careless manners. They do not seem to realize that   1157

by their dress and by their acts they make it hard for well-bred people to over-   1236

look plain cheapness. So they demand respect when they should command   1307

it—and there is a big difference.   1341

If time permits after you have met your goals for this lesson, practice selected control drills from pages 119 and 120.

LESSON 60
RECONSTRUCTION PRACTICE   *5 minutes*

Directions. Type on the stroke level.

"Mum, sum, gum, memory, maximum, dumb"—they all sound much like a   67
mimicry of childhood rhymes. Still, "jump, stump, lump, bump, mump,   136
thump" make a good drill for the reach from m to u and back again. There is   213
no gem of thought in this paragraph. Perhaps it would be better to write about   293
making more meaningful every thought and deed; or about experts who expect   368
experienced workers to express themselves exceedingly well. What difference   445
does it make just so the right reaches are involved? So here's the prize jingle   526
for the day: "Mum, sum, gum, memory, maximum, dumb." Yes, it is quite   598
"dumb."   605

Directions. Type the letter once.

Mr. P. H. Dreyer Snell Arcade Building Atlantic City, New Jersey Dear Sir On the 16th of last month, we wrote you that your check for $158.37 was being returned to the Union Deposit Bank. We certainly thought such an important matter would receive your immediate attention. To our amazement, we have not received any return from the bank. Failure to hear from the bank indicates that you have again failed to honor the check on its presentation. (P) We must insist that you take steps to honor this check immediately. Your bank has been given instructions to hold the check for five days in order to give you ample time in which to make arrangements for its payment. (P) We are very reluctant to place a client's account in the hands of our attorneys for collection; but in the event of your continued inattention to this matter, we shall have no other alternative. Yours very truly ELECTRIC MANU-FACTURERS, INC. M. R. Sleighter, Treasurer *(Strokes, 956; words, 145.)*

LESSON 63

RECONSTRUCTION PRACTICE   3 minutes

Directions. Use a 70-space line; single spacing. Type the sentence five times without error.

The rhythmic pattern established in typing this sentence will give control.

TECHNIQUE PRACTICE 63   7 minutes

Directions. 1. Use a 70-space line; single spacing.
2. Type each sentence five times without error, or for a one-minute writing.

	STROKES
After all, if you know that you have done right, you have your reward.	70
If there is a smile on our lips, those around us will smile with us.	68
He who holds a lofty vision, a high ideal, will one day realize it.	67
Sincerity, a deep, genuine sincerity, is a trait of the truly heroic.	69
If you have knowledge, you should let others light their candles by it.	71

EXERCISE 78   11 minutes

Directions. Type the letter once. The inside address and the closing lines are printed in problem form. Type them in the correct form for business letters.

mr l f reilly 4518 lancaster street newark new jersey subject: protested check dear sir (P) Your check for $864.29 has been returned protested, thus incurring protest fees of $2.50. We deposited your check on the day following its receipt in this office, so we are at a loss to understand why the check has been returned because of insufficient funds. We feel quite certain that the American National Bank of Newark, the bank on which this check was drawn, has made an error, although the check was marked "N. S. F." and returned to our bank without delay. (P) A draft for $866.79, to cover your returned check and the protest fees incurred, is being forwarded to the American National Bank, the bank on which your check was drawn. We shall expect you to protect this draft on its presentation. yours very truly electric manufacturers, inc m r sleighter, treasurer *(Strokes, 888; words, 141.)*

EXERCISE 79   20 minutes

Directions. 1. Use a 70-space line; double spacing.
2. Type for five minutes at a controlled rate. You have no definite speed goal to attain; your control goal is to type with an average of not more than one error for each four lines of typing.

3. When you have reached your control goal for five minutes of writing, type the paragraphs for ten minutes. Goal: an average of no more than one error for each three lines of typing.
4. You will be checked on your control and not your speed. MEET YOUR CONTROL GOAL.

TECHNIQUE PRACTICE 60 *5 minutes*

Directions. 1. Use a 70-space line; double spacing.

2. Type each sentence once; then check the five lines. Retype the sentences that were not typed without error. Goal: Each line without error and for each error an extra line typed accurately.

STROKES

John Zilbagy saw them have the trapeze quickly fixed for the show. 66

It is worth while to learn to do some work so well you can excel in it. 73

A brawny jaguar held fast till the quaking Zouave victim had expired. 69

Before you begin to type a test, get the right feel of the typewriter. 70

Bismarck proved equally just when excluding her from the Zollverein. 68

EXERCISE 74 *25 minutes*

Directions. 1. Use a 70-space line; double spacing.

2. Your speed goal is to type 10 words a minute slower than your normal speed rate. Your control goal is to type without error.

3. Determine the rate at which you are to type; then check the half-minute and minute goals.

4. Type for five minutes. If you achieve your goal, select a new speed goal but hold to your goal of errorless writing; type the material again for five minutes. If you type with not more than one error for each four lines, you are doing satisfactory work; but if you type without error, you are doing superior work.

STROKES

You can figure it out exactly for yourself. There are just so many hours 74

for work in each day. In an office one is paid a straight salary for the month. 156

Reduce your pay to the hour basis; then divide the amount of pay you get for 233

each hour of work by the number of letters you can transcribe in an hour. 308

You will then have a portion of the cost of letters. If you waste a large part 388

of the day, which should be given to work, the total correspondence cost goes 466

up. This is why employers never quit searching for better workers who will 542

do more and chatter less; who will help to lessen the jam of work that often 619

piles up toward the zero hour of closing time. This cost per letter can be 695

maintained with ease when there is consistent work and no loss of time 766

through chatter. 784

"Your tongues wag too much," said an employer the other day to two lazy 856

young workers. After he went to his office, I heard the wagging tongues say 933

pointed but probably false things about the "old crab," who was the "boss." 1010

The next time that man has to comment upon the waste of time caused by 1081

ELECTRIC

MANUFACTURERS, INC.

SERVING PRINCIPAL CITIES

BROUGHTON TERMINAL

NEWARK ○ NEW JERSEY

February 6, 194-

STROKES

17

Mr. Theodore L. Woodworth   43
Treasurer, Western Electric Company   79
1657-1659 W. 121st Street   105
New York, New York   124

Dear Sir   133

                Subject: Account No. 480-Y   161

        We have not received a check from you covering   208
last month's balance of $647.50. We must ask that   259
you take care of the account without further delay.   312

        Our Order Department reports that E. J. McNair,   360
representing this company in New York City, mailed   411
to us another order from you, Order No. 293. At the   464
time Mr. McNair sent the order in, he said that you   516
had explained to him the delay in paying your last   567
month's balance and that you promised to mail your   618
check to us promptly.   641

        We appreciate your business and want to continue   690
our mutually profitable relationship, but we must   740
have a remittance from you not later than the first   792
of next week. Your last order, No. 293, will then be   846
shipped without delay.   870

                        Yours very truly   887

                        ELECTRIC MANUFACTURERS, INC.   916

                        M. R. Sleighter, Treasurer   943

    hbf   946

(Strokes, 946; words, 145.)

Style Letter No. 6 — Modification of the Block Form of Letter with a Subject Line

[125]

office chatter, he is just as likely to tell those workers that they may have   1159

full time to devote to their talking as he is to give an ungentle hint that the   1239

office is no place for social talk. You can be quite as certain, too, that the   1319

classroom is no place for the chattering habit. There is a time and a place   1346

for all things, and the business office and the classroom are not places for   1473

idle talk.   1483

SPEED EMPHASIS   *8 minutes*

Select a fifteen-second goal that will call for a five-word increase in your five-minute writing rate on Exercise 74. When you have typed at the goal rate *without error*, type at the same rate for thirty seconds without error; then type at the same rate for a minute without error; then increase your time to two- and three-minute writings. Use the material of Exercise 74 for this speed emphasis practice. Each time you add fifteen seconds to the length of time you type, begin at the first of the paragraph so that the repetition typing will add to the ease with which you handle the words.

CONTROL DRILLS

If a control drill is to be functional, it must be selected to meet your known needs. Special practice procedures and special practice materials must be selected for use after a diagnosis of difficulty has revealed a particular need. Class unison drill has its place in teaching typewriting, although it is generally conceded that unison drill is of limited value. Control drills are peculiarly personal and they must, therefore, be typed at individual rates rather than at a directed class rate.

The drills that follow should not be timed, for their function is to eliminate faulty stroking and not to increase speed of stroking. These drills may be used effectively to reduce and overcome errors of the following kinds:

1. Adjacent key controls
2. Vowel confusion
3. Transposition of letters
4. Failure to start typing after carriage return
5. Faulty shifting

Adjacent Key Controls. If you are striking *r* for *t*, *m* for *n*, *a* for *s*, or other similar adjacent keys, select the word drills listed for the two adjacent keys and practice on the stroke level until you feel you have established some mastery of the reaches. Vigorously think or say aloud the adjacent letters as they appear in the words.

Vowel Confusion. When vowel confusion is noted in your work, fix your attention on letter combinations and type on the letter level until the finger pathway has been reconstructed; then return to the word level of typing. Practice the *a*, *e*, *i*, *o*, and *u* lines.

Transposition of Letters. Reading too far in advance of typing or the imperfect timing of your strokes will cause transposition of letters. Type the alphabetic sentences on the stroke level with particular attention to the timing of each stroke.

Failure to Start Typing After Carriage Return. This hesitancy so often noted in the work of student typists is caused by the feeling of uncertainty in returning the hand to typing position or to the failure to hold the eyes on the copy as the carriage is returned. Select sentence and paragraph drills for specific line timing and work for the smooth and continuous movement of the carriage.

Faulty Shifting. Many of these errors are caused by releasing the shift key too quickly or not depressing it firmly. Select the sentence drills for shift key control and practice typing the capitals with a lengthened one-count, depressing the shift key firmly and holding it down until the letter key has been struck and released.

EXERCISE 75

18 minutes

Directions. Type Style Letter No. 6 in the form shown on page 125. Note the following:

1. In the full open form of punctuation, punctuation is omitted after the salutation and the complimentary close as well as after the lines of the address.

2. If the street name is a number that can be represented only by three or more digits, write it in figures.

3. A subject is properly a part of the body of the letter. Unless the printed letterhead indicates the position of the subject, type it two single spaces below the salutation. Long subjects should be arranged in two lines. The subject is treated as a manuscript heading and is not followed by a period.

4. In introducing a name into the body of a letter, use the initials and the family name; after that, use the title *Mr.* with the family name. If the person has a title, such as *Dr.*, it must be used in both cases.

5. When the signature is the name of an incorporated firm, a comma usually separates the name from *Inc.*

EXERCISE 76

10 minutes

Directions. Type the letter once.

When the month is not used as a part of the date, the figures expressing the day should be followed by *th, d,* or *st.* (See the first paragraph of the letter.)

Lang Battery Service 418 Seventh Street Ridgewood, New Jersey Gentlemen Subject: Invoices Nos. 684 and 692 (P) We have not yet received a remittance from you to take care of our invoices Nos. 684 and 692, dated the 16th and 25th of last month; nor have we had a reply to our two letters concerning these invoices. In each of our letters we asked that you inform us when your account would be paid. In view of the fact that you have ignored our letters and invoices, we are necessarily forced to use more drastic means to effect a settlement. (P) Unless your check for $357.81, in payment of invoices Nos. 684 and 692, is received by the end of next week, we shall be compelled to send your account to our Legal Department for collection. (P) We shall expect to have a check from you without further delay. Yours very truly ELECTRIC MANUFACTURERS, INC. M. R. Sleighter, Treasurer *(Strokes, 891; words, 150.)*

LESSON 62

RECONSTRUCTION PRACTICE

5 minutes

Directions. Type Technique Practice 61 as directed.

TECHNIQUE PRACTICE 62

7 minutes

Directions. 1. Use a 70-space line; double spacing.

2. Center the heading, Technique Practice 62, in capitals. Triple-space after typing the centered heading.

3. Type each sentence once; then check the five lines. Retype the sentences that have errors. Goal: Each line without error and an extra line typed accurately for each error made.

	STROKES
The "-" is used to form compounds; and the "*" is used with footnotes.	70
FOR RENT: A 6-room apartment; steam heated; garage; $70 a month.	65
Did he write the article on "How Learning to Typewrite Takes Place"?	68
He wrote, "The meeting is at ten o'clock." I shall arrive at 8:30 a.m.	71
The women's clothing and the children's toys were shipped early in May.	71

CORRECTIVE DRILLS FOR ADJACENT KEY CONTROLS
AND VOWEL CONFUSION

Drill

(a) abeyance acclaim adamant aerial afraid aggravate ahead aidance ajar akin
A state leader made a characteristic statement after hearing that appeal.

(b) barber baffle battery baggage rubber tablet brother grabbed trouble both
Building big bridges brought Robert Brown to Burma to see his brother.

(c) cadence Cecil character circumstance click condescend credence currency
Cultivate charm, the lack of which can cause considerable practical harm.

(d) decided defended disagreed deducted drudgery demanded danced diamond
Don decided it was his duty to have the deed delivered to Dr. Davidson.

(e) earthen ebonize eccentrate educated effectuate egresses eighteenth eject
Every earnest endeavor does meet with some degree of measurable success.

(f) farther fearful fifty fluffy footfall frightful fulfill verify forfeit
Faith, not force, effectively fortifies one for life's difficult facts.

(g) great doing fighting brighter gingham grating guardian rightful ginger
Great good can be achieved by thinking and working for the good of all.

(h) highly handy hundred humbly history hardship headache holiday hyacinth
Hope, faith, and charity should have right emphasis in everything we do.

(i) insisting idealistic itemized impatient impartiality idiotic interview
I think this will bring him to emphasize his life principle in his will.

(j) January judged July joint juror jury jeopardize judgment journal jewel
Jealousy of the Journal's jobs jeopardized the adjustment on the project.

(k) Kansas knowledge keyboard kink knock knickers knuckle knack kickoff
Knowledge and skill and hard work make men great and keep life joyful.

(l) locally skillful slightly parallel limelight legally lightly legible
Learn to love your work fully as well as your play and you will do well.

(m) museums mummery murmured maximum hammer slump mysticism mushroom
Memories are sometimes more than merely remembering—they are reliving.

(n) nunnery running gunner nineteen kindly thinking notoriety narrow-minded
No one needs a finer understanding of punctuation than stenographers.

(o) opinion o'clock outlook orthodox outdoor offshoot overlook overcome loose
Only those who know how to work and who will work should hope to do well.

(p) period poise power person public appeal April pamphlet paragraph prophecy
Preparation for a profession will help you to gain respect of all people.

(q) quiz quit quick acquit quota quality quantity qualified acquire inquire
Quite frequently queer questions require quick insight and quiet thought.

BUDGET IV

LESSON 61

RECONSTRUCTION PRACTICE

4 minutes

Directions. 1. Use a 70-space line; double spacing.
2. Type this drill; operate the line-space lever twice and then type the technique practice on the same page.

bribery brambles barbecue cadence descend eccentric efficiency forgetful

gorgeous gurgling exaggerate hallelujah hyphen illicitly ill-willed July

knowledge kinsfolk lifelessly followed slightly maximum murmur Mohammedan

enunciation nutriment inundation phonograph perpetuate quartz acquired

TECHNIQUE PRACTICE 61

6 minutes

Directions. 1. Use a 70-space line; double spacing.
2. Center the heading, Technique Practice 61, in capitals. (Release the shift lock before typing the figures.) Triple-space after the centered heading.
3. Type each sentence once; then check the five lines. Retype sentences that have errors. Goal: Each line without error and an extra line typed accurately for each error made.
Study the following explanatory notes before typing any of the sentences:

Sentence 1. With *p.m.* or *a.m.* express time in figures. When a period follows a small letter abbreviation, no space follows the period within the abbreviation.
Sentence 2. A parenthetical word, phrase, or clause is set off by commas. Type round sums of money without the decimal and ciphers.
Sentence 3. When two unrelated groups of figures come together, separate them by a comma.
Sentence 4. Words in a series are separated by commas. Use figures for all numbers closely connected if the largest number cannot be expressed in one or two words.
Sentence 5. A parenthetical word, phrase, or clause is set off by commas. When two or more adjectives modify a noun, separate them by commas if they bear the same relation to the noun.

	STROKES
Mr. B. J. Kingsly of St. Cloud expects to be here today at 2:15 p.m.	68
Order #169-A will, without question, total more than $700, as he said.	70
In 1935, $985.75 in cash prizes was given away by Marxbergh & Johnson.	70
Max shipped 8 horses, 36 cows, and 145 sheep to the Cincinnati market.	70
Car PRR 482965 has been loaded, I believe, with luscious, ripe melons.	70

LETTER EXERCISES

2 minutes

The letters in this budget were dictated by Mr. M. R. Sleighter, treasurer of the Electric Manufacturers, Inc., of Newark, New Jersey. Mr. Sleighter uses open punctuation and a modification of the block form of letter. You will notice that the inside address is blocked at the left margin; the paragraphs are indented; the subject line is centered; and the complimentary close and the signatures are blocked in the position for the complimentary close. The dictator's name and the title are typed four spaces below the firm name. The reference initials consist of the stenographer's initials only.

Directions for Exercises 76, 77, and 78. 1. Refer to the placement table on page 86 for the margin adjustments.
2. Use single spacing; open punctuation; the modification of the block style of letter that is used for Style Letter No. 6.
3. Use current date; and substitute your initials for those of the stenographer who typed the original letter.

Drill

(r) **realize readily require remarks raffle rifler laggard leverage rarefy**
Read and write about the right and fear only to do wrong; then work hard.

(s) **sales scales sense shape short shows since sixth spaces styles spends**
Success comes to some through luck, but most often it comes through work.

(t) **testament transatlantic tittle-tattle top-heavy thirteenth tenant tacit**
Tests of conduct and tests of thought must be made quite often, it seems.

(u) **unusual untruthful humorous numerous mountain multitude multitudinous**
Unnumbered hundreds of thoughtful men question his soundness of judgment.

(v) **verify verve survived deliver vivacity fervidly virtual veritable grave**
Very few victors have the drive to go to the top without fervent approval.

(w) **watchword woodwork sworn switch swelter widowed swallow swift-winged**
Worthy work will win rewards for you when wishing without work will fail.

(x) **xylophone excessive fixture experience quixotic exhibit pretext examine**
He expressed pleasure in the experience of excelling in the extra exams.

(y) **youthfully hazy lazy quiz yesterday zephyr zealous dazzle quizzical your**
Years go by rapidly, and youth today quickly gives way to age tomorrow.

(z) **zinc zone size daze blaze zephyr zenith zealous prizes realize antagonize**
Zeal and zest for one's work may lift one to dazzling heights of growth.

CONTROL DRILLS FOR TRANSPOSITION OF LETTERS
(ALPHABETIC SENTENCES)

	STROKES
Pack my box with five dozen jars of liquid gum.	47
The puzzled judge soon became quite vexed at your wonderful knowledge.	70
A lazy stenographer will be vexed quickly if much poor work be rejected.	72
Galaxies of quaint larkspur blew jocundly above the garden maze.	64
Joe was quite amazed and perplexed by the vacant labyrinth of the king.	71
Dazzling jonquils heavy with dew make an extremely beautiful picture.	69

DRILLS FOR CALLING THE THROW

	STROKES
Good work can be done by all of us if we are willing to work.	61
It means we lack will if we give up when we have some trouble.	62
There are only four fingers on each hand to control when we type.	65
We are not all able to read or to work at the same rate of speed.	65
Habit is a cable. Each day we weave a thread of strength or weakness.	70
Learning to walk past failures is the meaning of real success in life.	70
Skill in typing is the sum total of doing many little things very well.	71
If we want practice to make perfect, we must practice in the right way.	71

D. ADDRESS

1. The official title in the address should be placed on the second line before the company name and should be followed by a comma. If the second line is very long, however, the official title may be typed on the first line and separated from the personal name by a comma and a space. A particularly long official title may be correctly placed on a separate line.
2. The first line of the address is typed even with the left margin.
3. In the indented style of letter, the second line of the address is indented five spaces from the left margin; the third, ten spaces.
4. Double-space between the last line of the address and the salutation.
5. Spell *Street* and *Avenue* in full, unless abbreviations are necessary for a balanced address.

E. ATTENTION LINE

1. This is typed two single spaces below the last line of the address and before the salutation.
2. In the indented form the line is either centered or begun at the paragraph point. In the block form of letter the attention line is typed even with the left margin.

F. SALUTATION

1. This is always typed even with the left margin, two single spaces below the address or the attention line.
2. In the business letter the salutation is followed by a colon when close or mixed punctuation is used. (No mark is used after the salutation when the letter is typed in the open punctuation form.)
3. Double-space between the salutation and the subject line or between the salutation and the first line in the body of the letter.

G. SUBJECT LINE

1. The subject is really a part of the body of the letter and the letterhead may indicate the place for it. If not, type the subject two single spaces below the salutation.
2. Arrange long subjects in two lines.
3. The subject is treated as a manuscript heading and is not followed by a period.

H. BODY OF LETTER

1. Letters that are single-spaced require double spacing between paragraphs.
2. Paragraphs are usually indented five spaces when the indented form is used. Ten-space indentations are permitted, although they are not generally used.

I. COMPLIMENTARY CLOSE

1. The first word only is capitalized.
2. In the indented and the modified block styles, the complimentary close usually begins 5 spaces to the left of the center of the letter (35 for pica and 45 for elite type). The longest of the closing lines of the letter must not extend beyond the right margin.

J. COMPANY SIGNATURE

1. This is typed in capital letters, two single spaces below the complimentary close.
2. In the indented form of letter, indent the company signature five spaces from the beginning of the complimentary close.
3. In the block form of letter, the company signature begins even with the complimentary close.

K. OFFICIAL TITLE

1. The official title is typed four single spaces below the company signature.
2. In the indented form of letter, the official title is indented five spaces from the beginning of the company signature, or it may be spaced so that it will end at the right margin of the letter.
3. The official title is typed in small letters, each word beginning with a capital.
4. If an official title is not used, the dictator's name may be typed in the position usually given to the official title.

L. REFERENCE INITIALS

1. The reference initials include the initials or the name of the dictator and the initials of the stenographer.

    If the dictator's name is typed in the signature, it is not necessary, although it is permissible, to include his initials in the reference line.

2. Reference initials are typed flush with the left margin of the letter, two single spaces below the official title.
3. If the letter does not carry an official title, the reference initials are typed four single spaces below the company signature.
4. If the letter has neither a company signature nor an official title, type the reference initials six to eight single spaces below the complimentary close.

M. ENCLOSURE

1. *Enclosure* is typed at the left margin, two single spaces below the reference initials.
2. More than one enclosure is indicated by the correct figure typed after the word *Enclosures.*

DRILLS FOR SHIFT-KEY CONTROL

	STROKES
Mary, Jack, and Jane will go to Maine or Maryland for the month of May.	71
Robert will take Albert Spaulding to San Antonio for a week in April.	69
Mark and James will go there in March. Is Jane in Maryland this week?	70
I know Larry, Harry, and Mark will want to live in Maine in the summer.	71
We wrote them to meet William and Frank at West Chester Sunday morning.	71
Nettie said, "Morris and I met James and Russell in Algiers last April."	72

CONTROL DRILL PARAGRAPHS

STROKES

The way you strike the keys is one technique that builds strength or weakness in your typing skill. Realize this and build for power by developing the right key stroking. Direct your stroke to the center of the key; just use a quick get-away stroke and keep the muscles of the forearm relaxed. Then you will achieve real typing power. — 73 / 152 / 235 / 311 / 337

If you want to know the joy that will come to you as an expert in typewriting, you must check the way you type as well as the quantity you write. The size of your day's production is important, of course; but equally important just now is the way in which you produce the work. Be very certain your work habits are correct—then your skill will grow. — 74 / 151 / 228 / 306 / 352

You cannot suddenly acquire the best typing skill of which you are capable. You must organize your effort for growth, establish fixed ways of reacting to stimuli, and follow the right sequence in the use of the practice procedures. A check of your work must be made so that you will know just what remedial drills to use. This is your work to do. — 77 / 155 / 236 / 309 / 349

Before you can expect to develop much skill in typewriting, you must check to see that you have quiet, almost motionless arms and wrists as you type. The finger movements should be made without permitting the hands to bounce in the air. Just try the use of light, poised fingers with quiet hand movements and you will realize how important these are for you. — 75 / 151 / 226 / 307 / 360

Do you use a quick key release with the fingers pulled slightly to the palm of the hand? Are your fingers curved so there will be very little hand motion when making the reaches? Make these adjustments in your technique now and you will not need to agonize over the problem of developing greater stroking power with usable control; you will have speed and accuracy. — 76 / 155 / 230 / 308 / 368

When you shift for capitals, use the hinge motion of the wrist so that the hand alignment with the keyboard will remain just the same. All excessive movements of hands, elbows, and wrists quite definitely act as hindrances to the development of typing power. You must automatize this control of the shift key so you can capitalize without error. — 75 / 150 / 227 / 301 / 407

PART II
OFFICE TYPEWRITING PROBLEMS

3 minutes

There are some duties of office workers that cannot be taught in school, but many specific habits of work and an understanding of the terminology and the office procedures that are common to office typing can be developed in the classroom. The units of instruction in Part II of this textbook have been organized to emphasize the following:

1. The understanding of business terminology through the use of letters, statements, and other business forms that have been taken from the files of successful businesses.
2. The development of businesslike attitudes through the study of traits that are common to outstandingly successful office workers.
3. The reconstruction and the improvement of skill in typewriting through the use of manipulation drills; sentence and paragraph practice; control drill paragraphs; and special drills designed for the teaching of syllabication, of methods of expressing numbers, and of correct punctuation and capitalization.

You are enrolled in the typewriting class so that you may learn to type. Other values you may consider as incidental outcomes, yet these incidental outcomes may be the very factors that will help you to demonstrate superior ability as an office worker. Type the drills, the paragraphs, and the exercises as well as you can, of course; in addition, learn all the related things taught with each budget of work. Know the rule for the use of a mark of punctuation, the reason for using a particular method of expressing numbers, and the basic principles of capitalization and syllabication. These are some of the incidental outcomes that will equip you to do superior office work.

UNIT VI — *THE BUSINESS LETTER*

1 minute

The letters given in the budgets of this unit will help you to gain an insight into the plan of work in a business office. In each office, workers must meet the demands and cope with the unexpected situations that arise daily. As letters are the personal representatives of a business, such letters must reflect the spirit of the organization. It is the responsibility of the dictator to determine the content of the letters; but the typist must assume responsibility for the details of form and for accuracy in spelling, punctuation, capitalization, and syllabication.

OUTLINE OF THE SETUP OF THE BUSINESS LETTER

A. LETTERHEAD
1. Standard page, 8½ by 11 inches.
2. Average depth of heading, 2 inches.

B. DATE LINE
1. On letterhead paper, type the date two single spaces below the city and state line.
2. The date line may be
   a. Centered under the city and the state.
   b. Indented five spaces to the right of the beginning of the city name.
   c. Begun under the first letter of the city.
   d. Placed so that it will end at approximately the right margin of the letter. This plan is followed if the letterhead is unusual in its arrangement.

3. In the date line, spell the month in full.
4. When the month, the day, and the year appear on one line, type the day and the year in figures and separate them by a comma.

C. SPACING BETWEEN THE DATE LINE AND THE ADDRESS
1. This is determined largely by the length of the letter.
2. Six single spaces between the date line and the first line of the address will usually give a satisfactory placement of letters of average length. Regardless of the length of the letter, have at least three single spaces between the date line and the inside address.

55/8
6